# EXPLANATORY NOTES

CRIMINAL JUSTICE ACT 2003

**GRAN*GIS* UK Publishing**

Adapted and published by GRANGIS (Grand Register Library).
Online: www.grangis.com
E-mail: contact@grangis.com


In this version:
ISBN: 979-8-88559-039-6

Note: This is the original version (as it was originally enacted). Title, sub-title and the generated date is as marked on the pages.

*These notes refer to the Criminal Justice Act 2003 (c.44)*

---

# EXPLANATORY NOTES

## CRIMINAL JUSTICE ACT 2003

Section 31: Removal of requirement to substantiate information on oath

**PART 5: DISCLOSURE**

Section 32: Initial duty of disclosure by prosecutor

Section 33: Defence disclosure

Section 34: Notification of intention to call defence witnesses

Section 35: Notification of names of experts instructed by defendant

Section 36: Further provisions about defence disclosure

Section 37: Continuing duty of disclosure by prosecutor

Section 38: Application by defence for disclosure

Section 39: Faults in defence disclosure

Section 40: Code of practice for police interviews of witnesses notified by accused

**PART 6: ALLOCATION AND TRANSFER OF OFFENCES**

Section 41: Allocation of offences triable either way, and sending cases to Crown Court

**Sending cases to the Crown Court etc.**

Section 42: Mode of trial for certain firearms offences ; transitory arrangements

**PART 7 : TRIALS ON INDICTMENT WITHOUT A JURY**

Section 43: Application by prosecution for certain fraud trials to be conducted without a jury

Sections 44 and 46: Application for prosecution for trial to be conducted without a jury where danger of jury tampering; discharge of jury because of jury tampering

*Section 45: Procedure for applications under sections 43 and 44.*

Section 47: Appeals

Section 48: Further provision about trials without a jury

Section 49: Rules of court

Section 50: Application of Part 7 to Northern Ireland

**PART 8 – LIVE LINKS**

Section 51: Live links in criminal proceedings

Section 52: Effect of, and rescission of, direction

Section 53: Magistrates' courts permitted to sit at other locations

Section 54: Warning to the jury

Section 164: Fixing of fines

Section 165: Remission of fines

Section 167: The Sentencing Guidelines Council

Section 168: Sentencing Guidelines Council supplementary provisions

Section 169: The Sentencing Advisory Panel

Section 170: Guidelines relating to sentencing and allocation

Section 171: Functions of Sentencing Advisory Panel in relation to guidelines

Section 172: Duty of court to have regard to sentencing guidelines

Section 173: Annual report by Council

Section 174: Duty to give reasons for, and explain effect of, sentence

Section 175: Duty to publish information about sentencing

Section 176: Interpretation of Chapter 1

**Chapter 2 : Community Sentences for offenders aged 16 or over**

Section 177: Community orders

Section 178: Power to provide for court review of community orders

Section 179: Breach, revocation or amendment of community order

Section 180: Transfer of community orders to Scotland or Northern Ireland

**Chapter 3 : Prison sentences of less than 12 months**

Section 181: Prison sentences of less than 12 months

Section 182: Licence conditions

Section 183: Intermittent custody

Section 184: Restrictions on power to make intermittent custody order

Section 185 Intermittent custody: licence conditions

Section 186: Further provisions relating to intermittent custody

Section 187: Revocation or amendment of order

Section 188: Transfer of custody plus order or intermittent custody order to Scotland or Northern Ireland

Section 189: Suspended sentences of imprisonment

Section 190: Imposition of requirements by suspended sentence order

Section 191: Power to provide for review of suspended sentence order

Section 242: Interpretation of sections 240 and 241

Section 243: Persons extradited to the United Kingdom

Section 244: Duty to release prisoners

Section 245: Restrictions on operation of section 244(1) in relation to intermittent custody Prisoners

Section 246: Power to release prisoners on licence before required to do so

Section 247: Release on licence of prisoner serving extended sentence under section 227 or 228

Section 248: Power to release prisoners on compassionate grounds

Section 249: Duration of licence

Section 250: Licence conditions

Section 251: Licence conditions on re-release of prisoner serving sentence of less than 12 months

Section 252: Duty to comply with licence conditions

Section 253: Curfew condition to be included in licence under section 246

Section 254: Recall of prisoners while on licence

Section 255: Recall of prisoners released under s.246

Section 256: Further release after recall

Section 257: Additional days for disciplinary offences

Section 258: Early release of fine defaulters and contemnors

Section 259: Persons liable to removal from the United Kingdom

Section 260: Early removal of prisoners liable to removal from United Kingdom

Section 261: Re-entry into United Kingdom of offender removed from prison early

Section 262: Prisoners liable to removal from United Kingdom: modifications of Criminal Justice Act 1991

Section 263: Concurrent terms

Section 264: Consecutive terms

Section 265: Restriction on consecutive sentences for released prisoners

Section 266: Release on licence, etc: drug testing requirements

Section 267: Alteration by order of relevant proportion of sentence

Section 268: Interpretation of Chapter 6

**Chapter 7: Effect of Life Sentence**

Section 269: Determination of minimum term in relation to mandatory life sentence

Section 270: Duty to give reasons

Section 271: Appeals

Section 272: Review of minimum term on reference by Attorney General

Section 273: Life prisoners transferred to England and Wales & Section 274: Further provisions about references relating to transferred life prisoners

Section 275: Duty to release certain life prisoners

Section 276: Mandatory life sentences : transitional cases

**Chapter 8: Other Provisions about sentencing**

Section 278: Deferment of Sentence

Section 279: Drug treatment and testing requirement in action plan order or supervision order

Section 280: Alteration of penalties for summary offences

Section 281: Alteration of penalties for other summary offences

Section 282: Increase in maximum term that may be imposed on summary conviction of offence triable either way

Section 283: Enabling powers: alteration of maximum penalties

Section 284: Increase in penalties for drug related offences

Section 285: Increase in penalties for certain driving-related offences causing deaths

Section 286: Increase in penalties for offences under section 174 of Road Traffic Act 1988

Section 287: Minimum sentence for certain firearms offences

Section 288: Certain firearms offences to be triable only on indictment

Section 289: Power to sentence young offender to detention in respect of certain firearms offences: England and Wales

Section 290: Power to sentence young offender to detention in respect of certain firearms offences: Scotland

Section 291: Power by order to exclude application of minimum sentence to those under 18

Section 292: Sentencing for firearms offences in Northern Ireland

Schedule 8 – Breach, revocation and amendment of community order

Schedule 9 – Transfer of community orders to Scotland or Northern Ireland

Schedule 10: Revocation or amendment of custody plus orders and amendment of intermittent custody orders

Schedule 11 – Transfer of custody plus orders or intermittent custody orders to Scotland or Northern Ireland

**PARTS 2 AND 3**

**PART 4**

Schedule 12: Breach, revocation and amendment of suspended sentence order, and effect of further conviction

Schedule 13 – Transfer of suspended sentence orders to Scotland or Northern Ireland

**PARTS 1 AND 2**

**PART 3**

**PART 4**

Schedule 14 – Persons to whom copies of requirements to be provided in particular cases

Schedule 18: Release of prisoners serving sentences of imprisonment or detention for public protection

Schedule 19: The Parole Board: supplementary provisions

Schedule 20: Prisoners liable to removal from the United Kingdom: modifications of the Criminal Justice Act 1991

Schedule 21: Determination of minimum term in relation to mandatory life sentences

Paragraph 4

Paragraph 5

Paragraphs 6 and 7

Paragraphs 8 to 12

Schedule 22 : Mandatory Life Sentences: Transitional Cases

Paragraph 1

**Existing prisoners notified by Secretary of State: Paragraphs 2, 3 and 4**

**Existing prisoners not notified by Secretary of State: Paragraphs 5 to 8**

**Sentences passed on or after commencement date in respect of offences committed before that date: Paragraphs 9 and 10**

Paragraph 11

Paragraphs 12 to 18

Schedule 23: Deferment of sentence

Schedule 24: Drug treatment and testing requirement in action plan order or supervision order

Schedule 25: Summary offences no longer punishable with imprisonment

Schedule 26: Increase in maximum term for certain summary offences

Schedule 27: Enabling powers: alteration of maximum penalties etc.

Schedule 28: Increase in penalties for drug-related offences

Schedule 30: Disqualification from working with children

Schedule 31: Default orders: modification of provisions relating to community orders

Schedule 32: Amendments relating to sentencing

Schedule 33: Jury service

Paragraphs 2, 3, 14 and 15

Paragraphs 4 to 11

Schedule 34: Parenting Order attached to Referral Order

Schedule 38: Transitory, transitional and savings provisions

## HANSARD REFERENCES

*These notes refer to the Criminal Justice Act 2003 (c.44) which received Royal Assent on 20th November 2003*

# CRIMINAL JUSTICE ACT 2003

---

## EXPLANATORY NOTES

### INTRODUCTION

1. These explanatory notes relate to the Criminal Justice Act 2003 which received Royal Assent on 20th November. They have been prepared by the Home Office in order to assist the reader in understanding the Act. They do not form part of the Act and have not been endorsed by Parliament.

2. The notes need to be read in conjunction with the Act. They are not, and are not meant to be, a comprehensive description of the Act. So where a section or part of a section does not seem to require any explanation or comment, none is given.

### SUMMARY AND BACKGROUND

3. In July 2002 the Government published a White Paper outlining its plans for the criminal justice system, from crime prevention through to the punishment and rehabilitation of offenders. *Justice for All* (Cm 5563) focused particularly on reforms to court procedure and sentencing, to make trials faster and to deliver clear, consistent and appropriate sentencing. On these issues the White Paper built on the proposals in two consultation documents: *Review of the Criminal Courts of England and Wales* by Sir Robin Auld (2001) and *Making Punishment Work: report of a review of the sentencing framework of England and Wales* (2001) by John Halliday.

4. This Act is intended to introduce reforms in these two areas. With regard to court procedure, the Act aims to improve the management of cases through the courts by involving the Crown Prosecution Service in charging decisions, by reforming the system for allocating cases to court, and by increasing magistrates' sentencing powers so that fewer cases have to go to the Crown Court. It will enable action to be taken to reduce breaches of bail by introducing a new presumption against bail in certain circumstances.

5. The Act is designed to ensure that criminal trials are run more efficiently and to reduce the scope for abuse of the system. It will reform the rules on advance disclosure of evidence and will allow for judge-alone trial in cases involving threats and intimidation of juries, and paves the way for judge-alone trial in exceptionally long, complex serious fraud cases. It will ensure the wider involvement of the community as a whole by reforming rules on jury service. Rules on evidence will be changed to allow the use of previous convictions where relevant, and to allow the use of reported (hearsay) evidence where there is good reason why the original source cannot be present, or where the judge otherwise considers it would be appropriate. It will enable any witness to give evidence using live links. A right of appeal for the prosecution against judicial decisions to direct or order an acquittal before the jury has been asked to consider the evidence will be introduced to balance the defendant's right of appeal against both conviction and sentence. The Act will also make it possible in certain very serious cases for a retrial to take place despite an earlier acquittal if there is new and compelling evidence of an accused's guilt.

6. The Act aims to provide a sentencing framework which is clearer and more flexible than the current one. The purposes of sentencing of adults are identified in statute for the first time, as punishment, crime reduction, reform and rehabilitation, public protection and reparation. The principles of sentencing are set out, including that any previous convictions, where they are recent and relevant, should be regarded as an aggravating factor which will increase the severity of the sentence. A new Sentencing Guidelines Council will be established. Sentences will be reformed, so that the various kinds of community order for adults will be replaced by a single community order with a range of possible requirements; custodial sentences of less than 12 months will be replaced by a new sentence, (described in the Halliday report as "custody plus"), which will always involve a period of at least 26 weeks post-release supervision in the community; and sentences over 12 months will be served in full, half in custody, half in the community, with supervision extended to the end of the sentence rather than the ¾ point as now. Serious violent and sexual offenders will be given new sentences which will ensure that they are kept in prison or under supervision for longer periods than currently. At the other end of the custodial scale, several "intermediate" sanctions will be introduced. These include intermittent custody and a reformed suspended sentence in which offenders have to complete a range of requirements imposed by the court. The intention is for the court to be able to provide each offender with a sentence that best meets the need of the particular case, at any level of seriousness, and for sentences to be more effectively managed by the correctional services who will need to work together closely in delivering the new sentences.

7. The Act also addresses a number of other areas. It contains a number of provisions on drug related offending, including extending to those aged 14 and above the provisions to test persons in police detention and at other points in the criminal justice system for specified Class A drugs. It establishes a new scheme under which the court, rather than the Home Secretary, will determine the minimum term to be served in prison by a person convicted of murder. It will establish a 5 year mandatory minimum custodial sentence for unauthorised possession of a prohibited firearm. It will increase the maximum penalty for causing death by dangerous driving from 10 to 14 years and retain the power of arrest for the possession of cannabis or cannabis resin following their proposed reclassification from Class B to Class C drugs. Finally, in relation to juveniles, the Act extends the use of parenting orders by making them available at an earlier stage and introduces individual support orders, requiring young people with anti-social behaviour orders to undertake education-related activities.

8. In general the Act extends only to England and Wales.

9. The Act is in fourteen parts. Part 1 contains provisions on the Police and Criminal Evidence Act. Part 2 contains provisions on bail. Part 3 contains provisions on conditional cautions. Part 4 contains provisions on charging. Part 5 contains provisions on disclosure. Part 6 contains provisions on allocation and sending of offences. Part 7 contains provisions on trials on indictment without a jury. Part 8 contains provisions on live links. Part 9 contains provisions on prosecution appeals. Part 10 contains provisions enabling retrial for serious offences following acquittal (double jeopardy). Part 11 contains provisions on evidence of bad character (Chapter 1) and provisions on hearsay evidence (Chapter 2). Part 12 contains provisions on sentencing and is split into a number of Chapters. Chapter 1 contains general provisions about sentencing. Chapter 2 contains provisions on community orders for offenders aged 16 or over. Chapter 3 contains provisions on prison sentences of less than 12 months. Chapter 4 contains further provisions on orders under Chapters 2 and 3. Chapter 5 contains provisions on dangerous offenders. Chapter 6 contains provisions on release of prisoners on licence. Chapter 7 deals with the effect of life sentences. Chapter 8 contains other provisions about sentencing. Chapter 9 contains supplementary provisions. Part 13 contains miscellaneous provisions and Part 14 contains general provisions.

## Part 1 – Amendments of Police and Criminal Evidence Act 1984

10. Part 1 amends the Police and Criminal Evidence Act 1984 (PACE). The Act extends the definition of prohibited articles under section 1 of PACE so that it includes an article made, adapted or intended for use in causing criminal damage. The effect is to give police officers the power to stop and search where they have reasonable suspicion that a person is carrying any such item. It also makes new provision for warrants to enter and search. At present, persons who accompany constables executing search warrants are able to do so merely in an advisory or clerical capacity. The Act allows those accompanying the police under a warrant to actively assist in searching premises.

11. The Act enables the immediate grant of bail from the scene of arrest ("street bail") where there is no immediate need to deal with the arrested person at a police station. It gives police the discretion to decide when and where an arrested person should attend a police station for interview. It also enables reviews of the continuing need for detention without charge to be conducted over the telephone rather than in person at the police station as is currently the case. Where video conferencing facilities are available they should be used in preference to the telephone.

12. The Act extends to persons who are aged 14 and above the provisions in the Police and Criminal Evidence Act 1984 enabling officers to detain a person after charge to test for specified class A drugs, subject to conditions in section 63B of PACE (as introduced by Section 57 of the Criminal Justice and Court Services Act 2000). An appropriate adult is required to be present during the testing procedure for those under the age of 17. The Secretary of State may alter the minimum age by order subject to the affirmative resolution procedure.

13. The Act extends the time for which someone may be detained without charge, under the authority of a superintendent, from 24 to 36 hours for any arrestable offence, rather than for any serious arrestable offence as the law currently stands. At present a custody officer is required to record everything a detained person has with him on entering custody. *Section 8* of the Act changes the law so that whilst the custody officer still has a responsibility to ascertain what the person has with him, any recording and where it is made will be at his discretion.

14. The Act makes fundamental changes to the process for establishing and amending codes of practice under PACE. At present codes cover stop and search, searching of premises, detention, identification, and the recording of interviews. Issuing a new code or revising an existing one requires extensive public consultation and an active process of parliamentary consideration. The amendments provide for a targeted consultation process and for a level of parliamentary scrutiny proportionate to the amendments proposed. The introduction of any new code will remain subject to the affirmative procedure.

15. The Act extends the powers of the police to enable them to take fingerprints and a DNA sample from a person whilst he is in police detention following his arrest for a recordable offence. Fingerprints can now be taken electronically and the police will be able to confirm in a few minutes the identity of a suspect where that person's fingerprints are already held on the National Fingerprint Database. It will prevent persons who may be wanted for other matters avoiding detection by giving the police a false name and address. Fingerprints taken under this provision will be subject to a speculative search across the crime scene database to see if they are linked to any unsolved crime. The DNA profile of an arrested person will be loaded onto the National DNA Database and will be subject to a speculative search to see whether it matches a crime scene stain already held on the Database. This will assist the police in the detection and prevention of crime.

16. *Section 12* introduces Schedule 1 which deals with amendments related to this Part of the Act.

## Part 2 – Bail

17. This Part gives effect to the Law Commission's recommendation that minor amendments should be made to the Bail Act 1976 to ensure that its compliance with the ECHR is beyond dispute. The provision which purports to make it an exception to the right to bail that an offence appears to have been committed while the defendant was on bail for another offence is repealed, and replaced with a presumption that bail will not be granted in these circumstances to a defendant aged 18 or over unless the court is satisfied that there is no significant risk of his re-offending on bail. There is also a presumption that a defendant aged 18 or over who without reasonable cause has failed to surrender to custody will not be granted bail, unless the court is satisfied that there is no significant risk that he would so fail if released.

18. This Part also gives effect to recommendations of Lord Justice Auld in his *Review of the Criminal Courts of England and Wales* for simplifying the bail appeals system, including removing the High Court's bail jurisdiction where it is concurrent with that of the Crown Court. The right of the prosecution to appeal to the Crown Court against a decision by magistrates to grant bail is extended to cover all imprisonable offences, and not just those carrying a maximum penalty of 5 years or more as at present.

19. This Part creates a presumption that bail will not be granted for a person aged 18 or over who is charged with an imprisonable offence, and tests positive for a specified Class A drug, if he refuses to undergo an assessment as to his dependency or propensity to misuse such drugs, or following an assessment, refuses any relevant follow-up action recommended unless the court is satisfied that there is no significant risk of his re-offending on bail.

## Part 3 – Conditional Cautions

20. This Part allows for a caution with specific conditions attached to it to be given where there is sufficient evidence to charge a suspect with an offence which he or she admits, and the suspect agrees to the caution. It would be for the prosecutor to decide whether a conditional caution was appropriate, and in most cases for the police to administer it. If the suspect failed to comply with the conditions, he or she would be liable to be prosecuted for the offence. The Act provides for the publication of a Code of Practice for conditional cautions.

## Part 4 – Charging etc

21. This Part amends the Police and Criminal Evidence Act 1984 to provide that, where a custody officer decides that there is sufficient evidence to charge a suspect who is in police detention, he is to have regard to guidance issued by the DPP in determining whether the suspect should be released without charge but on bail, released without charge and without bail, or charged. Where, pursuant to that guidance, a case is referred to the Crown Prosecution Service to determine whether proceedings should be instituted (and if so on which charge), the defendant will be released on police bail with or without conditions.

22. This Part also makes provision for a new method of initiating public prosecutions, to replace laying an information and issue of a summons. The police, the CPS and other named public prosecutors will instead issue a written charge, which will be accompanied by a 'requisition' informing the defendant when he is to appear in court to answer to it.

## Part 5 – Disclosure

23. This Part amends some of the provisions in the Criminal Procedure and Investigations Act 1996 that govern the disclosure of unused prosecution material to the defence and the provision of a defence case statement. It replaces the present two stage test with a new objective single test for the disclosure of unused prosecution material

to the defence, requiring the prosecutor to disclose prosecution material that has not previously been disclosed and which might reasonably be considered capable of undermining the case for the prosecution against the accused, or of assisting the case for the accused. It replaces the present secondary disclosure stage with a revised continuing duty on the prosecutor to disclose material that meets the new test. The prosecutor is specifically required to review the prosecution material on receipt of the defence statement and to make further disclosure if required under the continuing duty.

24. It also amends the defence disclosure requirements, requiring the accused to provide a more detailed defence statement than currently required. The main changes are that the defence will be required to set out the nature of his defence including any particular defences on which he intends to rely and indicate any points of law he wishes to take, including any points as to the admissibility of evidence or abuse of process. Other new provisions are a requirement for the judge to warn the accused about any failure to comply with the defence statement requirements, placing cross service of defence statements on a statutory footing, a requirement for service of an updated defence statement to assist the management of the trial, requiring the accused to serve, before the trial, details of any witnesses he intends to call to give evidence (other than himself) and also details of all experts instructed including those not called to give evidence. The new obligation on the defence to provide details of the witnesses it intends to call will be accompanied by a code of practice governing the conduct of any interviews by the police or non-police investigators with defence witnesses disclosed in accordance with the requirement.

25. Other provisions include a requirement that the judge must warn the defence about disclosure failures and judicial discretion to disclose the defence statement to the jury. The procedure for enabling the jury to draw adverse inferences from defence disclosure failures in respect of the defence statement is simplified.

## Part 6 – Allocation and sending of offences

26. This Part of the Act (with *Schedule 3*) amends the procedure to be followed by magistrates' courts in determining whether cases triable either way should be tried summarily or on indictment, and provides for the sending to the Crown Court of those cases which need to go there. The new procedures are designed to enable cases to be dealt with in the level of court which is appropriate to their seriousness, and to ensure that they reach that court as quickly as possible.

27. These provisions give effect to a number of recommendations from Lord Justice Auld's *Review of the Criminal Courts*, including making magistrates aware, when they determine allocation, of any previous convictions of the defendant; removing the option of committal for sentence in cases which the magistrates decide to hear; allowing defendants in cases where summary trial is considered appropriate to seek a broad indication of the sentence they would face if they were to plead guilty at that point; and replacing committal proceedings and transfers in serious fraud and child witness cases with a common system for sending cases to the Crown Court, based on the present arrangements for indictable-only cases.

28. Provision is made for defendants aged under 18 to give, for certain offences, an indication of plea, along the lines of the procedure which applies in adult cases. This should help to avoid cases involving young defendants being sent to the Crown Court unnecessarily. Provision is made for defendants under 18 who are charged with certain firearms offences to be sent to the Crown Court for trial.

## Part 7 – Trials on indictment without a jury

29. This Part of the Act sets out the circumstances in which criminal trials that currently take place on indictment in the Crown Court before a judge and jury will in future be conducted by a judge sitting alone.

30. This Part makes provision for the prosecution to apply for a trial of a serious or complex fraud case to proceed in the absence of a jury. The judge may order the case to be conducted without a jury if he is satisfied that the length or complexity of the case (having regard to steps which might reasonably be taken to reduce it) is likely to make the trial so burdensome upon the jury that the interests of justice require serious consideration to be given to conducting the trial without a jury.

31. This Part provides for a trial to be conducted without a jury where there is a real and present danger of jury tampering, or continued without a jury where the jury has been discharged because of jury tampering. The court must be satisfied that the risk of jury tampering would be so substantial (notwithstanding any steps, including police protection, that could reasonably be taken to prevent it) as to make it necessary in the interests of justice for the trial to be conducted without a jury. In trials already under way where the jury has been discharged because of jury tampering, the trial will continue without a jury unless the judge considers it necessary in the interests of justice to terminate the trial. In that event, he may order a retrial, and if he does he will have the option of ordering that the retrial should take place without a jury.

32. This Part provides a right of appeal to the Court of Appeal for both prosecution and defence against a determination made by a court on an application for a trial without a jury, and against a court order to continue a trial in the absence of a jury, or to order a retrial without a jury, because of jury tampering.

33. Where a trial is conducted or continued without a jury and a defendant is convicted, the court will be required to give its reasons for the conviction.

### Part 8 – Live links

34. This Part provides powers for the courts to hear evidence by way of a live television link from outside the court building. The court will be able to exercise these powers where they believe it to be in the interests of the efficient or effective administration of justice. Under the law as it stands at present witnesses are generally required to attend the court in person. The law does however currently provide for the use of live links in limited cases, such as in the case of young, disabled, vulnerable or intimidated witnesses under the Youth Justice and Criminal Evidence Act 1999.

35. Sir Robin Auld during his Review of the Criminal Courts, which reported in October 2001, considered evidence given by experts and recommended provision for the use of live links in this context. The provisions of this Part extend live link provision to any witness, other than the defendant, where it is in the interests of efficiency or effectiveness, to hear that witness's evidence by way of a live link.

### Part 9 – Prosecution appeals

36. Under current legislation, the defendant has a right of appeal at the end of the trial against both conviction and sentence but the prosecution has no equivalent right of appeal against an acquittal, whether as a result of a jury's decision or a judge's ruling that has the effect of bringing trial to an end early. This Part introduces an interlocutory prosecution right of appeal against two categories of ruling by a Crown Court judge. The first group comprises a ruling that has the effect of terminating the trial made either at a pretrial hearing or during the trial, at any time up until the start of the judge's summing up. This includes both rulings that are terminating in themselves and those that are so fatal to the prosecution case that the prosecution proposes to treat them as terminating and, in the absence of the right of appeal, would offer no or no further evidence. The second group relates to an evidentiary ruling or series of rulings made in certain trials for qualifying offences listed in *Schedule 4*. This right of appeal is limited to those rulings that significantly weaken the prosecution case and may only be exercised up to the opening of the defence case.

37. Leave to appeal must be obtained either from the judge or the Court of Appeal. Depending upon the circumstances of the case the judge will decide whether the appeal follows either an expedited route, where the trial is adjourned pending the conclusion of the appeal, or a non-expedited route, where any jury that has been empanelled may be discharged. In both cases any judicial ruling effectively acquitting the defendant or otherwise terminating the trial will not take effect while the prosecution is considering whether to appeal and, if an appeal is pursued, until the conclusion of the appeal or its abandonment. When appealing a terminating or effectively terminating ruling the prosecution must agree to the acquittal of the defendant(s) for the offence(s) to which the ruling applies, if leave to appeal is not granted or the appeal is abandoned. This does not apply to appeals against significantly weakening evidentiary rulings where the trial will usually continue or a fresh trial will take place, whatever the outcome of the appeal.

38. The Court of Appeal will be able to confirm, reverse or vary the ruling appealed against. Where it confirms a terminating or effectively terminating ruling, the Court of Appeal must order the acquittal of the defendant(s) for the offence(s) to which the appeal applies and it has the discretion to do so where it reverses or varies the ruling. Where it reverses or varies a terminating or effectively terminating ruling, the Court of Appeal may only order that proceedings in the Crown Court should continue or that a fresh trial should take place if this is necessary in the interests of justice. In the case of prosecution appeals against evidentiary rulings, after confirming, reversing or varying the ruling(s) appealed against, the Court of Appeal may order the continuation of the proceedings in the Crown Court or a fresh trial to take place. But where the prosecution indicates that it does not intend to continue with the prosecution the Court of Appeal may order the acquittal of the defendant. Under both categories of appeal, both the prosecution and the defence will have a further right of appeal to the Houses of Lords on a point of law of general public importance.

39. This Part also provides for restrictions on reporting the proceedings associated with the appeal and the appeal itself, until after the conclusion of the trial. The aim is to ensure that, if the appeal is successful, matters prejudicial to the continuing or fresh trial are not reported. This restriction will cover reports in England and Wales, Scotland and Northern Ireland. Contravention will be a summary offence subject to a maximum penalty of a level 5 fine.

## Part 10 – Retrial for serious offences

40. This Part of the Act reforms the law relating to double jeopardy, by permitting retrials in respect of a number of very serious offences, where new and compelling evidence has come to light. At present the law does not permit a person who has been acquitted or convicted of an offence to be retried for that same offence – this risk of retrial is known as "double jeopardy". There are two principles arising from the common law which prevent this. The first is known by the legal terms *autrefois acquit* and *autrefois convict*. These principles provide a bar to the trial, in respect of the same offence, of a person who has previously been either acquitted or convicted of that offence. In addition, the courts may consider it an *abuse of process* for additional charges to be brought, following an acquittal or conviction, for different offences which arose from the same behaviour or facts. There are certain exceptions to this rule.

41. The Government considers that the law should be reformed to permit a re-trial in cases of serious offences where there has been an acquittal in court, but compelling new evidence subsequently comes to light against the acquitted person. This is in line with, but drawn more widely than, recommendations of the Law Commission and those set out in Lord Justice Auld's review of the Criminal Courts, published in 2001. Examples of new evidence might include DNA or fingerprint tests, or new witnesses to the offence coming forward. The measures amend the law to permit the police to re-investigate a person acquitted of serious offences in these circumstances, to enable the prosecuting authorities to apply to the Court of Appeal for an acquittal to be quashed, and for a re-trial to take place where the Court of Appeal is satisfied that the new evidence is highly

probative of the case against the acquitted person. The measures provide safeguards aimed at preventing the possible harassment of acquitted persons in cases where there is not a genuine question of new and compelling evidence, by requiring the personal consent of the Director of Public Prosecutions (DPP) both to the taking of significant steps in the re-opening of investigations – except in urgent cases – and to the making of an application to the Court of Appeal. The DPP will take into account both the strength of the evidence and the public interest in determining whether a re-investigation or application to the Court is appropriate.

42. The new arrangements will apply only in respect of serious offences. These are offences which carry a maximum sentence of life imprisonment, and for which the consequences for victims or for society as a whole are particularly serious. The offences are listed in Schedule 5 to the Act and include, for example, murder, manslaughter and rape. They do not include all offences for which life imprisonment is the maximum punishment, because this would catch a number of common law offences which may not have such serious consequences, and for which a life sentence would rarely be imposed.

43. Where the Court of Appeal quashes an acquittal, a new indictment for the same offence may then be preferred by the prosecuting authorities, and a retrial will follow. The retrial will take account of all the evidence available in the case. The Court of Appeal may refuse to quash an acquittal in cases where the evidence is not new and compelling, or where it is not considered in the interests of justice to proceed with a retrial.

## Part 11 – Evidence

44. Chapter 1 deals with the admissibility in criminal proceedings of evidence of a person's bad character. Under the law as it currently stands, there is an exclusionary rule which prevents the prosecution generally from producing evidence in a trial of a defendant's previous misconduct. This includes the fact that they have previously been convicted of an offence and any other evidence that might show a disposition in that person to break the law or act in particular way. This rule is an exception to the general principle that all relevant evidence is admissible and is itself subject to a number of exceptions. These include the "similar fact rule", which allows the prosecution to rely on evidence of a defendant's previous misconduct as part of its case against him in certain circumstances. There are also statutory exceptions such as section 1(3) of the Criminal Evidence Act 1898, which allows a defendant to be asked questions about his past in cross-examination where he has claimed to be of good character or has himself attacked the character of a prosecution witness or given evidence against a co-defendant. There are, however, no comparable rules governing the introduction of a witness's previous misconduct, which is therefore admissible provided that it is relevant.

45. This area of the law has been the subject of a comprehensive study by the Law Commission, who published a report of their conclusions and recommendations for reform in October 2001: "Evidence of Bad Character in Criminal Proceedings" (Report No. 273). It was also considered by Sir Robin Auld during his Review of the Criminal Courts, which also reported in October 2001. Both offered substantial criticism of the present rules.

46. The Government's approach has been closely informed by both reports and was set out in the Criminal Justice White Paper "Justice for All" (Cm 5563, July 2002). The Act's provisions are intended to provide a comprehensive set of rules for the admissibility of this sort of evidence in respect both of witnesses and defendants. Accordingly, the existing common law rules are abolished and other statute law substantially repealed.

47. Chapter 2 makes further changes to the rules of evidence by reforming the law relating to the admissibility of hearsay evidence in criminal proceedings.

48. The common law rule against the admission of hearsay evidence is generally accepted as meaning that 'an assertion other than one made by a person while giving oral evidence in the proceedings is inadmissible as evidence of any fact or opinion asserted'.

This means that only a statement given by a witness *orally* in court proceedings is admissible as evidence of the facts as they represent them. The main implication of this rule is that witnesses *must* give oral evidence in court from first-hand knowledge, and may not repeat what other people have told them. For example:

- Written records are inadmissible evidence of the matters they contain;
- Witnesses must give oral evidence and a written statement cannot be a substitute for their personal appearance in the witness box;
- Witnesses must give evidence from first hand knowledge and may not repeat what other people have told them; and
- Previous out of court oral statements made by the witness themselves are inadmissible evidence of the matters they contain.

49. There are several exceptions to this rule, some of which are found in common law and some in statute. Both the common law rule and the way in which the exceptions operate, however, have been the subject of considerable criticism.

50. This area of the law was the subject of a Law Commission Report *Evidence in Criminal Proceedings: Hearsay and Related Topics* (Report No 245) in 1997, which included 50 recommendations for reform and incorporated a draft Bill. This area of law was again considered by Sir Robin Auld as part of his Review. Sir Robin Auld concluded that we should move away from the strict rule against the admission of hearsay evidence in criminal proceedings, to a more flexible position where we admit such evidence and instead trust fact-finders to assess the weight of the evidence.

51. The provisions in Chapter 2 of Part 11 are intended, so far as necessary, to codify the law relating to the admissibility of out of court statements in criminal proceedings. They aim to simplify the law and to provide greater certainty as to the circumstances when such evidence will be admitted. The main provisions (in *Sections 114 and 115)* remove the old common law rule against the admission of hearsay evidence and provide that such evidence *will* be admissible (on behalf of the prosecution and defence) provided certain safeguards are met.

52. Chapter 2 also provides the court with an additional statutory discretion to allow an out of court statement to be admitted as evidence where it would be in the interests of justice to do so. In addition, witness's previous statements will be more widely admissible at trial (as proof of the facts contained within). Chapter 3 provides that certain witnesses in serious cases may use their video recorded statements in place of their main evidence.

## Part 12 – Sentencing

53. Chapter 1 sets out general sentencing provisions. Many of these re-enact existing provisions, which are currently contained in the Powers of Criminal Courts (Sentencing) Act 2000.

54. *Sections 142 to 146* make provision for matters to be taken into account in sentencing. These include the purposes of adult sentencing, principles for determining the seriousness of an offence, reduction in sentences for early guilty pleas and aggravating factors where the offence was motivated by the offender's race, religion, disability or sexual orientation. The purposes of sentencing are set out in statute for the first time. They are: punishment, crime reduction, reform and rehabilitation, public protection and reparation.

55. *Sections 147 to 151* specify when community sentences can be used and set out general restrictions on imposing community sentences. *Sections 152 and 153* perform a similar function in relation to custodial sentences. *Sections 154 to 155* amend the existing limits on magistrates' court's powers to impose custodial sentences. *Sections 156 to 160* set out the procedural requirements for imposing community and custodial sentences.

They deal, in particular, with pre-sentence reports and other requirements in the case of mentally disordered offenders. For adult offenders pre-sentence reports are written by the probation service on the basis of their analysis of the offender's behaviour, criminal history and needs. They suggest to the court the kind of punishment and rehabilitation that would be appropriate in each particular case and make recommendations as to the particular sentence that should be passed. In the case of mentally disordered offenders the court has to obtain a medical report before imposing a custodial sanction. *Section 161* provides for pre-sentence drug testing when the court is considering imposing a community sentence or a suspended sentence. The test is intended to help the court to decide whether drug treatment and testing is necessary. *Sections 162 to 165* deal with the court's powers to impose and remit fines. *Section 166* re-enacts existing provisions about mitigation and about dealing with mentally disordered offenders.

56. *Sections 167 to 173* set up the Sentencing Guidelines Council, a new body which will produce sentencing guidelines for all criminal courts and guidelines on the allocation of cases between courts. Sentencing guidelines enable courts to approach sentence in any case from a common starting point. They are also intended to enable practitioners and the public generally to know what that starting point will be. The Act creates a new Council to promulgate those guidelines and provides for the existing Sentencing Advisory Panel to tender its advice to that Council. The Council will create guidelines across a wide range of issues that are relevant to sentencing and Courts will be obliged to take the guidelines into account when deciding a sentence. The Council will be chaired by the Lord Chief Justice and will consist of 7 further judicial members and 4 non-judicial members. In addition, the Home Secretary will appoint an observer who will bring to the Council experience of sentencing policy and the administration of sentences

57. *Section 174* replaces the existing duties on courts to provide reasons for sentence, with a new overarching duty to provide reasons and explain the sentence. The court is required to give reasons if it departs from a recommended guideline. *Section 175* expands the existing duty on the Home Secretary in section 95 of the Criminal Justice Act 1991 to publish information on the effectiveness of sentencing.

58. Chapter 2 provides for community orders for offenders aged 16 or over. There are currently a number of different community orders: community rehabilitation orders, community punishment orders, community punishment and rehabilitation orders, curfew orders, drug treatment and testing orders, drug abstinence orders (being piloted), and exclusion orders (not yet commenced). This Act creates a single generic community sentence, which combines requirements currently available under different community sentences.

59. The range of requirements available with a generic community sentence will be:

- Compulsory (unpaid) work;
- Participation in any specified activities;
- Programmes aimed at changing offending behaviour;
- Prohibition from certain activities;
- Curfew;
- Exclusion from certain areas;
- Residence requirement;
- Mental health treatment (with consent of the offender);
- Drug treatment and testing (with consent of the offender);
- Alcohol treatment (with consent of the offender);
- Supervision;

- Attendance centre requirements (for those under 25).

60. Schedules 8 and 9 make provision for breaches of community sentences and their transfer to Scotland or Northern Ireland.

61. Chapter 3 contains new provisions in relation to short prison sentences of less than 12 months. Currently an offender serving a prison sentence of less than 12 months is released automatically at the half way point of the sentence, and the second half of the sentence is not subject to any licence conditions. Following the recommendations of the Halliday Report 'Making Punishments Work', new sentences of less than 12 months have been developed which are designed to provide a more effective framework within which to address the needs of offenders.

62. *Sections 181 and 182* make provision for the new sentence (described in the Halliday report as "custody plus"), that will replace all short prison sentences of under 12 months (with the exception of intermittent custody). It will be made up of a short period in custody of up to 3 months (to fulfil the punishment purpose of the sentence) followed by a longer period under supervision in the community (to fulfil the reparation and crime reduction purposes of the sentence) of a minimum of 6 months. At the point of sentence the court will specify the lengths of the two parts and attach specific requirements, based upon those available under the generic community sentence, to the supervision part of the sentence so as to address the rehabilitative needs of the offender.

63. If the court deems it appropriate, and the offender consents, the custodial part of the sentence can be served intermittently. *Sections 183 to 186* outline this sentence. Where an intermittent custody order is made the custodial periods will be served in short blocks of a few days at a time, while the licence period runs between the blocks (and may continue after the last custodial period). Intermittent custody will enable offenders to maintain jobs, family ties or education, all of which have been shown to play a part in reducing re-offending. This will be a new type of sentence in England and Wales, although there are similar systems in Europe. It will be piloted in two sites before a decision is made on whether to implement it more widely. If an offender fails to comply with the terms of the community part of the sentence he will be returned to custody. As with all recalls, the Parole Board will decide when he is to be re-released.

64. Schedules 10 and 11 set out the provisions for dealing with revocation and amendment of custody plus and intermittent custody orders, and for their transfer to Scotland and Northern Ireland.

65. *Sections 189 to 194* deal with suspended sentences. At present a custodial sentence can be suspended for between one and two years provided that the offence warrants custody and the suspension is justified by the "exceptional circumstances" of the case. A suspended sentence can be combined with a fine or compensation order, but not with a community sentence (although a supervision order can be attached). The custodial sentence is activated by the committal of another imprisonable offence. This Act replaces this sentence with an amended version which is designed to be more widely available and more effective in correcting offending behaviour. The key change is that the court may suspend a short custodial sentence (as described in *Section 181*) for between six months and two years on condition that the offender undertakes activities in the community. These activities are chosen by the court from the list available under the generic community sentence. If the offender breaches the terms of the suspension the suspended sentence will be activated. The commission of a further offence during the period of suspension will also count as a breach, and the offender's existing suspended sentence will normally be activated when the court sentences him for the new offence. The provisions dealing with breaches of suspended sentences are set out in Schedule 12 and arrangements for their transfer to Scotland or Northern Ireland in Schedule 13.

66. This Act provides the courts with a discretionary power to review an offender's progress under a suspended sentence. Courts already have the power to review drug treatment

and testing orders (see section 54(6) of the Powers of Criminal Courts (Sentencing) Act 2000). The court can amend any requirement or provision of the drug treatment and testing order based on the progress of the offender under the sentence. The court will continue to have this power in relation to a drug treatment and testing requirement of a community sentence. It will also have the power to review the progress of an offender on a suspended sentence, if it chooses, whether or not a drug rehabilitation requirement forms part of the order, and alter the requirements accordingly. This more general power of review is limited to the new suspended sentence in this Act, but may be extended further if it proves successful.

67. Chapter 4 contains the provisions common to community sentences and short prison sentences. *Sections 197 and 198* describe the duties of the "responsible officer". A responsible officer is an employee of the local probation board, an electronic monitoring provider (if electronic monitoring of a curfew or exclusion requirement is the only requirement on the order), and if the offender is under 18 it can be either a probation officer or a Youth Offending Team member. The responsible officer has overall control of an offender on a community sentence or the licence period of a custodial sentence. *Sections 199 to 214* describe in detail the requirements available in relation to community orders, custody plus orders, suspended sentence orders and intermittent custody orders. *Section 215* provides that electronic monitoring can be attached to any of the requirements. *Sections 216 to 220* set out general procedural requirements for community orders and short prison sentences, such as ensuring that people receive relevant information concerning each order. *Sections 221 to 223* set out the powers of the Secretary of State in relation to various requirements, including provisions as to whom copies of relevant orders should be provided to which are set out in Schedule 14.

68. Chapter 5 provides measures for dealing with dangerous offenders. The Halliday report criticised the existing disparate set of provisions for sexual and violent offenders and identified a need for a more coherent sentencing structure to deal with this type of offender. The Act introduces a new scheme of sentences for offenders who have been assessed as dangerous and have committed a specified sexual or violent offence. Under the new scheme, dangerous offenders who have been convicted of a trigger sexual or violent offence (listed in Schedule 15) for which the maximum penalty is between two and ten years will be given an extended sentence (*Section 227*). This sentence will be a determinate sentence served in custody to the half way point. Release during the whole of the second half of the sentence will be on recommendation of the Parole Board. In addition extended supervision periods of up to five years for violent offenders and eight years for sexual offenders must be added to the sentence.

69. If an offender has been assessed as dangerous and has been convicted of a sexual or violent trigger offence (listed in Schedule 15) whose maximum sentence length is ten years or more, he will receive either a sentence of imprisonment for public protection (*Section 225*) or a discretionary life sentence. In cases where the offender has been assessed as dangerous and has been convicted of a trigger offence carrying a maximum sentence of life imprisonment the court must consider the seriousness of the offence when deciding upon which of the two possible sentences to impose. For both sentences the court will specify a minimum term which the offender is required to serve in custody. After this point the offender will remain in prison until the Parole Board is satisfied that their risk has sufficiently diminished for them to be released and supervised in the community. Following release, those serving a sentence of imprisonment for public protection would be able to apply to the Parole Board to have their licence rescinded after ten years had elapsed. Offenders serving a discretionary life sentence would be on licence for the rest of their lives. The Act makes similar provisions for juveniles enabling the sentence of detention for public protection (*Section 226*) and the extended sentence (*Section 228*) to be passed for offenders aged under 18 who have committed a specified sexual or violent offence (listed in Schedule 15) and have been assessed by the courts as dangerous.

70. Chapter 6 deals with the arrangements for prisoners' release on licence, recall to prison following breach of licence requirements, and further re-release. It also contains provisions for calculating remand time, calculating how sentences should be served and drug testing requirements on licence.

71. *Sections 240 to 243* enable the court to deduct any time spent on remand from the custodial part of the sentence that it passes.

72. *Sections 244 to 253* provide for the release of offenders from custody. Under the present system only half of a prison sentence of between 12 months and 4 years has to be served in prison. Following release the offender will be subject to licence conditions until the three-quarter point of his sentence. If the sentence is of 4 years or more then the offender may be released between the half and two thirds point of the sentence subject to a recommendation by the Parole Board. At the two-thirds point release is automatic and the prisoner is subject to licence conditions until the three-quarter point and remains on licence until the end of his sentence.

73. Under the new framework, offenders serving sentences of 12 months or more will be released automatically on licence at the half-way point of their sentence (subject to early release on home detention curfew (HDC) which will remain available). Upon release, the second half of their sentence will be subject to standard licence conditions and any combination of the additional prescribed conditions that the Secretary of State may determine by order. New custodial sentences of 12 months or more will therefore be served in full and licence conditions may be imposed right up to the end of the sentence.

74. If an offender fails to comply with a licence condition or commits an offence on licence he is liable to be recalled to prison, as described in *Sections 254 and 255*. This Act makes recall to custody an executive decision – by the prison and probation services - rather than by the Parole Board, as at present. The offender will have the right of appeal to the Parole Board, and even if the offender chooses not to exercise this right the Parole Board will nonetheless scrutinise all recall decisions, to ensure they are fairly taken. By allowing the Parole Board to focus on assessing decisions of recall, the Act removes the anomaly by which the Parole Board currently both advise on recalls and act as an appeal body against those same recalls.

75. When determining an appeal against recall, or scrutinising the validity of a recall decision, the Parole Board will consider the issue of re-release, as laid out in *Section 256*. It will either set a date for re-release or for a review of re-release a further date for considering re-release if setting a date is not feasible.

76. *Section 257* provides the Secretary of State with the power to add days to prison sentences, under prison rules, where disciplinary offences are committed whilst in custody.

77. *Sections 259 to 262* provide for a new early removal scheme from prison for foreign national prisoners liable to removal from the UK. Eligible prisoners may be removed up to 135 days early provided the custodial part of the sentence is at least 6 weeks and a specified proportion of the sentence has been served. The provisions will apply to all determinate sentence prisoners. The provisions introduce an order-making power to allow the Secretary of State, inter alia, to reduce or increase the reference to 135 days as well as to alter the provisions specifying the minimum custodial part of the sentence and the proportion of the sentence that must have been served. *Section 260* provides that, if a foreign national prisoner who has been removed from prison and from the UK in these circumstances re-enters the UK then he is liable to be detained in pursuance of his sentence for the period he would have served if he had not been removed early from prison or his sentence expiry date, whichever is earlier. *Section 262* gives effect to a new schedule (Schedule 20) which makes provisions for a similar scheme to apply in advance of the commencement of this Act.

78. *Sections 263 and 264* set out the principles for calculating the time offenders must spend in custody and on licence where several sentences are passed on the same or different occasions, and are ordered to be served concurrently (at the same time) or consecutively (one after the other).

79. *Section 266* amends section 64 of the Criminal Justice and Court Services Act 2000 (release on licence etc. drug testing requirements) to require a young offender aged 14 and above, to be tested for specified Class A drugs if a responsible officer believes that the offender is likely to misuse any specified class A drug and that such misuse has caused or contributed to any offence for which he was convicted, or may cause him to commit further offences. An appropriate adult is required to be present during the testing procedure for those under the age of 17. The requirement for a trigger offence to have been committed is removed.

80. Chapter 7 establishes a new scheme under which the court, rather than the Home Secretary, will determine the minimum term to be served in prison by a person convicted of murder. The length of this minimum term is to be determined by reference to a new statutory framework set out in Schedule 21. Once the minimum term has expired, the Parole Board will consider the person's suitability for release, and if appropriate, direct his release. These provisions respond to two court judgements, the judgement of the European Court of Human Rights in May 2002 in *Stafford*, and the judgement of the House of Lords in *Anderson* in November 2002.

81. Chapter 8 contains additional sentencing provisions. One of these relates to deferred sentences. Currently a court can defer passing a sentence pending the good behaviour of the offender, as long as the offender consents and the court believes that deferring the sentence is in the interests of justice. If the offender commits another offence during the deferment period the court will deal with both sentences at once. This Act will require more of the offender on a deferred sentence. The power to defer passing sentence is only exercisable if the offender undertakes to comply with any requirements as to his conduct that the court considers it appropriate to impose. He may have to complete undertakings in the community as set by the court. These can be activities such as reparation to the community. The probation service or other responsible body will monitor the offender's compliance with the requirements and will prepare a report for the court at the point of sentence. Failure to comply with a requirement will result in the offender being brought back to court early for sentence. As now, if the offender commits another offence during the deferment period the court will deal with both sentences at once.

82. *Section 279* introduces Schedule 24 which enables a requirement as to drug treatment and testing to be included in an action plan order or a supervision order.

83. *Sections 280 to 284,* in conjunction with Schedules 25, 26, 27 and 28 make the necessary alterations to the maximum penalties available for certain offences so as to ensure that they are compatible with the new sentencing framework. The Act creates a new sentence of less than 12 months, custody plus, that will replace all short custodial sentences currently available (see *Sections 181 and 182*). The maximum length of a sentence of custody plus, in relation to a single offence, will be 51 weeks. Therefore, in order to ensure that a full sentence of custody plus may be passed for a certain offence, this offence must have a maximum penalty of 51 weeks imprisonment or more. Currently there are a number of offences, triable only in the magistrates' court, that carry maximum penalties of six months imprisonment or less. These penalties will have no practical application under the new sentencing framework, therefore *Sections 280 and 281* make the necessary alterations to the maximum penalties for such offences by either raising them to 51 weeks or lowering them to non custodial penalties. Similarly, *Section 282* makes the necessary alterations to the penalties for certain triable-either-way offences on summary conviction so that they may be compatible with the new sentencing framework. *Section 283* also amends those powers in other legislation that provide for the creation of new summary or triable either way offences, so as to ensure that any offences created under these enabling powers will have maximum penalties

that are compatible with the new sentencing framework. *Section 284* and Schedule 28 increase the penalties for certain drug-related offences.

84. In July 2002, the Government published its Report on the Review of Road Traffic Penalties and proposed to increase the maximum penalties for the offences of causing death by dangerous driving, causing death by careless driving under the influence of drink or drugs and aggravated vehicle taking where the aggravating feature is that, owing to the driving of the vehicle, an accident occurs and death results. Concerns had been expressed in response to the Review about the level of the maximum penalties and some sentences had been passed at, or close to, the maximum. *Section 285* of the Act provides that each of these three offences should have the same maximum penalty of 14 years imprisonment, an increase from 5 years for the aggravated vehicle taking offence and from 10 years for the other two offences. This will provide consistency in approach for driving offences where death results.

85. *Sections 287 to 293* make provision for establishing a mandatory minimum sentence for anyone who is convicted, on indictment, of illegal possession or distribution of prohibited firearms.

86. *Section 299* and Schedule 30 insert two new sections into Part 2 of the Criminal Justice and Court Services Act 2000 which deal with disqualifying unsuitable people from working with children. New *section 29A* extends the court's powers by adding a discretion to make an order if it is satisfied that it is likely a further offence against a child will be committed, even though the sentence threshold specified in the Act is not met. N*ew section 29B* provides that where a court was under a duty to consider the issue of a disqualification order, by virtue of convicting the offender of a relevant offence and passing a sentence which met the threshold specified, but appeared not to have done so, the prosecution may subsequently apply to a senior court for a disqualification order to be made.

87. *Sections 300 and 301* provide a power to impose an unpaid work or curfew requirement on a fine defaulter or to disqualify them from driving, rather than sending them to prison. Schedule 31 sets out the equivalent number of hours of unpaid work or days of curfew in relation to amounts of fine defaulted.

88. Chapter 9 sets out the principal repeals and deals with the interpretation of Part 12.

## Part 13- Miscellaneous

89. *Section 306* amends Schedule 8 to the Terrorism Act 2000.

90. *Section 307* provides for the maximum prison sentences for offences arising from EC Regulations on the protection of wild fauna and flora to be increased from two years to five years.

91. *Section 308* extends the cases in which a defendant in the magistrates' court can plead guilty and be dealt with in his absence.

92. *Sections 309 to 312* extend the scope of statutory preparatory hearings and *sections 313 to 319* make changes to criminal appeal procedures.

93. *Section 320* adds the common law offence of "outraging public decency" to the list of offences at Schedule 1 of the Magistrates' Courts Act 1980. This will have the effect of making it triable summarily, as well as on indictment. At the present time, this offence is triable on indictment only.

94. The Act amends the principal statute governing jury service, the Juries Act 1974, to abolish (except in the case of mentally disordered persons) the categories of ineligibility for, and excusal "as of right" from jury service, currently set out in that Act. This means that certain groups who currently must not, or need not, do jury service, will, when these provisions are brought into force, be required to do so unless they can show good reason

not to. The Act also makes amendments to the category of those disqualified from jury service to reflect developments in sentencing legislation, including those made by the Act itself.

95. *Sections 322 and 323* provide for an Individual Support Order, aimed at preventing further anti-social behaviour, to be available for use where an anti-social behaviour order has already been granted against a person under 18. The Individual Support Order may require the young person to undertake activities to tackle the underlying causes of their anti-social behaviour.

96. *Section 324* and Schedule 34 amend the Parenting Order provisions in the Crime and Disorder Act 1998 and the Referral Order provisions in the Powers of Criminal Courts (Sentencing) Act 2000 to enable courts to make a Parenting Order when a Referral Order is being made. In such cases the court must first obtain a report indicating requirements proposed for the Order, the reasons for these, and, where the offender is aged under 16 years, information about the family circumstances. If a Parenting Order is not made at the same time as a Referral Order, the provision will also allow Youth Offending Panels to refer parents to the court where a parent has failed to attend panel meetings. The measure will allow Parenting Orders to be issued to parents of first time offenders who plead guilty.

97. *Sections 325 to 327* build upon the provisions in the Criminal Justice and Court Services Act 2000 that place a requirement upon the responsible authority to establish arrangements for the management of certain high-risk offenders in the community. The responsible authority was defined as the local probation board and the chief officer of police and the Act extends this definition to include the Minister of State exercising functions in relation to prisons. The Act also places a new duty upon certain named bodies (e.g. local housing authorities and health authorities) to co-operate with the responsible authority as necessary to enable it to undertake its statutory duties effectively. The Act requires the responsible authority to regularly review its effectiveness in undertaking its duties and to recruit two lay advisers to oversee this task.

98. *Section 328* and Schedule 35 amend Part 5 of the Police Act 1997 which sets out the statutory framework under which the Criminal Records Bureau (CRB) provides criminal record disclosures for employment vetting purposes. The changes give effect to a number of the recommendations of the Independent Review Team appointed in September 2002 to take a fundamental look at the operations of the CRB. The amendments to the 1997 Act are designed to improve the efficiency and effectiveness of the CRB so that it can provide greater protection for children and vulnerable adults whilst ensuring that the disclosure process does not act as a bar to speedy recruitment.

99. Section 329 makes new provision about cases where a person who has been convicted of an imprisonable criminal offence takes civil action for damages for trespass to the person against the victim of the offence or against a third party who has intervened, for example to protect the victim or to protect or recover property. It requires that, where a claimant convicted of an imprisonable offence wishes to sue someone for damages for a trespass to the person which is committed on the same occasion as the offence, he must first obtain the permission of the court. Permission may only be given if there is evidence that certain conditions relating to the defendant's perceptions and reasons for doing the act which amounted to trespass to the claimant's person are not met, or that in all the circumstances the defendant's act was grossly disproportionate. The defendant will not be liable at the trial if he can prove that the relevant conditions are met and that in all the circumstances the action was not grossly disproportionate.

## TERRITORIAL APPLICATION

100. The Act's effect in Wales is the same as in England. It contains no provisions which relate exclusively to Wales, or affect the National Assembly for Wales.

## COMMENTARY ON SECTIONS

### Part 1: Amendments of Police and Criminal Evidence Act 1984

#### *Section 1: Extension of powers to stop and search*

101. This Section extends the definition of prohibited articles under section 1 of the Police and Criminal Evidence Act 1984 (PACE) so that it includes articles made, adapted or intended for use in causing criminal damage. It does this by amending the list of offences in section 1(8) of PACE to include offences under section 1 of the Criminal Damage Act 1971. The effect is to give police officers power to stop and search where they have reasonable suspicion that a person is carrying, for example, a paint spray can which they intend to use in producing graffiti.

102. Section 1(1) of the Criminal Damage Act 1971 makes it a criminal offence for a person to destroy or damage any property belonging to another without lawful excuse if he intends to destroy or damage that property or is reckless as to whether that property would be destroyed or damaged. Section 1(2) of that Act creates a related offence of destroying or damaging property with intent to endanger life.

#### *Section 2: Warrants to enter and search*

103. This Section enhances the powers of persons authorised to accompany constables executing search warrants. Section 16(2) of PACE allows a search warrant to authorise persons to accompany any constable who is executing the warrant.

104. New subsection (2A) provides that any such person has the same powers as the constable whom he is accompanying in relation to executing the warrant and seizing anything to which the warrant relates. Subsection (2B) ensures that the person can only exercise these powers when he is accompanied by a constable and under that constable's supervision.

105. This addition to PACE will ensure that persons who accompany police officers in the execution of warrants can play an effective role in searching and seizure. For example, it will often be necessary for someone who is expert in computing or financial matters to assist a constable in searching premises where particular types of records are likely to be found. This provision enables such experts to take an active role in carrying out searches and in seizing material, rather than being present in a merely advisory or clerical capacity.

#### *Section 3: Arrestable offences*

106. Section 3 add, the following offences to the list of specified offences which are arrestable offences:-

- the offence of making a false application for a passport;
- the offence of possession of cannabis or cannabis resin (which are controlled drugs);
- the offence of making a false application for a driving licence, etc;

In relation to drugs, this provision allows the police to continue to arrest without a warrant persons in possession of cannabis or cannabis resin following the drugs' reclassification from Class B to Class C under the Misuse of Drugs Act 1971. The date of reclassification is 29 January 2004.

#### *Section 4: Bail elsewhere than at a police station*

107. This Section amends section 30 of PACE to enable police officers to grant bail to persons following their arrest without the need to take them to a police station. It provides the police with additional flexibility following arrest and the scope to remain

on patrol where there is no immediate need to deal with the person concerned at the station. It is intended to allow the police to plan their work more effectively by giving them new discretion to decide exactly when and where an arrested person should attend at a police station for interview.

108. *Subsections (2) to (6)* amend section 30 to take account of the new power to grant bail. The basic principle remains that a person arrested by a constable or taken into custody by a constable after being arrested by someone else must be taken by a constable to a police station as soon as practicable. However, this is subject to the provisions dealing with release either on bail or without bail.

109. *Subsection (4)* expands existing section 30(7) of PACE to provide that a constable must release the person concerned without bail if, before reaching the police station, he is satisfied that there are no grounds for keeping him under arrest or releasing him on bail under the new provisions.

110. *Subsection (5)* replaces existing sections 30(10) and (11) of PACE to make it clear that a constable may delay taking an arrested person to a police station or releasing him on bail if that person's presence elsewhere is necessary for immediate investigative purposes. The reason for such delay must be recorded either on arrival at the police station or when the person is released on bail.

111. *Subsection (6)* adapts some existing exclusions in section 30(12) of PACE to take account of the new arrangements for granting bail.

112. *Subsection (7)* inserts a series of new sections into PACE which provide police officers with the framework of powers to grant bail following arrest. *Section 30A* provides that a constable has power to release a person on bail at any time prior to arrival at a police station. It specifies that the person released on bail must be required to attend a police station and that any police station may be specified for that purpose. No other requirement may be imposed on the person as a condition of bail.

113. *Section 30B* requires that the constable must give the person bailed a written notice, prior to release, setting out the offence for which he was arrested and the ground on which that arrest was made. It must tell him that he is required to attend a police station and may specify the relevant station and time. If these details are not specified in that initial notice, they must be set out in a further notice provided to the person at a later stage. Police have the capacity to change the specified station or time if necessary and the person concerned must be given written notice of any such change.

114. *Section 30C* contains various supplemental provisions. *Section 30C(1)* allows for the police to remove a requirement to attend a police station to answer bail, provided they give the person a written notice to that effect.

115. *Section 30C(2)* makes it clear that where someone attends a non-designated police station to answer bail following arrest he must be released or taken to a designated police station within 6 hours of his arrival. Designated stations are those nominated by chief officers as suitable for detention purposes and are generally stations with appropriate facilities to cater for extended periods of custody.

116. *Section 30C(3)* specifies that nothing in the Bail Act 1976 applies in relation to bail under these new arrangements. The law which applies to this form of bail is set out in PACE as amended by the Act.

117. *Section 30C(4)* clarifies that a person who has been released under the new bail provisions may be rearrested if new evidence justifying that has come to light since their release.

118. *Section 30D* deals with failure to answer to bail under the new arrangements. *Section 30D(1)* allows a constable to arrest without a warrant a person who fails to attend the police station at the specified time. *Section 30D(2)* states that a person arrested in

such circumstances must be taken to a police station as soon as practicable after the arrest. *Section 30D(3)* defines the station relevant for the purposes of subsection (1) as whichever station is defined in the latest notice provided to the person concerned. *Section 30D(4)* clarifies that such an arrest for failure to answer to bail is to be treated as an arrest for an offence for certain PACE purposes.

### *Section 5: **Drug Testing for under eighteens***

119. Section 57 of the Criminal Justice and Court Services Act 2000 inserted new provisions in the Police and Criminal Evidence Act 1984 (PACE), enabling custody officers after charge, to detain a person to enable a sample to be taken to test for the presence of any specified class A drug, subject to the conditions detailed in section 63B of PACE. The conditions include that the person concerned has attained the age of 18. The provisions currently apply only within certain police areas where section 57 has been brought into force.

120. *Section 5* amends these provisions in PACE (in respect of section 63B and section 38) to enable persons under the age of 18 to be tested for specified Class A drugs and for custody officers to detain a person after charge to enable a sample to be taken for that purpose. The person concerned must have attained the age of 14. The Section also makes provision for an appropriate adult to be present during the testing procedure in the case of a person who is under 17 years old. The Secretary of State is given power by order (under the draft affirmative procedure) to change the minimum age.

### *Section 6: **Use of telephones for review of police detention***

121. This provision enables reviews of the continuing need for detention without charge carried out under section 40 of PACE to be conducted over the telephone rather than in person at the police station. Such reviews have to be carried out by an officer of at least inspector rank. PACE currently only allows telephone reviews where it is not reasonably practicable for the reviewing officer to be present at the police station.

122. New *section 40A(1)* allows a review to be carried out by means of a discussion over the telephone with one or more persons at the police station where the arrested person is held. In practice, the reviewing officer would normally speak to the custody officer at the police station, as well as to the detained person or their legal representative if they wanted to exercise their right to make representations about the continuing need for detention.

New *section 40A(2)* specifies that telephone reviews are not applicable where it is reasonably practicable to carry out the review using video conferencing facilities in accordance with regulations under section 45A of PACE. Where such video conferencing facilities are readily available, it is appropriate that they should be used.

### *Section 7: **Limits on periods of detention without charge***

123. This provision extends the scope for an officer of at least superintendent rank to authorise detention without charge up to a maximum of 36 hours. As the law currently stands, an officer of superintendent rank or above can extend detention without charge up to an overall period of 36 hours if satisfied that detention is necessary to secure, preserve or obtain evidence, that the investigation is being conducted diligently and expeditiously and that the relevant offence is a serious arrestable offence. Serious arrestable offences are defined in section 116 of PACE and are either offences which are specified to be "always serious" (e.g. murder) or offences which give rise to serious consequences.

124. The amendment will allow detention to be extended for up to an overall period of 36 hours where the relevant offence is an arrestable offence, provided the other conditions are satisfied. Section 24 of PACE defines an arrestable offence as (a) any offence for which the sentence is fixed by law, (b) any offence for which a sentence of

imprisonment of 5 years or more may be imposed or (c) any offence specifically listed in Schedule 1A to PACE.

125. This broadened capacity for extended detention without charge will assist the police in dealing effectively with a range of offences, for example robbery, where it will sometimes be extremely difficult or impossible to complete the necessary investigatory processes within 24 hours.

### *Section 8: **Property of detained persons***

126. This provision removes the requirement on the custody officer, currently in section 54(1) of PACE, to record or cause to be recorded everything a detained person has with him on entering custody. The custody officer will still be under a duty to ascertain what the person has with him, but the nature and detail of any recording will be at the custody officer's discretion. He will also have discretion as to whether the record is kept as part of the custody record or as a separate record. This seeks to reduce the serious burden on officers which can arise from recording large volumes of property. Clearly, it will still be necessary to make records, not least to ensure against claims that property has been mishandled or removed. However, it will now be open to the police to make judgements about how to balance the need for recording against the amount of administrative work involved.

### *Section 9: **Taking fingerprints without consent***

127. This Section extends the circumstances in which the police may take a person's fingerprints without consent to include taking fingerprints from a person arrested for a recordable offence and detained in a police station.

128. Section 61 of PACE currently provides powers for taking fingerprints from those in police detention without consent in the following circumstances:

- following charge with a recordable offence or notification that a suspect will be reported for such an offence;
- on the authority of an inspector, which can only be given where the officer has reasonable grounds for believing the suspect is involved in a criminal offence and the fingerprints will tend to confirm or disprove his involvement or facilitate the ascertainment of his identity;
- an authorisation may only be given for the purpose of facilitating the ascertainment of the person's identity where the person has either refused to identify themselves or the authorising officer has reasonable grounds to suspect they are not who they claim to be.

129. Fingerprints may also be taken from a person convicted of a recordable offence or cautioned, warned or reprimanded in respect of such an offence.

130. *Subsection (2)* replaces the existing provisions about the taking of fingerprints on the authority of an Inspector with a wider power to take fingerprints from any person detained in consequence of his arrest for a recordable offence.

131. The existing requirement to give a person whose fingerprints are taken without consent reasons for doing so and for recording the reason as soon as practical applies to the new power (see subsection (5) of section 9).

132. This amendment to section 61 of PACE will prevent persons who come into police custody and who may be wanted on a warrant or for questioning on other matters from avoiding detection by giving the police a false name and address. Using Livescan technology, which enables the police to take fingerprints electronically and which is linked to the national fingerprint database (NAFIS), the police will be able to confirm a person's identity whilst he is still in police detention if his fingerprints have been taken

previously. It will also assist in enabling vulnerable or violent people to be identified more quickly and dealt with more effectively. A speculative search of the fingerprint crime scene database will also reveal if the person may have been involved in other crimes.

### *Section 10: Taking non-intimate samples without consent*

133. This Section extends the circumstances in which the police may take without consent a non-intimate sample from a person in police detention to include taking such a sample from a person arrested for a recordable offence.

134. Section 63 of PACE provides powers for taking a non-intimate sample without consent from a person in the following circumstances:

- following charge with a recordable offence or notification that the person will be reported for such an offence;
- if the person is in police detention (or is being held in custody by the police on the authority of a court), on the authority of an inspector which can only be given where the officer has reasonable grounds for believing the suspect is involved in a recordable offence and the sample will tend to confirm or disprove his involvement;
- following conviction for a recordable offence.

135. In relation to a person in police detention, *subsections (2) and (3)* replace the existing provisions about the taking of a non-intimate sample on the authority of an inspector with a wider power to take a non-intimate sample from any person in police detention in consequence of his arrest for a recordable offence. This is conditional on him not having had a sample of the same type and from the same part of the body taken already in the course of the investigation or if one has that it proved insufficient for the analysis.

136. The new power is available whether or not the sample is required for the investigation of an offence in which the person is suspected of being involved. But of course the police will be able to use the new power to obtain samples in cases where under the present law an inspector's authorisation would be given (for example, in a rape investigation, to obtain a foot impression, a hair sample and a mouth swab).

137. The existing requirement to give a person from whom a non-intimate sample is taken without consent the reason for doing so and for recording the reason as soon as practicable applies to the new power. (see subsection (5) of Section 10).

138. The amendments do not affect the existing powers to take samples from persons held in custody by the police on the authority of a court.

139. DNA profiles extracted from non-intimate samples taken from arrested persons will be added to the samples already held on the National DNA Database and checked for matches with DNA taken from crime scenes.

### *Section 11: Codes of practice*

140. This section makes fundamental changes to the process for establishing and amending codes of practice under PACE. At present there are codes covering stop and search, searching of premises, detention, identification, and the recording of interviews. The amendments provide for a less bureaucratic and more targeted consultation process for new and revised codes and for a simpler process of seeking parliamentary approval for minor or straightforward changes to existing codes. The amendment to section 67 of PACE will maintain the requirement for an order bringing a new code into operation to be laid before Parliament and approved by each House.

141. *Subsection (1)* establishes a new procedure whereby orders bringing revisions into operation to the codes may be either laid before Parliament or subject to the draft affirmative procedure. The Government has undertaken (see Hansard, 7 July 2003, col.

45) to be bound by the advice of the Home Affairs Select Committee on the appropriate procedure to be followed for proposed changes.

142. *Subsections (2) to (4)*amend the procedure for making and revising codes of practice applicable to the military police to require codes and revisions simply to be laid before Parliament. .

### *Section 12: Amendments related to Part 1*

143. This section introduces Schedule 1, which deals with amendments related to this Part of the Act.

## Part 2 : Bail

### *Section 13: Grant and conditions of bail*

144. *Subsection (1)* makes a number of changes to section 3(6) of the Bail Act 1976 to enable bail conditions to be imposed for a defendant's own protection or welfare, in the same circumstances that he or she might have been remanded in custody for that purpose.

145. *Subsection (2)* makes similar changes to section 3A(5), and *subsection (3)* to paragraph 8(1) of Part 1 of Schedule 1 to the 1976 Act.

146. *Subsection (4)* amends paragraph 5 of Part 2 of Schedule 1 to the Bail Act 1976 so that, where a defendant charged with a non-imprisonable offence is arrested under section 7, bail may be refused only if the court is satisfied that there are substantial grounds for believing that if released on bail (whether subject to conditions or not) he or she would fail to surrender to custody, commit an offence whilst on bail, or interfere with witnesses or otherwise obstruct the course of justice.

### *Section 14: Offences committed on bail*

147. *Subsection (1)* requires the court to refuse bail to an adult defendant who was on bail in criminal proceedings at the date of the offence, unless the court is satisfied that there is no significant risk that he would commit an offence if released on bail. This replaces paragraph 2A of Part I of Schedule 1 of the Bail Act 1976 (which provides that a defendant need not be granted bail if he was on bail at the time of the alleged offence).

148. *Subsection (2)* adds a new paragraph 9AA to Part 1 of Schedule 1 to the Bail Act 1976, which provides that where a defendant under the age of 18 is on bail in criminal proceedings on the date an offence was committed particular weight can be given to this fact when the court is deciding whether he or she would be likely to re-offend if released on bail.

### *Section 15: Absconding by persons released on bail*

149. *Subsection (1)* requires the court to refuse bail to an adult defendant who failed without reasonable cause to surrender to custody in answer to bail in the same proceedings, unless the court is satisfied that there is no significant risk that he would so fail if released.

150. *Subsection (2)* requires the court, in the case of defendants under 18, to give particular weight to the fact that they have failed to surrender to bail, in assessing the risk of future absconding.

151. *Subsection (3)* disapplies section 127 of the Magistrates' Court Act 1980 (which prevents summary proceedings from being instituted more than 6 months after the commission of an offence) in respect of offences under section 6 of the Bail Act, and instead provides that such an offence may not be tried unless an information is laid either within 6 months of the commission of the offence, or within three months of the defendant's surrender to custody, arrest or court appearance in respect of that offence.

This will ensure that a defendant cannot escape being prosecuted for the Bail Act offence merely by succeeding in absconding for more than six months.

### *Section 16: Appeal to Crown Court*

152. *Section 16* creates a new right of appeal to the Crown Court against the imposition by magistrates of certain conditions of bail. The conditions which may be challenged in this way are requirements relating to residence, provision of a surety or giving a security, curfew, electronic monitoring or contact. This complements the removal by *Section 17* of the existing High Court power to entertain such appeals.

### *Section 17: Appeals to the High Court*

153. *Section 17* abolishes the jurisdiction of the High Court in respect of bail where it duplicates that of the Crown Court.

### *Section 18: Appeal by prosecution*

154. *Section 18* amends section 1 of the Bail (Amendment) Act 1993 so that the prosecution's right of appeal to the Crown Court against a decision by magistrates to grant bail is extended to cover all imprisonable offences.

### *Section 19: Drug users: restriction on bail*

155. Evidence suggests that there is a link between drug addiction and offending. In addition, it is widely accepted that many abusers of drugs fund their misuse through acquisitive crime. There is thus a real concern that if such offenders who have been charged with an imprisonable offence are placed on bail, they will merely re-offend in order to fund their drug use.

156. Under this Section, an alleged offender aged 18 or over who has been charged with an imprisonable offence will not be granted bail (unless the court is satisfied that there is no significant risk of his committing an offence while on bail), where the three conditions below exist:

(i) there is drug test evidence that the person has a specified Class A drug in his body (by way of a lawful test obtained under section 63B of the Police and Criminal Evidence Act 1984 or Section 161 of this Act);

(ii) either the offence is a drugs offence associated with a specified Class A drug or the court is satisfied that there are substantial grounds for believing that the misuse of a specified Class A drug caused or contributed to that offence or provided its motivation; and

(iii) the person does not agree to undergo an assessment as to his dependency upon or propensity to misuse specified Class A drugs or, has undergone such an assessment but does not agree to participate in any relevant follow-up offered.

157. The assessment will be carried out by a suitably qualified person, who will have received training in the assessment of drug problems. If an assessment or follow-up is proposed and agreed to, it will be a condition of bail that they be undertaken. The provision can only apply in areas where appropriate assessment and treatment facilities are in place.

### *Section 20: Supplementary amendments to the Bail Act 1976*

158. *Section 20* makes supplementary amendments to the Bail Act 1976.

### *Section 21: Interpretation of Part 2*

159. *Section 21* defines various terms used in this Part of the Act.

## Part 3: Conditional Cautions

### *Section 22: Conditional cautions*

160. *Section 22* defines a conditional caution and provides that it may be given to an adult offender if the five requirements in *section 23* are met. The conditions which may be imposed are restricted to those aimed at reparation for the offence, or at the rehabilitation of the offender. A conditional caution may be given by an authorised person as defined in subsection (4).

### *Section 23: The five requirements*

161. *Section 23* sets out the requirements which need to be met for a conditional caution to be given. The requirements are that there is evidence against the offender; that a 'relevant prosecutor' (as defined in *section 27)* considers that the evidence would be sufficient to charge him or her and that a conditional caution should be given; that the offender admits the offence; that the offender has been made aware of what the caution (and failure to comply with it) would mean; and that he or she signs a document containing details of the offence, the admission, the offender's consent to the caution, and the conditions imposed.

### *Section 24: Failure to comply with the conditions*

162. *Section 24* provides that if the offender fails without reasonable excuse to satisfy the conditions attached to the conditional caution he or she may be prosecuted for the offence. If proceedings are commenced the document referred to in *Section 23* is admissible in evidence, and the conditional caution ceases to have effect.

### *Section 25: Code of practice*

163. This section makes provision for the Home Secretary, with the consent of the Attorney General, to publish a Code of Practice setting out the criteria for giving conditional cautions, how they are to be given and who may give them, the conditions which may be imposed and for what period, and arrangements for monitoring compliance.

164. The Home Secretary is required to publish the Code in draft and to consider any representations regarding it. The completed Code must then be laid before Parliament.

### *Section 26: Assistance of National Probation Service*

165. *Section 26* amends the Criminal Justice and Court Services Act 2000 to extend the statutory duties of the National Probation Service to cover offenders who are given (or being considered for) a conditional caution.

### *Section 27: Interpretation of Part 3*

166. *Section 27* defines various terms used in this Part of the Act.

## Part 4: Charging Etc

### *Section 28: Charging or release of persons in police detention*

167. *Section 28* introduces *Schedule 2* which makes additional provision for the charging or release of people in police detention. It amends section 37 of the Police and Criminal Evidence Act 1984 and inserts new sections 37A-37D. New section 37A enables the Director of Public Prosecutions to issue guidance to which custody officers are to have regard in deciding whether, in cases where they consider that there is sufficient evidence to charge a suspect, they should release the suspect without charge but on bail, release him or her without charge and without bail, or charge him.

168. It is envisaged that the DPP's guidance will set out the circumstances in which it will be appropriate for the police to charge or otherwise deal with a suspect without reference to the Crown Prosecution Service; this is likely to include minor cases (such as the majority of road traffic offences), cases where there is an admission by the suspect and which could be disposed of by the magistrates' court, and cases where there is a need to bring the suspect before a court with a view to seeking a remand in custody. In other cases it will be appropriate for the police to release the suspect without charge but on bail while (as required by section 37B) the case is referred to the CPS.

169. Section 37B provides that, if a suspect is released without charge but on bail, it is then for the CPS to determine, if they agree that the evidence is sufficient, whether the suspect should be charged, and if so with what offence; or whether he should be given a caution (and if so in respect of what offence). The suspect is then to be charged, cautioned, or informed in writing that he is not to be prosecuted.

170. Section 37C makes provision for dealing with breach of any conditions attached to police bail granted pending the CPS decision as to charge. *Paragraph 5 of Schedule 2* amends section 46A of the Police and Criminal Evidence Act 1984 to confer a power of arrest on reasonable suspicion that bail conditions have been broken. *Paragraph 6(3)* of that Schedule amends section 47(1A) of that Act to enable conditions to be imposed where a person is released on bail pending consultation with the CPS.

### *Section 29:* ***New method of instituting proceedings***

171. This section provides for a new method of instituting criminal proceedings which is available to a public prosecutor as defined in subsection (5). It consists in the issue to the person to be prosecuted of a written charge, together with a written requirement ('a requisition') for him or her to appear before a magistrates' court to answer to the charge.

172. *Subsection (3)* requires the written charge and the requisition to be served on the person named and to be copied to the court.

173. *Subsection (4)* prohibits public prosecutors from laying an information for the purpose of obtaining the issue of a summons under section 1 of the Magistrates' Courts Act 1980. They may still do so, however, for the purpose of obtaining the issue of a warrant (Section*30(4)*).

### *Section 30:* ***Further provision about new method***

174. This section makes further provisions about the new method of instituting proceedings as described in *section 29*.

175. *Subsection (1)* provides that rules of court may be made as necessary especially in relation to the form, content, recording, authentication and service of written charges or requisitions.

176. *Subsection (4)* provides that nothing in *section 29* affects the power of a person who is not a public prosecutor to lay an information for the purpose of obtaining the issue of a summons under section 1 of the Magistrates' Courts Act, or the power to charge a person whilst he or she is in custody.

### *Section 31:* ***Removal of requirement to substantiate information on oath***

177. *Section 31* abolishes the need for applications for warrants under section 1 of the Magistrates' Court Act 1980 to be substantiated on oath.

## Part 5: **Disclosure**

178. This Part amends some of the provisions in the Criminal Procedure and Investigations Act 1996 (the 1996 Act) that govern the disclosure of unused prosecution material to the defence and the provision of a defence case statement.

### *Section 32: **Initial duty of disclosure by prosecutor***

179. This Section amends section 3 of the 1996 Act and introduces a new objective single test for the disclosure of unused prosecution material to the defence. It replaces the current two tests that apply at the primary and secondary disclosure stages of the present scheme.

180. The new test will require the prosecutor to disclose to the accused:

> "‘….any prosecution material which has not previously been disclosed to the accused and which might reasonably be considered capable of undermining the case for the prosecution against the accused, or of assisting the case for the accused."

### *Section 33: **Defence disclosure***

181. This Section amends the defence disclosure requirements in section 5 of the 1996 Act.

182. *Subsection (1)* amends section 5 of the 1996 Act to provide for the cross service of defence statements following an order of the court. The court may make such an order of its own motion or on the application of any party (new *sub-section 5(B)*).

183. *Subsection (2)* inserts a new section 6A in the 1996 Act. The new section prescribes the content of a defence statement. It replaces subsections (6) to (9) of section 5 of the 1996 Act (which are repealed).

184. At present the accused is required to set out in general terms the nature of his defence. The effect of the new section is to require the accused to provide a more detailed defence statement. The present requirements contained in section 5(6)(b) and (c) of the 1996 Act are replicated in the new section 6A(1)(b) and (c) and the alibi notification provisions in section 5(7) and (8) are replicated in the new section 6A(2) and (3). The main changes are that the accused will, in the future, be required to set out the nature of his defence, including any particular defences on which he intends to rely, and indicate any points of law he wishes to take. Details of alibi witnesses must include the witness's date of birth.

185. *Subsection (1)* of the new section 6A defines a defence statement for the purposes of Part 1 of the 1996 Act. The accused will be required to provide a written statement setting out the nature of his defence, including any particular defences on which he intends to rely. The statement must also indicate any facts on which the accused takes issue with the prosecution, setting out in respect of which matter the reason why he takes issue with the prosecution and indicating any point of law he wishes to take, including the admissibility of evidence and abuse of process points, and any authority on which he intends to rely for that purpose.

186. *Subsection (2)* of the new section 6A provides that if the statement discloses an alibi, the accused must include particulars of the alibi in the statement. These are to include the name, address and date of birth of any witness the accused believes is able to give evidence in support of the alibi, if the accused knows these details, when the defence statement is given. If the accused does not have this information, the particulars are to include any information in his possession that might assist in identifying or finding any such witness.

187. *Subsection (3)* of the new section 6A defines evidence in support of an alibi for the purpose of section 6A as evidence tending to show that by reason of the presence of the accused at a particular place or in a particular area at a particular time, he was not, or was unlikely to have been, at the place where the offence is alleged to have been committed at the time of its alleged commission. This definition reproduces the definition of evidence in support of an alibi given in section 11(8) of the Criminal Justice Act 1967.

188. *Subsection (4)* of the new section 6A gives the Secretary of State power to prescribe in regulations further details that are to be contained in defence statements. Such regulations will be subject to the affirmative resolution procedure.

189. *Subsection (3)* of the Section inserts a new Section 6B in to the 1996 Act which requires the accused to provide an updated defence statement within a period specified in regulations made under section 12 of the 1996 Act. However, if the accused has nothing to add to his earlier defence statement, he may instead give a written statement to that effect.

190. Updated defence case statements must comply with the requirements applicable to defence statements.

191. *Subsections (5)* and *(6)* of the new section 6B provide for the cross service of updated statements following an order of the court (made either of its own motion or on application by any party). This mirrors new sub section (5B) of section 5 of the 1996 Act (inserted by Section 28(1)) that provides for the cross service of the initial statement.

### *Section 34*: ***Notification of intention to call defence witnesses***

192. This Section inserts a new section 6C in the 1996 Act which imposes a new requirement on the accused to serve, before the trial, a notice giving details of any witnesses he intends to call to give evidence at his trial. Details of the witnesses' name, address and date of birth must be given to the court and the prosecutor within a time limit specified in regulations made under section 12 of the 1996 Act. If the address is not known, the accused must provide any information that might assist in identifying or finding the witness. The Section does not require the accused to provide advance notice that he personally intends, or does not intend, to give evidence at the trial.

193. *Subsection (2)* of the new section 6C provides that if details of any alibi witnesses have already been provided as part of the defence statement in accordance with new section 6A(2), further details do not have to given under this provision.

194. *Subsection (4)* of the new section 6C requires the accused to give an amended notice if he subsequently decide to call a witness who is not in the notice, decides not to call someone who is on the list or discovers any information on the whereabouts of the witness.

### *Section 35*: ***Notification of names of experts instructed by defendant***

195. This Section inserts a new section 6D into the 1996 Act, which imposes a new requirement on the accused to serve, before the trial, a notice giving details of the name and address of any expert witness consulted. A notice will be required in respect of each expert consulted.

196. *Subsection (2)* of the new section 6D provides that if details of the expert have already been provided under new section 6C (notification of intention to call defence witnesses), a notice is not required under this section.

### *Section 36*: ***Further provisions about defence disclosure***

197. This Section inserts a new section 6E into the 1996 Act.

198. *Subsection (1)* of new section 6E provides that a defence statement served under sections 5,6 or 6B of the 1996 Act on behalf of an accused, by his solicitor, is deemed to have been given on the authority of the accused, unless the contrary is proved.

199. *Subsections (2)* and *(3)* of the new section 6E provides that where it appears to the judge at a pre trial hearing (as defined in Part 4 of the 1996 Act) that the accused has not fully complied with the requirements set out in sections 5 (defence statement), 6B

(updated defence statement) or 6C (witness list), the judge must warn him that there is the possibility of comment being made or inferences being drawn.

200. *Subsections (4), (5)* and *(6)* of section 6E apply where there is a trial before judge and jury. They enable the judge, either of his own motion or on the application of any party, to give to the jury a copy of the defence statement and, if he does so, to direct that it be edited to exclude any inadmissible material. The defence statement that is given to the jury is the updated defence statement where this has been provided. Where no updated defence statement has been given it is the initial defence statement.

### *Section 37: **Continuing duty of disclosure by prosecutor***

201. This Section inserts a new section 7A in the 1996 Act. The new section 7A replaces the existing sections 7 and 9 of the 1996 Act (which are repealed). The new section 7A imposes a continuing duty on prosecutors to disclose unused material.

202. *Subsection (1)* of the new section 7A provides that the section applies at all times after the prosecutor has provided initial prosecution disclosure under section 3, or has purported to do so. This duty continues until the accused is acquitted, convicted or the prosecutor decides not to continue with the case.

203. *Subsection (2)* of the new section 7A requires the prosecutor to keep under review the question of whether there is any material that meets the new disclosure test in set out in section 3 (material that might reasonably be considered capable of undermining the case for the prosecution or of assisting the case for the accused and has not been disclosed to the accused).

204. *Subsection (3)* of the new section 7A provides that if there is any such material the prosecutor must disclose it to the accused as soon as is reasonably practicable or within any time limit specified in regulations made under section 12 of the 1996 Act.

205. *Subsection (4)* of the new section 7A provides that when complying with the requirement to review the unused prosecution material the prosecutor must take account of the state of affairs as it stands at the time, including the prosecution case.

206. *Subsection (5)* of the new section 7A provides that where the prosecutor receives a defence statement served under sections 5, 6 or 6B and as a result of that statement is required to make further disclosure in accordance with section 7A, he must do so within the relevant period specified in regulations made under section 12 of the 1996 Act or give a written statement that that no disclosure is required.

207. *Subsection (6)* of the new section 7A defines prosecution material for the purposes of the section as material which is in the prosecutor's possession, or which he has been allowed to inspect in pursuance with a Code of Practice issued under Part 2 of the 1996 Act.

208. *Subsection (7)* of the new section 7A provides that the prosecutor should disclose material under this section as he does so when carrying out initial prosecution disclosure in accordance with section 3 of the 1996 Act.

209. *Subsection (8)* of the new section 7A provides that material must not be disclosed to the accused under this section if the court, on application by the prosecutor concludes that it is not in the public interest to disclose it, and has ordered accordingly.

210. *Subsection (9)* of the new section 7A provides that material must not be disclosed to the accused under this section if disclosure is prohibited under section 17 of the Regulation of Investigatory Powers Act 2000.

### *Section 38: Application by defence for disclosure*

211. This Section replaces subsections (1) and (2) of section 8 the 1996 Act. Section 8 enables the accused to apply to the court for further disclosure of unused prosecution material if certain conditions are met.

212. *New subsection (1)* of section 8 provides that the section applies when the defence has given a defence statement under sections 5, 6 or 6 B and the prosecutor has complied with his continuing duty to disclose or purported to comply with it or has failed to comply with it.

213. *New subsection (2)* of section 8 enables the accused to apply to the court for an order requiring the prosecutor to disclose material, to the accused, if the accused has reasonable cause to believe that there is prosecution material that should have been, but has not been, disclosed to the accused pursuant to the prosecutor's continuing duty to disclose.

### *Section 39: Faults in defence disclosure*

214. This Section substitutes a new section 11 for existing section 11 of the 1996 Act. The new section 11 extends the existing list of defence disclosure failures and removes the leave requirement for making comment in respect of some of these.

215. New section 11 provides that a court or jury may draw inferences from certain faults in relation to disclosure by the accused in deciding whether he is guilty.

216. *Subsection (1)* of section 11 provides that this section applies in three sets of circumstances, as set out in subsections (2), (3) and (4).

217. *Subsection (6)* provides that in the case of a failure to mention a point of law in a defence statement, comment by another party may only be made with the leave of court.

218. *Subsection (7)* provides that in the case of failures in relation to witness lists, comment by another party may only be made with the leave of the court.

219. *Subsection (10)* provides that a person cannot be convicted solely on an inference under this section.

### *Section 40: Code of practice for police interviews of witnesses notified by accused*

220. *Section 40* should be read in conjunction with *section 34*. It inserts a new section 21A into the 1996 Act. New section 21A provides for a code of practice, which will apply where the police, or non-police investigators, interview a person whose details have been disclosed under new section 6A(2) or 6C of the 1996 Act.

221. *Subsection (1)* of new section 21A requires the code to be prepared by the Secretary of State.

222. *Subsection (2)* specifies a number of matters on which the code must provide guidance, for example, the attendance of the interviewee's solicitor at such an interview. The list is not exclusive.

223. *Subsection (3)* requires police officers and non-police investigators conducing such interviews to have regard to the code of practice.

224. *Subsection (4)* requires the Secretary of State to consult the persons specified in the subsection when the code is being prepared. The persons to be consulted vary, depending on whether the code is to apply to England and Wales or Northern Ireland. The lists are not exclusive, in that the Secretary of State may consult anybody else, if he thinks fit.

225. *Subsection (5)* provides for the code to be brought into operation by the Secretary of State by order.

226. *Subsection (6)* enables the Secretary of State to revise the code from time to time and applies the same consultation requirement, and provision for it to enter into operation by order, to the revised as to the initial code.

227. *Subsections (7) to (10)* set out the Parliamentary procedures that will apply when an order is made to bring a code or revised code into operation. Under subsection (10), any consultation requirements must have been discharged before an order is made.

228. *Subsection (11)* makes it clear that a failure to have regard to the code cannot, in itself, render the person responsible for the failure liable to criminal or civil proceedings.

229. *Subsection (12)* makes the code admissible in evidence in all criminal and civil proceedings and *subsection (13)* requires all courts to take the code, or a failure to have regard to it, into account where the code or the failure appears to be relevant to a questions before them in any criminal or civil proceedings.

## Part 6: Allocation and Transfer of Offences

### *Section 41: Allocation of offences triable either way, and sending cases to Crown Court*

230. *Section 41* introduces *Schedule 3*, Part 1 of which sets out (through amendments to existing statutes) how it is to be decided whether cases triable either way should be tried summarily or on indictment, and provides for the sending to the Crown Court of those cases which need to go there.

*Amendments to the Magistrates' Courts Act 1980.*

231. Paragraphs 3 and 4 of Schedule 3 clarify that the preliminary stages of an either-way case, including the plea before venue and allocation procedures, may take place at a hearing before a single justice. But a single justice may not conduct a contested trial, nor – whilst he may take a guilty plea – may he impose a sentence on the offender. Paragraph 3 also limits the sentence that may be imposed where a person pleads guilty to a low-value offence.

232. Paragraph 5 substitutes section 19 of the Magistrates' Courts Act 1980, which makes provision for the procedure to be followed by a magistrates' court in deciding whether a case involving an offence triable either way to which the defendant has not indicated a guilty plea should be tried summarily or on indictment. The new procedure ('allocation') differs from the present one in that the court is to be informed about, and take account of, any previous convictions of the defendant in assessing whether the sentencing powers available to it are adequate. The court is to have regard, not only (as now) to any representations made by the prosecution or defence, but also to allocation guidelines which may be issued by the Sentencing Guidelines Council under section 170.

233. Paragraph 6 substitutes section 20 of the Magistrates' Courts Act 1980 which sets out the procedure to be followed by the magistrates' court where it decides that a case is suitable for summary trial. As now, defendants will be told that they can either consent to be tried summarily or, if they wish, be tried on indictment. In making that decision they may be influenced by the knowledge that, since it will generally no longer be possible to be committed for sentence to the Crown Court once the magistrates have accepted jurisdiction, they cannot receive a sentence beyond the magistrates' powers. Moreover, defendants are to have the opportunity of requesting an indication from the magistrates whether, if they pleaded guilty at that point, the sentence would be custodial or not.

234. The magistrates' court will have a discretion whether or not to give an indication to a defendant who has sought one. Where an indication is given, defendants will be given the opportunity to reconsider their original indication as to plea. Where a defendant then decides to plead guilty, the magistrates' court will proceed to sentence. A custodial

sentence will be available only if such a sentence was indicated, and if so – unlike after a guilty plea indication under s17A or 17B – the option of committal to the Crown Court for sentence under s3 of the Powers of Criminal Courts (Sentencing) Act 2000 will not be available, although committal for sentence under section 3A of that Act will be available where the criteria for an extended sentence or a sentence for public protection appear to be met.

235. Otherwise (i.e. where the defendant declines to reconsider his plea indication, or where no sentence indication is given) the defendant will be given the choice between accepting summary trial or electing trial on indictment, as at present. Where an indication of sentence is given and the defendant does not choose to plead guilty on the basis of it, the sentence indication is not binding on the magistrates who later try the case summarily, or on the Crown Court if the defendant elects trial on indictment.

236. Paragraph 7 substitutes section 21 in the Magistrates' Courts Act 1980 so that, where the court decides that trial on indictment appears more suitable, it will proceed to send the case to the Crown Court in accordance with section 51(1) of the Crime and Disorder Act 1998.

237. Paragraph 10 adds four new sections (24A-24D) to the Magistrates' Courts Act 1980 which apply a procedure akin to that in sections 17A-17C ('plea before venue') to cases involving defendants who are under 18. It would apply in certain cases where it falls to the court to decide whether the defendant should be sent to the Crown Court for trial, whether in his or her own right, or for joint trial with an adult defendant.

238. Paragraph 11 amends section 25 of the Magistrates' Courts Act 1980. The current power to switch between summary trial and committal proceedings is abolished, and in its place there is a new power for the prosecution to apply for an either-way case which has been allocated for summary trial to be tried on indictment instead.

## Sending cases to the Crown Court etc.

239. Paragraphs 15-20 amend the Crime and Disorder Act 1998, Paragraph 17 sets out the order in which a magistrates' court is to apply various procedures in respect of either-way offences.

240. Paragraph 18 substitutes section 51 of the Crime and Disorder Act 1998 so that it applies not only (as now) to indictable-only offences (and cases related to such offences), but also where an either-way case involving an adult defendant is allocated for trial on indictment. The provisions for sending to the Crown Court related cases against the same defendant or another defendant (including one under 18) are preserved.

241. Paragraph 18 also inserts into the Crime and Disorder Act 1998 new section 51A, which replaces the existing provisions for moving cases where the principal defendant is under 18 to the Crown Court for trial; and new sections 51B and 51C, which subsume the transfer provisions now in section 4 of the Criminal Justice Act 1987 (serious fraud cases) and section 53 of the Criminal Justice Act 1991 (child witness cases) respectively. The procedure in sections 51B and 51C is initiated, as it is now, by the issue of a notice by the prosecutor.

242. Paragraph 19 makes provision for reporting restrictions.

243. Paragraphs 21 to 28 amend the Powers of Criminal Courts (Sentencing) Act 2000. The most important of these concerns the committal to the Crown Court for sentence of offences triable either-way. This power will no longer be available in cases where the magistrates' court has dealt with the case having accepted jurisdiction (whether as a contested case or a guilty plea) but will be limited to cases where a guilty plea has been indicated at plea before venue.

244. If a defendant is charged with a number of related either-way offences, pleads guilty to one of them at plea before venue and is sent to the Crown Court to be tried for the

rest, the existing power in section 4 of the Powers of Criminal Courts (Sentencing) Act 2000 to send the offence to which he has pleaded guilty to the Crown Court for sentence is retained.

245. Part 2 of Schedule 3 contains minor and consequential amendments to various statutes.

### *Section 42: Mode of trial for certain firearms offences ; transitory arrangements*

246. This Section makes interim arrangements to allow defendants under 18 to be sent to the Crown Court for trial where they have committed certain firearms offences (and were aged 16 or over at the time). The interim arrangements will be replaced by permanent arrangements when the new allocation and sending procedure is introduced.

## Part 7 : Trials on Indictment Without a Jury

247. This Part of the Act sets out the circumstances in which a trial on indictment in the Crown Court must, or may, be heard by a judge sitting alone without a jury.

### *Section 43: Application by prosecution for certain fraud trials to be conducted without a jury*

248. *Section 43* makes provision for the prosecution to apply for a serious or complex fraud trial on indictment in the Crown Court to proceed in the absence of a jury. The court would need to be satisfied that the length or complexity (or both) of the trial is likely to make it so burdensome upon the jury that the interests of justice require serious consideration to be given to conducting the trial without a jury *(subsection (5)).* Where the court is so satisfied, it has a discretion to order that the trial should be conducted without a jury, but such an order requires the approval of the Lord Chief Justice or a judge nominated by him *(subsection (4)).*

249. *Subsections (6) and (7)* require the judge to consider whether there is anything that can reasonably be done to make the trial less complex and lengthy. Particularly relevant in this context will be the provision made for the preparatory hearing procedure under section 7 of the Criminal Justice Act 1987 or section 29 of the Criminal Procedure and Investigations Act 1996. However, in so doing the court is not to regard as reasonable any measures which would significantly disadvantage the prosecution. For example, the prosecution may be disadvantaged by the severing of an indictment or by the exclusion of relevant and important evidence simply on jury management grounds.

250. Commencement of section 43 is by affirmative resolution procedure (see section 330(5)).

### *Sections 44 and 46: Application for prosecution for trial to be conducted without a jury where danger of jury tampering; discharge of jury because of jury tampering*

251. *Sections 44 and 46* provide for a trial on indictment in the Crown Court to be conducted without a jury where there is a danger of jury tampering, or continued without a jury where the jury has been discharged because of jury tampering.

252. The power of a judge to discharge a jury on the grounds of jury tampering exists at common law. The phrase "jury tampering" is intended to be understood from that context as covering a range of circumstances in which the jury's independence is, may be or may appear to be compromised, for example, because of actual or attempted harm or threats to, or intimidation or bribery of, a jury or any of its members. It could also include improper approaches to a juror's family or friends, or threats etc in respect of a juror's property.

253. *Section 44* allows the prosecution to make an application for a juryless trial. For this to be granted, the court must be satisfied that there is evidence of a real and present danger that jury tampering would take place (*subsection (4)*); this echoes the test in considering whether police protection should be ordered in respect of a jury. In addition, the court

must be satisfied that the danger of jury tampering is so substantial, notwithstanding any steps (including police protection) that could reasonably be taken to prevent it, as to make it necessary in the interests of justice for the trial to be conducted without a jury.

254. *Subsection (6)* sets out examples of what might constitute evidence of a real and present danger of jury tampering.

255. *Section 46* concerns trials already under way where jury tampering has, or appears to have, occurred. In these circumstances, if the judge is minded to discharge the jury (in exercise of his common law powers) he must notify the prosecution and defence that he is so minded, explain his reasons for doing so, and hear what each party has to say on the matter (*subsection (2)*). If the judge then decides to discharge the jury (in the exercise of his common law powers) and is satisfied that tampering has occurred, he may order that the trial should continue without a jury if he is satisfied that this would be fair to the defendant (*subsection (3)*). *Subsection (4)* provides that where the judge considers it necessary in the interests of justice to terminate the trial, he must terminate it. In that event, he may order a retrial, and if he does so, he will have the option of ordering that the retrial should take place without a jury (*subsection (5)*). However, if he is to order the retrial is to take place without a jury, he will need to have satisfied himself that both the conditions in *section 44* are likely to be met in respect of the retrial.

### *Section 45*: ***Procedure for applications under sections 43 and 44.***

256. This section prescribes the procedure for determining applications for a trial to be conducted without a jury under *section 43* (serious or complex fraud trials) and *44*(danger of jury tampering); this provision is likely to be supplemented by rules of court.

257. *Subsection (2)* makes clear that any such application will be determined at a preparatory hearing. Provisions governing preparatory hearings are contained in the Criminal Justice Act 1987 and the Criminal Procedure and Investigations Act 1996. *Section 45* builds on and amends these provisions to allow for applications for non-jury trial to be considered either at a preparatory hearing ordered under the existing provisions of those Acts, or at a preparatory hearing ordered particularly for that purpose.

258. The effect of *subsections (5) and (9)* is that an appeal will lie to the Court of Appeal for both prosecution and defendant against the determination made by the court at a preparatory hearing on any application for a trial without a jury under *section 43 or 44*.

### *Section 47*: ***Appeals***

259. This section provides a right of appeal to the Court of Appeal against:

- an order made under *section 46(3)* to continue a trial in the absence of a jury and
- an order made under *section 46(5)* for a retrial to be conducted in the absence of a jury

following the discharge of a jury because of jury tampering.

### *Section 48*: ***Further provision about trials without a jury***

260. These provisions ensure that, where a court orders a trial to be conducted (under *sections 43, 44 or 46(5)*) or continued (under *section 46(3)*) without a jury, the trial will proceed in the usual way, except that the functions which would otherwise have been performed by a jury can be fully performed by the judge sitting alone, with suitable allowance for the obvious requirements of the change of context.

261. Where a trial is conducted or continued without a jury, and a defendant is convicted, *subsection (5)(a)* requires the court to give its reasons for the conviction.

262. *Subsection (6)* provides that the functions of a jury in determining fitness to plead are unchanged.

### *Section 49: Rules of court*

263. *Section 49* makes provision for the making of rules of court.

### *Section 50: Application of Part 7 to Northern Ireland*

264. *Section 50* provides that Part 7 applies in Northern Ireland subject to the modifications made by this section. *Subsection (2)* provides that Part 7 does not apply to a trial to which section 75 of the Terrorism Act 2000 applies.

## Part 8 – Live Links

### *Section 51: Live links in criminal proceedings*

265. This section enables a court to authorise witnesses, other than the defendant, to give evidence through a live link in certain criminal proceedings. "Live link" is defined in *section 56(2)* and will usually mean a closed circuit television link, but could apply to any technology with the same effect such as video conferencing facilities or the internet.

266. *Subsections (4)(a) and (4)(b)* provide that a court may only authorise the use of a live link if:

- it is in the interests of the efficient or effective administration of justice for the witness to give evidence by way of a live link (for example, a witness may be able to give evidence from his place of work in a different part of the United Kingdom rather than have to travel to court); and
- the court has been notified by the Secretary of State that suitable facilities are available in the area where the proceedings are to take place: this will allow for phased implementation of the facilities required for live links. The responsibility for ensuring that there are facilities in the remote location from which the witness intends to give evidence falls to the parties and is therefore not covered by this section.

267. *Subsection (6)* directs the court to consider all the circumstances of the case when deciding whether to authorise the use of a live link and *subsection (7)* points out some of the most important considerations the court must take into account.

### *Section 52: Effect of, and rescission of, direction*

268. This section provides that where a direction for a live link has been given that witness must give all their evidence through a live link. This makes it clear that any cross-examination of the witness is also to be given by live link, although the court can rescind a direction if it seems to be in the interests of justice to do so. A party may only apply for the direction to be rescinded if there has been a material change of circumstances since the decision was made. An example of when a direction might be rescinded is where problems with the live link technology arise after a direction has been given.

### *Section 53: Magistrates' courts permitted to sit at other locations*

269. Lack of facilities in particular areas or courts should, as far as possible, not frustrate the aims of this Part. *Section 53* therefore allows a magistrates' court to move temporarily to a different location where the necessary live link facilities are available.

### *Section 54: Warning to the jury*

270. This section allows the judge to give directions to the jury, if necessary, to ensure that they give the same weight to evidence given through a live link as they would, had the evidence been given by the witness in person in court.

### *Section 55: Rules of court*

271. The rule-making power provided by this section will enable rules of court to be made governing the procedure to be followed when an application is made for evidence to be given through a live link. Such rules may also make provision as to the arrangements which must be put in place in connection with the operation of live links.

### *Section 56: Interpretation of Part 8*

272. *Subsection (5)* makes clear that the provisions in this Part of the Act are not intended to affect the inherent discretion of the court to authorise evidence to be heard by live link in circumstances not covered by *section 51*, or to make to make any other directions or orders in relation to witnesses, including the defendant.

## Part 9: Prosecution Appeals

### *Section 57: Introduction*

273. This section sets out certain basic criteria for a prosecution appeal under this Part of the Act. The right of appeal arises only in trials on indictment and lies to the Court of Appeal.

274. *Subsection (2)* sets out two further limitations on appeals under this Part. It prohibits the prosecution from appealing rulings on discharge of the jury and those rulings that may be appealed by the prosecution under other legislation, for example, appeals from preparatory hearings against rulings on admissibility of evidence and other points of law.

275. *Subsection (4)* provides that the prosecution must obtain leave to appeal, either from the judge or the Court of Appeal.

### *Section 58: General right of appeal*

276. This section sets out the procedure that must be followed when the prosecution wishes to appeal against a terminating ruling. The section covers both rulings that are formally terminating and those that are de facto terminating in the sense that they are so fatal to the prosecution case that, in the absence of a right of appeal, the prosecution would offer no or no further evidence. It applies to rulings made at an applicable time during a trial (which is defined in *subsection (13)* as any time before the start of the judge's summing up to the jury).

277. By virtue of *subsection (4)*, following the ruling, the prosecution must either inform the court that it intends to appeal or request an adjournment to consider whether to appeal *(subsection (4)(a))*. If such an adjournment is requested, the judge has the discretion to grant it (*subsection (5)*) but that discretion will be exercised in accordance with rules of court or other guidance. It is likewise envisaged that the period of any adjournment will be specified in rules of court. Following such an adjournment the prosecution must advise the court whether or not it intends to appeal *(subsection (4)(b))*. Under *subsection (6)*, a ruling which affects more than one offence need not be appealed against insofar as it affects all the offences. It can be appealed against, if the prosecutor wishes, only insofar as it affects one or more of the offences.

278. *Subsections (3), (10) and (11)* provide that the judge's ruling has no effect while the prosecution follows the procedure in *subsection (4)* in order to consider whether to appeal or is pursuing an appeal.

279. It is only possible for the prosecutor to appeal under this section against a single ruling. However, under *subsection* (7), where the ruling that is the subject of the appeal is a ruling of no case to answer the prosecutor may nominate other rulings that relate to the offence that is the subject of the appeal, for the Court of Appeal to consider at the same time. These rulings will also be regarded as the subject of the appeal.

280. Where the prosecution fails to obtain leave to appeal or abandons the appeal, the prosecution must agree that an acquittal follow by virtue of *subsections (8) and (9).*

### *Section 59: Expedited and non-expedited appeals*

281. This section provides two alternative appeal routes, an expedited (fast) route and a non-expedited (slower) route. The judge must determine which route the appeal will follow (*subsection (1))*. In the case of an expedited appeal the trial may be adjourned (*subsection (2))*. If the judge decides that the appeal should follow the non-expedited route he may either adjourn the proceedings or discharge the jury, if one has been sworn (*subsection (3)). Subsection (4)* gives both the judge and the Court of Appeal power to reverse a decision to expedite an appeal, thus transferring the case to the slower non-expedited route. If a decision is reversed under this subsection, the jury may be discharged.

### *Section 60: Continuation of proceedings for offences not affected by ruling*

282. This provision deals with cases where the trial involves more than one offence but the appeal does not apply to all of those offences. *Subsection (2)* enables proceedings to continue in relation to any offence to which the appeal does not apply. A ruling may affect several offences and several defendants, but the prosecutor may only wish to appeal against the ruling insofar as it affects one or more of those offences or defendants. This section enables proceedings to continue, at the discretion of the trial judge, against any offences affected by the ruling but not by the appeal.

### *Section 61: Determination of appeal by Court of Appeal*

283. This section sets out the powers of the Court of Appeal when determining a prosecution appeal. This needs to be read in conjunction with *section 67.*

284. *Subsection (1)* authorises the Court of Appeal to confirm, reverse or vary a ruling appealed against. The section is drafted to ensure that, after the Court of Appeal has ordered one or other of these disposals, it must then always make it clear what is to happen next in the case.

285. When the Court of Appeal confirms a ruling, *subsection (3)* and *(7)* provide that it must then order the acquittal of the defendant(s) for the offence(s) which are the subject of the appeal.

286. When the Court of Appeal reverses or varies a ruling, *subsections (4) and (8)* provide that it must *either* order a resumption of the Crown Court proceedings or a fresh trial, *or* order the acquittal of the defendant(s) for the offence(s) under appeal. By virtue of *subsections (5) and (8)*, the Court of Appeal will only order the resumption of the Crown Court proceedings or a fresh trial where it considers it necessary in the interests of justice to do so.

### *Section 62: Right of appeal in respect of evidentiary rulings*

287. This section provides that the prosecution may appeal either a single or two or more qualifying evidentiary rulings. Like the right of appeal in *section 58* this right of appeal will only be available to the prosecution.

288. *Subsection* (2) defines a qualifying evidentiary ruling as one made by a judge in relation to a trial on indictment at any time before the opening of the case of the defence (defined in *subsection (8)).*

289. *Subsections (3) and (4)* limit the right of appeal to a qualifying ruling or rulings that relate to qualifying offences, regardless of whether the ruling also relates to other (non-qualifying) offences.

290. *Subsections (5), (6) and (7)* set out the procedure that must be followed when the prosecution is seeking to appeal against a single or two or more qualifying evidentiary rulings.

291. Before the opening of the case for the defence, the prosecution must inform the court that it intends to appeal and give details of the ruling or rulings and the offences, including the qualifying offences to which the appeal relates.

292. *Subsection (9)* makes clear that the term "evidentiary ruling" includes rulings that relate both to the admissibility and the exclusion of any prosecution evidence. It also defines a qualifying offence as one listed in Schedule 4.

### *Section 63*: ***Condition that evidentiary ruling significantly weakens prosecution case***

293. This section provides that leave to appeal a qualifying evidentiary ruling may not be given unless the judge or the Court of Appeal is satisfied that the relevant condition is met. This relevant condition is that a single ruling (or two or more rulings taken together) significantly weakens the prosecution case in relation to the offence or offences that are the subject of the appeal.

### *Section 64*: ***Expedited and non-expedited appeals***

294. As in the case of appeals against terminating rulings this section provides two alternative appeal routes for appeals against evidentiary rulings, an expedited (fast) route and a non-expedited (slower) route.

### *Section 65*: ***Continuation of proceedings for offences not affected by ruling***

295. This provision deals with cases where the trial involves more than one offence but the appeal does not apply to all of them. Subsection (2) enables proceedings to continue in relation to any offence to which the appeal does not apply.

### *Section 66*: ***Determination of appeal by Court of Appeal***

296. This section sets out the powers of the Court of Appeal when determining a prosecution appeal against an evidentiary ruling. This needs to be read in conjunction with section 67.

297. *Subsection (1)* authorises the Court of Appeal to confirm, reverse or vary a ruling appealed against. The section is drafted to ensure that, after the Court of Appeal has ordered one or other of these disposals, it must then always make it clear what is to happen next in the case.

298. When the Court of Appeal confirms, reverses or varies a ruling, *subsection (2)* provides that it must order a resumption of the Crown Court proceedings or a fresh trial, *or* order the acquittal of the defendant(s) for the offence(s) under appeal. By virtue of *subsection (3),* the Court of Appeal may only order an acquittal if the prosecution has indicated that it does not intend to continue with the prosecution of that offence. This is intended to cater for the situation where the prosecution considers that effect of the ruling or rulings on the prosecution case is so damaging that they do not wish to proceed with the prosecution.

### *Section 67: **Reversal of rulings***

299. This section sets out the criteria that have to be satisfied before the Court of Appeal can overturn a judge's ruling. This applies to both the general right of appeal and appeals against evidentiary rulings.

### *Section 68: **Appeals to the House of Lords***

300. *Subsection (1)* amends section 33(1) of the Criminal Appeal Act 1968 to give both the prosecution and defence a right of appeal to the House of Lords from a decision by the Court of Appeal on a prosecution appeal against a ruling made under this Part of the Act.

301. *Subsection (2)* amends section 36 of the Criminal Appeal Act 1968 to prevent the Court of Appeal from granting bail to a defendant who is appealing, or is applying for leave to appeal, to the House of Lords from a Court of Appeal decision made under this Part of the Act. Bail will continue to be a matter for the trial court.

### *Section 69: **Costs***

302. *Subsections (2) and (3)* amend sections 16(4A) and 18 of the Prosecution of Offences Act 1985 to give the Court of Appeal power, on an appeal under this Part, to award costs to and against the defendant.

### *Section 70: **Effect on time limits in relation to preliminary stages***

303. Section 22 of the Prosecution of Offences Act 1985 enables overall and custody time limits to be set which apply during the preliminary stages of criminal proceedings, although not to the trial itself. If the prosecution were to appeal against a ruling made prior to the commencement of the trial, the time limits set under section 22 of the 1985 Act would continue to run pending the outcome of the appeal. *Section 70* addresses this problem by inserting a new subsection (6B) into section 22 of the 1985 Act. Subsection (6B) disapplies the overall time limit and the custody time limit for the period during which proceedings are adjourned pending a prosecution appeal under this Part of the Act.

### *Section 71: **Restrictions on reporting***

304. *Subsection (1)* contains a general prohibition on the reporting of appeals arising under this Part of the Act. This general prohibition is qualified by *subsections (7) and (8)* which provide that the restriction ends at the conclusion of the trial and does not apply to various matters including details of the court, the defendants, witnesses, legal representatives and the offences at issue.

305. *Subsections (2), (3) and (4)* give the judge, the Court of Appeal and the House of Lords respectively, power, by order, to lift the reporting restriction under *subsection (1)* either completely or to a specified extent. If the defendant(s) object to the making of such an order, such an order may only be made if it would be in the interests of justice to do so (*subsections (5) and (6)*).

306. *Subsection (10)* ensures that any other restrictions on the reporting of court proceedings are preserved.

### *Section 72: **Offences in connection with reporting***

307. *Section 72* sets out the summary offences created by the new reporting restrictions under *section 71* and the penalties which may be imposed on conviction. Prosecutions under this section may only be bought in England and Wales by or with the consent of the Attorney General or, where instituted in Northern Ireland, by or with the consent of the Attorney General for Northern Ireland or, after the Justice (Northern Ireland) Act 2002 comes into force, the Director of Public Prosecutions for Northern Ireland.

### *Section 73* ***Rules of court***

308. This section makes clear that rules of court may be made governing the procedure to be followed. It is envisaged that these rules will address the time limits that will apply, and the powers of a single judge of the Court of Appeal, in respect of appeals under Part 9.

### *Section 74:* ***Interpretation of*** *Part 9*

309. *Subsection* (3) prevents the same ruling from being appealed against more than once. *Subsection* (4) provides that where a ruling relates to more than one offence any appeal does not affect the ruling in relation to an offence that is not the subject of the appeal. *Subsection (5)* provides that two defendants charged jointly with the same offence are to be treated as charged with separate offences. This, when read in conjunction with, say, *section 58 (6)*, will mean that an appeal will be possible against a ruling so far as it relates to only one of the defendants.

## Part 10: Retrial for Serious Offences

### *Section 75:* ***Cases that may be retried***

310. *Section 75* sets out the cases which may be retried under the exception to the normal rule against double jeopardy. These cases all involve serious offences which in the main carry a maximum sentence of life imprisonment, and which are considered to have a particularly serious impact either on the victim or on society more generally. The offences to which the provisions apply are called "qualifying offences", and are listed in Schedule 5 to the Act.

311. The cases which may be re-tried are those in which a person has been acquitted of one of the qualifying offences, either on indictment or following an appeal, or of a lesser qualifying offence of which he could have been convicted at that time. This takes into account cases of "implied acquittals", in which, under the current law, an acquittal would have prevented a further prosecution being brought for a lower level offence on the same facts. For example, an acquittal for murder may also imply an acquittal for the lower level offence of manslaughter, but new evidence may then come to light which would support a charge of manslaughter. A person may only be re-tried in respect of a qualifying offence.

312. In certain circumstances cases may also be tried where an acquittal for an offence has taken place abroad, so long as the alleged offence also amounted to a qualifying offence and could have been charged as such in the UK. This would include for example offences such as War Crimes, and murder committed outside the UK, for which the courts in England and Wales have jurisdiction over British citizens abroad. Such cases are likely to be rare. Subsection *(5)* recognises that offences may not be described in exactly the same way in the legislation of other jurisdictions.

313. The law in Scotland is not being changed in this respect at present, so this Part of the Act is not applied to acquittals which take place in Scotland.

### *Section 76:* ***Application to Court of Appeal***

314. *Section 76* allows a prosecutor to apply to the Court of Appeal for an order which quashes the person's acquittal and orders him to be retried for the qualifying offence. A "prosecutor" means a person or body responsible for bringing public prosecutions, such as the Crown Prosecution Service or HM Customs and Excise. Where a person has been acquitted outside the United Kingdom the Court will need to consider whether or not the acquittal would act as a bar to a further trial here and, if it does, the Court can order that it must not be a bar.

315. Applications to the Court of Appeal require the personal written consent of the Director of Public Prosecutions (DPP). This provides a safeguard to ensure that only those cases

in which there is sufficient evidence are referred to the Court of Appeal. The DPP will also consider whether it is in the public interest to proceed. This section also recognises any international obligations arising under the Treaty of the European Union, under which negotiations are taking place to support the mutual recognition of the decisions of the courts in other EU member states.

316. Applications may also be brought by public prosecuting authorities if new evidence arises in cases which have previously been tried by means of a private prosecution.

317. Only one application for an acquittal to be quashed may be made in relation to any acquittal.

### *Section 77: Determination by Court of Appeal*

318. *Section 77* sets out the decisions which the Court of Appeal may make in response to an application for an acquittal to be quashed. The Court must make an order quashing an acquittal and ordering a retrial if it considers that the requirements set out in *Sections 78 and 79* of the Act are satisfied, namely that there is new and compelling evidence in the case, and that it is in the interests of justice for the order to be made. The Court must dismiss an application where it is not satisfied as to these two factors.

319. Where an acquittal has taken place outside the United Kingdom, the Court must decide whether that acquittal provides a bar to prosecution. A "bar" means that the Court would not allow a further prosecution to proceed. If it does not provide a bar, then the Court must make a declaration to that effect. If the acquittal does provide a bar, then the Court must make an order that the acquittal is not to be a bar to a trial in respect of the qualifying offence, if it is satisfied that, as above, the requirements in *Sections 78 and 79* are met. If it is not satisfied, then the Court must make a declaration that the acquittal remains a bar to retrial.

### *Section 78: New and compelling evidence*

320. *Section 78* sets out the requirement for there to be new and compelling evidence against the acquitted person in relation to the qualifying offence, and defines evidence which is "new and compelling". Evidence is "new" if it was not adduced at the original trial of the acquitted person. Evidence is "compelling" if the Court considers it to be reliable and substantial and, when considered in the context of the outstanding issues, the evidence appears to be highly probative of the case against the acquitted person. The Court is thus required to make a decision on the strength of the new evidence. So for example, new evidence relating to identification would only be considered "compelling" if the identity of the offender had been at issue in the original trial. It is not intended that relatively minor evidence which might appear to strengthen an earlier case should justify a re-trial.

321. This applies equally to acquittals abroad. In such cases it will be for the prosecution to provide the Court with information relating to the evidence available and the issues in the trial.

### *Section 79: Interests of justice*

322. *Section 79* sets out the requirement that in all the circumstances it is in the interests of justice for the Court to quash an acquittal and order a re-trial. In determining whether it is in the interests of justice, the Court will consider in particular: whether there are existing factors which make a fair trial unlikely (for example, the extent of adverse publicity about the case); the length of time since the alleged offence was committed; and whether the police and prosecution acted with due diligence and expedition in relation to both the original trial and any new evidence. The Court may take into account any other issues it considers relevant in determining whether a retrial will be in the interests of justice.

323. Both *sections 78 and 79* apply where a previous prosecution case may have been led by a private rather than public prosecutor.

### *Section 80: Procedure and evidence*

324. *Section 80* sets out a number of technical and evidential procedures to be followed in bringing an application for an acquittal to be quashed. These provide for a notice of the application to be made to the Court of Appeal and served on the acquitted person within 2 days of the application being made (a longer time may be allowed where the service has to be made overseas); that there will be a Court of Appeal hearing to consider the application; that the acquitted person is entitled to attend the hearing (except where he is in lawful custody abroad); and that he is entitled to be represented at the hearing.

### *Section 81: Appeals*

325. *Section 81* allows appeals on a point of law to be made to the House of Lords from decisions made by the Court of Appeal on an application, for example to order or refuse a retrial, or to make a declaration with regard to whether an acquittal is a bar to further proceedings, or to decline to order a retrial on the grounds of admissibility of evidence or points of law. It amends the Criminal Appeal Act 1968 accordingly.

### *Section 82: Restrictions on publication in the interests of justice*

326. *Section 82* makes provisions for reporting restrictions to apply in respect of matters surrounding the application for a retrial, until either the end of the re-trial or to any point at which it is clear that the acquitted person can no longer be re-tried. These provisions are aimed at ensuring that a fair trial can take place by limiting the extent to which the media can report on the proceedings under this Part of the Act, to ensure that any potential jury is not influenced by these developments. Reporting restrictions may be sought only by the Director of Public Prosecutions or made by the Court of its own motion and may be imposed by order of the Court of Appeal at any stage after a new investigation into the acquitted person has commenced. The restrictions may apply to any information in respect of the investigation and to the re-publication of matters previously published. The Court will decide whether such restrictions are required, and their content and duration, according to what is necessary in the interests of justice. .

### *Section 83: Offences in connection with publication restrictions*

327. *Section 83* sets out the summary offences created by the new reporting restrictions under section 82 and the penalties which may be imposed upon conviction. Prosecutions under this Section may only be brought in England and Wales by or with the consent of the Attorney General, or where instituted in Northern Ireland, by or with the consent of the Attorney General for Northern Ireland, or after the Justice (Northern Ireland) Act 2002 comes into force, the Director of Public Prosecutions for Northern Ireland.

### *Section 84: Retrial*

328. *Section 84* makes provisions relating to the holding of retrials. An acquitted person may only be retried on an indictment preferred by the direction of the Court of Appeal. Arraignment on this indictment must be made within two months of the date on which the Court ordered a retrial, unless the Court allows a longer period. The Court can only extend this period if it is satisfied that the prosecutor has acted with due expedition since the order was made, and that there is still a good and sufficient reason to hold the retrial despite any additional lapse of time.

329. If the acquitted person is not arraigned for the retrial within the two months or any further time allowed, then he can apply to the Court of Appeal to set aside the order for retrial and restore the previous acquittal; or in the case of people acquitted outside the United Kingdom, for a declaration that the acquittal constitutes a bar to any trial for the qualifying offence.

330. An indictment may relate to more than one offence or to more than one person, including offences for which the accused has not been tried before.

331. This section also brings the provisions for retrial into line with changes to the law in respect of hearsay evidence and the use of depositions made elsewhere in this Act. It provides that evidence given orally at an original trial must be given orally at the retrial unless an exception in *subsection (6)* applies.Section 85: Authorisation of investigations

332. *Section 85* relates to the authorisation and conduct of police investigations. It requires the police to obtain the consent of the Director of Public Prosecutions before taking certain steps in the re-investigation of cases where new evidence has come to light, or where there are reasonable grounds to believe that further investigation will give rise to new evidence. The DPP must consider whether the previous acquittal constitutes a bar to a further prosecution. If the DPP certifies that in his opinion it does not constitute a bar, then there are no restrictions on police investigations into the offence. Where the previous acquittal does constitute a bar, the DPP's consent is required for the taking of specified steps which impinge directly on the acquitted person, where police wish to interview or arrest him, search his person, vehicle or premises occupied by him, seize evidence or take fingerprints or samples from him, in connection with the qualifying offence. It does not permit such actions to take place without authorisation even with the consent of the acquitted person, as this would provide a means of carrying out re-investigations without using appropriate police powers. This provides a safeguard against any potential harassment of acquitted persons. The requirement for the DPP's consent is not intended to hamper the police making other enquiries which do not directly impact on the life of the individual, for example by interviewing new or previous witnesses, or comparing fingerprint or DNA samples with records which they already hold.

333. An application for the DPP's consent must be made in writing by an officer of Commander rank or above in the Metropolitan and City Police forces, or Assistant Chief Constable or above in other police forces or bodies of constables. It can be made where new evidence has already been obtained, or where he has reasonable grounds to believe that new evidence is likely to be obtained if the investigation proceeds. There must therefore be some "trigger" for the application; it is not intended that the re-investigation of an acquitted person can take place without any element of new evidence.

334. The DPP can only give his consent if he is satisfied that there is sufficient new evidence to justify the re-investigation, or that such new evidence is likely to come to light if the investigation goes ahead, and that it is in the public interest for the investigation to proceed. In giving his consent, the DPP may also recommend to the chief officer of the force requesting the consent, that another force should conduct the re-investigation. It will then be for the chief officer to make appropriate arrangements with another force which can provide an appropriate level of investigative expertise.

335. The section applies similarly to investigators of HM Customs and Excise who are responsible for investigating a number of the qualifying drugs offences.

### *Section 86: Urgent investigative steps*

336. *Section 86* makes complementary provisions to *Section 85*, in circumstances where the police need to act urgently to prevent the investigation being substantially and irrevocably prejudiced, for example by securing evidence immediately. Urgent action may be needed in cases where new evidence is found during the course of other investigations, or where information provided to the police indicates that new evidence is temporarily at a particular location.

337. In such cases, urgent police action may be authorised by an officer of the rank of Superintendent or above. A Superintendent can only do this if there has been no undue delay in seeking the DPP's consent, and consent has not previously been refused. If the authorisation is not given in writing, it must be recorded in writing as soon as possible.

It also allows an individual officer to act immediately where necessary without any advance authorisation, and to obtain a confirming authorisation by a Superintendent later.

### *Section 87: Arrest and charge*

338. *Section 87* allows for the arrest of a person in respect of a qualifying offence by warrant, if the DPP's consent has not previously been obtained and the police are acting under the urgent procedures. A justice of the peace may issue a warrant where he is satisfied that new evidence against the acquitted person has been obtained. This does not affect his arrest in respect of any matter other than the qualifying offence. Where a person is arrested, the Section provides that he may be charged with the offence for which he has been arrested in accordance with the provisions of the Police and Criminal Evidence Act 1984 (PACE), if an officer of the rank of Superintendent or above, who has not been involved with the investigation, considers that there is sufficient evidence available for the case to be referred to a prosecutor in order to consider making an application for the acquittal to be quashed in accordance with this Part of the Act. This is the equivalent stage to bringing a criminal charge under PACE in normal proceedings, but provides the additional safeguard that the evidence must be considered at Superintendent level or above.

339. This Section also requires the Custody Officer to ensure that any relevant evidence which becomes available during the investigation is made available to the relevant officer at Superintendent rank or above to enable him to reach such a decision, and allows the Superintendent (or above) to direct that a charge shall be brought where there is sufficient evidence to do so.

### *Section 88: Bail and custody before application*

340. *Section 88* provides for a decision on bail or remand in custody to be made, in cases where an acquitted person has been charged under *Section 87*. The person must be brought before the Crown Court within 24 hours (excluding Sundays, bank holidays etc). This provision enables the courts either to bail the individual, or to remand him in custody, for a period not greater than 42 days (or such longer period as the court may, for good and sufficient cause, impose), whilst the application to the Court is prepared. It is subject to the same safeguards as other decisions on bail set out in the Bail Act 1976.

341. A power to remand in custody is considered necessary for the courts in those cases where there may be a risk of absconding prior to the application to the Court of Appeal being made or heard. It recognises that it will take some time for the police and prosecutors to formulate the appropriate application to the Court of Appeal, but this time should not be disproportionate. The bail or custody decision will be taken by the Crown Court who may either bail the person, with conditions on bail if necessary, or remand him in custody, either to a time at which the Court will review the decision, or to the time at which notice of the application is made to the Court of Appeal. If no notice of application to the Court of Appeal is made within the maximum 42 days, the prosecutor may ask the Court for an extension provided that there is good and sufficient cause to do so, and that the prosecution has acted expeditiously up to that point.

### *Section 89: Bail and custody before hearing*

342. *Section 89* similarly sets out the arrangements for bail or remand in custody once the notice of application is made to the Court of Appeal. At this stage, if the acquitted person is in custody, the Crown Court will make a further decision regarding bail or remand in custody pending the Court of Appeal hearing.

### *Section 90: Bail and custody during and after hearing*

343. *Section 90* makes similar provision for bail or remand in custody during and after the Court of Appeal hearing. At this stage decisions on bail or remand will be made by the

Court of Appeal, which will need to take into account its own decision in relation to the application. The Court may decide either to bail the person or remand him in custody until a retrial can be held, or until any appeal against the Court's ruling is determined.

### *Section 91*: *Revocation of bail*

344. *Section 91* provides for circumstances in which the court revokes a person's bail but the person is not in court. The court may order the person to surrender to the custody of the court and, should he fail to do so, the person may be arrested without warrant and must be brought before the court within 24 hours.

### *Section 92*: *Functions of the DPP*

345. *Section 92* disapplies for the purposes of Part 10 the provision of the Prosecution of Offences Act 1985 which allows the DPP's functions to be exercised by a Crown Prosecutor. In these cases it is intended that the DPP will take decisions personally as to when consent to re-investigate or to apply to the Court should be given. However, this section does allow for another person to be nominated by the DPP to take these decisions in cases where he is unavoidably absent.

### *Section 93*: *Rules of Court*

346. *Section 93* enables rules of court to be made in respect of the various court procedures set out in this Part.

### *Section 94*: *Armed Forces*: *Part 10*

347. *Section 94* ensures that section 31 of the Armed Forces Act 2001 will apply to Part 10 of the Act as it applies to "criminal justice enactments". Under section 31(3) the Secretary of State may by order make provisions for the armed forces' system of justice equivalent (subject to any modification) to those of "criminal justice enactments". Under section 31(2)"criminal justice enactments" broadly covers Acts relating to conduct, procedure and powers in relation to criminal investigations and trials; for example arrest, custody, evidence and sentence. Part 10 might by contrast be considered to affect the substantive criminal law.

348. Under *Section 94(*2) the Secretary of State is empowered to use section 31 to apply provisions equivalent to Part 10 to such offences under service law as he thinks fit. Service offences likely to be specified include such serious offences as assisting the enemy and mutiny.

349. *Section 31* applies to persons subject to service law wherever they are. This Section will have the same extent of application as that section.

350. An order under *Section 31* is generally subject to negative resolution procedure in Parliament. If however it alters the text of an Act (under *section 31(6)(c)*), such an order is subject to affirmative resolution procedure.

### *Section 95*: *Interpretation of Part 10*

351. *Section 95* defines various terms which appear in this Part of the Act, and provides that the jurisdiction of the Court of Appeal is exercised by the Criminal Division of the Court.

### *Section 96*: *Application of Part 10 to Northern Ireland*

*Section 96* applies Part 10 of the Act to Northern Ireland, subject to modifications which take account of the different legal procedures and arrangements in that jurisdiction.

### *Section 97: Application of Criminal Appeal Acts to proceedings under Part 10*

352. *Section 97* provides that the Secretary of State may make an order in relation to proceedings before the Court of Appeal under this Part which corresponds to any provisions which are contained in the Criminal Appeal Act 1968 and equivalent Northern Ireland legislation.

## Part 11 - Evidence

### *Chapter 1 : Evidence of Bad Character*

### *Section 98: Bad Character and Section 99: Abolition of common law rules*

353. *Section 98* defines the sort of evidence whose admissibility is to be determined under the new statutory scheme. The definition covers evidence of, or of a disposition towards, misconduct. The term "misconduct" is further defined in section 112 as the commission of an offence or other reprehensible behaviour. This is intended to be a broad definition and to cover evidence that shows that a person has committed an offence, or has acted in a reprehensible way (or is disposed to do so) as well as evidence from which this might be inferred.

354. The definition is therefore intended to include evidence such as previous convictions, as well as evidence on charges being tried concurrently, and evidence relating to offences for which a person has been charged, where the charge is not prosecuted, or for which the person was subsequently acquitted. This reflects the state of the current law. On the latter point, in the case of *Z* ([2000] 2 AC 483), the House of Lords held that there was no special rule that required the exclusion of evidence that a person had been involved in earlier offences, even if they had been acquitted of those crimes, provided that that evidence was otherwise admissible. Thus, if there were a series of attacks and the defendant were acquitted of involvement in them, evidence showing or tending to show that he had committed those earlier attacks could be given in a later case if it were admissible to establish that he had committed the latest attack. The Act preserves the effect of this decision.

355. Evidence not related to criminal proceedings might include, for example, evidence that a person has a sexual interest in children or is racist.

356. The scheme does not affect the admissibility of evidence of the facts of the offence. This is excluded from the definition, as is evidence of misconduct in connection with the investigation or prosecution of the offence. This evidence is therefore not governed by the new statutory rules.

357. Thus, if the defendant were charged with burglary, the prosecution's evidence on the facts of the offence – any witnesses to the crime, forensic evidence etc – would be admissible outside the terms of these provisions. So too would evidence of an assault that had been committed in the course of the burglary, as evidence to do with the facts of the offence. Evidence that the defendant had tried to intimidate prosecution witnesses would also be admissible outside this scheme as evidence of misconduct in connection with, as appropriate, the investigation or the prosecution of the offence, as would allegations by the defendant that evidence had been planted. However, evidence that the defendant had committed a burglary on another occasion or that a witness had previously lied on oath would not be evidence to do with the facts of the offence or its investigation or prosecution and would therefore be caught by the definition in section 98 and its admissibility would fall to be dealt with under the Act's provisions.

358. The intention is that this Part of the Act will provide a new basis for the admissibility of previous convictions and other misconduct. Accordingly, *section 99* abolishes the common law rules governing the admissibility of such evidence. (Statutory repeals are dealt with in Part 5 of Schedule 37.) This abolition does not extend to the rule that allows a person's bad character to be proved by his reputation. This common law

rule is preserved as a category of admissible hearsay in *section 118(1)*. However the admissibility of a person's bad character, in circumstances where it was being proved by reputation, would fall to be determined under this part of the Act.

### *Section 100* – *Non-defendant's bad character*

359. *Section 100* sets out the circumstances in which, outside the alleged facts of the offence and its investigation and prosecution, evidence can be given of the previous misconduct of a person other than a defendant in the proceedings. This might be a witness in the case or a victim but extends to any other person as well. Evidence of their bad character is not to be given without the permission of the court - *Section 100(4)* - and can only be given if it meets one of three conditions. These are:

- it is important explanatory evidence,
- it is of substantial probative value to a matter in issue and that issue is one of substantial importance in the case, or
- the prosecution and defence agree that the evidence should be admitted.

360. The term "explanatory evidence" is used to describe evidence which, whilst not going to the question of whether the defendant is guilty, is necessary for the jury to have a proper understanding of other evidence being given in the case by putting it in its proper context. An example might be a case involving the abuse by one person of another over a long period of time. For the jury to understand properly the victim's account of the offending and why they did not seek help from, for example, a parent or other guardian, it might be necessary for evidence to be given of a wider pattern of abuse involving that other person.

361. For evidence to be admissible as "important explanatory evidence", it must be such that, without it, the magistrates or jury would find it impossible or difficult to understand other evidence in the case – *Section 100(2)*. If, therefore, the facts or account to which the bad character evidence relates are largely understandable without this additional explanation, then the evidence should not be admitted. The explanation must also give the court some substantial assistance in understanding the case as a whole. In other words, it will not be enough for the evidence to assist the court to understand some trivial piece of evidence.

362. Evidence is of probative value to a matter in issue where it helps to prove that issue one way or the other. In respect of non-defendants, evidence of bad character is most likely to be probative where a question is raised about the credibility of a witness (as this is likely to affect the court's assessment of the issue on which the witness is giving evidence). The evidence might, however be probative in other ways. One example would be to support a suggestion by the defendant that another person was responsible for the offence.

363. Evidence which is of probative value is admissible if it meets an "enhanced relevance" test – *Section 100(1)(b)*. That is, it must be of substantial probative value and the matter in issue to which it relates must be of substantial importance in the context of the case. Thus evidence which has no real significance to an issue or is only marginally relevant would not be admissible, nor would evidence that goes only to a trivial or minor issue in the case.

364. *Section 100(3)* directs the court to take into account a number of factors when assessing the probative value of evidence of a non-defendant's bad character. These include the nature and number of the events to which it relates and when those events occurred. When considering evidence that is probative because of its similarity with evidence in the case (for example, to suggest that the alleged victim had acted in a particular way), the court is directed by *subsection (3)(c)* to consider the nature and extent of the similarities and dissimilarities. Similarly, where the evidence is being tendered to suggest a particular person was responsible, *subsection (3)(d)* requires the court to

consider the extent to which the evidence shows or tends to show that the same person was responsible each time.

### *Sections 101 to 108: defendants*

365. At present evidence of a defendant's bad character is generally inadmissible, subject to a number of restricted common law and statutory exceptions discussed in the 'Summary and Background' section (above). *Sections 101 to 108* set out the circumstances in which such evidence is to be admissible in future. In summary, these provide an inclusionary approach to a defendant's previous convictions and other misconduct or disposition, under which relevant evidence is admissible but can be excluded in certain circumstances if the court considers that the adverse affect that it would have on the fairness of the proceedings requires this. *Section 101* sets out the gateways through which this evidence can be admitted, whilst *Sections 102 to 106* provide additional definitional material. *Section 107* provides an important safeguard where this sort of evidence has been influenced by other witnesses or evidence in the case and is consequently false or misleading. *Section 108* deals with the admissibility of convictions for offences committed by a person under the age of fourteen in proceedings for offences committed by a person over the age of twenty-one.

### *Section 101: Defendant's bad character*

366. *Section 101(1)* provides that evidence of a defendant's bad character is admissible in the following circumstances:

- all the parties agree to it being given;
- the defendant introduces the evidence himself or it is given in response to a question put by the defendant (or his counsel) that is intended to elicit it;
- it is important explanatory evidence;
- it is relevant to an important issue between the defendant and prosecution;
- it has substantial probative value in relation to an important issue between the defendant and a co-defendant;
- it corrects a false impression given by the defendant about himself;
- the defendant has attacked the character of another person.

367. This is subject to an application by the defendant to have the evidence excluded if admitting it would have such an adverse effect on the fairness of the trial that it ought to be excluded (*Section 101(3))*. The circumstances in which such an application can be made are where the evidence is relevant to an issue in the case between the defendant and prosecution or has become admissible because of the defendant's attack on another person.

368. The test to be applied is designed to reflect the existing position under the common law, as section 78 of the Police and Criminal Evidence Act 1984 does, under which the judge assesses the probative value of the evidence to an issue in the case and the prejudicial effect of admitting it, and excludes the evidence where it would be unfair to admit it. The intention is for the courts to apply the fairness test set out here in the same way. In applying the test, the courts are directed specifically under *section 101(4)* to take account of the amount of time that has elapsed since the previous events and the current charge.

### *Section 102: "Important explanatory evidence"*

369. *Section 102* defines what is meant by important explanatory evidence. The definition mirrors that used in the context of non-defendants (see "non-defendant's bad character": section 100).

### *Section 103: "Matter in issue between the defendant and the prosecution"*

370. *Section 103* relates to evidence of a defendant's bad character that is admissible because it is relevant to an important matter at issue between the defendant and the prosecution (see *section 101(1)(d))*. Evidence might be relevant to one of a number of issues in a case. For example, it might help the prosecution to prove the defendant's guilt of the offence by establishing their involvement or state of mind or by rebutting the defendant's explanation of his conduct. Only prosecution evidence is admissible on this basis – section 103(6) – and the defendant may apply to have the evidence excluded under section 101(3).

371. *Section 103(1)(a)* makes it clear that evidence that shows that a defendant has a propensity to commit offences of the kind with which he is charged can be admitted under this head. For example, if the defendant is on trial for grievous bodily harm, a history of violent behaviour could be admissible to show the defendant's propensity to use violence. Evidence is not, however, admissible on this basis if the existence of such a propensity makes it no more likely that the defendant is guilty. This might be the case where there is no dispute about the facts of the case and the question is whether those facts constitute the offence (for example, in a homicide case, whether the defendant's actions caused death).

372. Where propensity is an issue, subsection (2) provides that this propensity may be established by evidence that the defendant has been convicted of an offence of the same description or category as the one with which he is charged. This is subject to subsection (3), which provides that the propensity may not be established in this way if the court is satisfied that due to the length of time since the previous conviction or for any other reason that would be unjust.

373. An offence of the same description is defined by reference to how the offence appears on an indictment or written charge. It therefore relates to the particular law that has been broken, rather than the circumstances in which it was committed. An offence will be of the same category as another if they both fall within a category drawn up by the Secretary of State in secondary legislation. An order establishing such categories will be subject to the affirmative procedure (see *section 330(5)*). The categories must contain offences that are of the same type (*section 103(4*)), for example, offences involving violence against the person or sexual offences.

374. *Section 103(1)(b)* makes it clear that evidence relating to whether the defendant has a propensity to be untruthful (in other words, is not to be regarded as a credible witness) can be admitted. This is intended to enable the admission of a limited range of evidence such as convictions for perjury or other offences involving deception (for example, obtaining property by deception), as opposed to the wider range of evidence that will be admissible where the defendant puts his character in issue by for example, attacking the character of another person. Evidence will not be admissible under this head where it is not suggested that the defendant's case is untruthful in any respect, for example, where the defendant and prosecution are agreed on the facts of the alleged offence and the question is whether all the elements of the offence have been made out.

### *Section 104: "Matter in issue between the defendant and a co-defendant"*

375. *Section 104* relates to evidence that is relevant to issues between the defendant and a co-defendant (*section 101(1)(e))*. Evidence is only admissible on this basis by (or at the behest of) a co-defendant: see *Section 104(2)* – the prosecution therefore cannot avail themselves of this provision. A co-defendant may wish to adduce evidence of a defendant's bad character if his defence is, for example, that it was the defendant, rather than himself, who was responsible for the offence. Under *Section 101(1)(e)* evidence is admissible on issues between the defendant and a co-defendant if it has substantial probative value in relation to an important issue in the case. In other words, evidence that has only marginal or trivial value would not be admissible, nor would it be admissible if the issue it related to were marginal or trivial in the case

as a whole. However, once this threshold is passed, there is no power for the courts to exclude the evidence. This ensures that defendants are able to put forward the widest range of evidence in their defence and reflects the current position. *Section 104* restricts the admissibility of evidence of a defendant's bad character that only shows that he has a propensity to be untruthful (that is, is not credible as a witness) to circumstances in which the defendant has undermined the co-defendant's defence. In these circumstances, his credibility may well have a bearing on resolving the issues in the case.

### *Section 105: "Evidence to correct a false impression"*

376. *Section 105* relates to evidence that is admissible under *Section 101(1)(f)* to correct a false impression given by the defendant. For this provision to apply, the defendant must have been responsible for an assertion that gives a false or misleading impression about himself. This might be done expressly, for example, by claiming to be of good character when this is not the case, or implied, for example, by leading evidence of his conduct that carries an implication that he is of a better character than is actually the case. It may also be done non-verbally, through his conduct in court, such as his appearance or dress *(Section 105(4) and (5))*. For example, if a defendant were to give a false impression by suggesting he were a priest, he could not escape this provision simply by not making such an assertion verbally but choosing to wear a clerical collar.

377. *Section 105(2*) sets out the circumstances in which a defendant is to be treated as being responsible for an assertion. These include the defendant making the assertion himself, either in his evidence or in his representative's presentation of his case or, if used in evidence, when being questioned under caution or on being charged with the offence. It also includes assertions made by defence witnesses, those by any witness if responding to a question by the defendant that was intended (or likely to) elicit it and out of court assertions made by anybody if adduced by the defendant.

378. In correcting the impression, the prosecution (and only the prosecution – see *Section 105(7))* may introduce evidence of the defendant's misconduct that has probative value in correcting it, in other words, is relevant to correcting the false impression. Exactly what evidence is admissible will turn on the facts of the case, in particular, the nature of the misleading impression he has given. Evidence is only admissible to the extent that it is necessary to correct that impression: *section 105(6*). A defendant may withdraw or disassociate himself from a false or misleading impression. Evidence to correct the impression is not then admissible: *section 105(3)*. In light of this, *section 101(3),* under which a defendant may apply to have evidence of his bad character excluded, does not apply to this evidence.

### *Section 106: "Attack on another person's character"*

379. *Section 106* deals with evidence that becomes admissible as a result of the defendant attacking another person's character (see *section 101(1)(g)*). A defendant attacks another person's character if he gives evidence that they committed an offence (either the one charged or a different one) or have behaved in a reprehensible way – *section 106(1)(a*) and *106(2)*. This is similar to the definition of evidence of bad character in *section 98* but it also includes evidence relating to the facts of the offence charged and its investigation and prosecution. Thus, a defendant would be attacking a prosecution witness if he claimed that they were lying in their version of events or adduced evidence of their previous misconduct to undermine their credibility. But a suggestion that a witness is mistaken is not intended to engage this provision.

380. A defendant also attacks another person's character if he or his representative ask questions that are intended (or are likely) to elicit evidence of this sort or if the defendant makes an allegation of this nature when questioned under caution or on being charged with the offence and this is heard in evidence – (*section 106(1)(b) and (c))*.

381. Where a defendant has attacked another person's character, evidence of his own bad character becomes admissible (but only by the prosecution – see *section 106(3))*. Evidence admissible on this basis may, however, be excluded under *section 101(3*).

382. Evidence admissible under section 101(1)(g) – as under section 101(1)(f) - will primarily go to the credit of the defendant. Currently a jury would be directed that evidence admitted in similar circumstances, under the 1898 Act, goes only to credibility and is not relevant to the issue of guilt. Such directions have been criticised and the new statutory scheme does not specify that this evidence is to be treated in such a way. However, it is expected that judges will explain the purpose for which the evidence is being put forward and direct the jury about the sort of weight that can be placed on it.

### *Section 107: Stopping the case where evidence contaminated*

383. *Section 107* deals with circumstances in which bad character evidence has been admitted but it later emerges that the evidence is contaminated, that is, has been affected by an agreement with other witnesses or by hearing the views or evidence of other witnesses so that it is false or misleading (see *Section 107(5))*.

384. Ordinarily it is for the jury to decide whether or not to believe evidence and decide on the weight to be placed on it. In cases where a question of contamination has arisen, the current position is that the judge must draw that matter to the jury's attention and warn them that if they are not satisfied that the evidence can be relied on as free of collusion, then they cannot rely on it against the defendant. If it becomes apparent that the evidence is so contaminated that it could not reasonably be accepted as free from collusion, the judge should go further and direct the jury not to rely on the evidence for any purpose adverse to the defence. This will continue to be the case.

385. However, there may be cases where it is not possible to expect the jury to put this evidence completely out of their mind. There are existing common law powers for the judge to withdraw a case from the jury at any time following the close of the prosecution case. *Section 107* builds on these powers by conferring a duty on the judge to stop the case if the contamination is such that, considering the importance of the evidence to the case, a conviction would be unsafe. This is intended to be a high test and if the judge were to consider that a direction along the lines described above would be sufficient to deal with any potential difficulties, then the question of safety does not arise and the case should not be withdrawn.

386. Having stopped the case the judge may consider that there is still sufficient uncontaminated evidence against the defendant to merit his retrial or may consider that the prosecution case has been so weakened that the defendant should be acquitted. *Section 107(1)* provides for the judge to take either of these courses. If, however, an acquittal is ordered then the defendant is also to be acquitted of any other offence for which he could have been convicted, if the judge is also satisfied that the contamination would affect a conviction for that offence in the same way (*Section 107(2)). Section 107(3*) extends the duty to the situation where a jury is determining under the Criminal Procedure (Insanity) Act 1964 whether a person, who is deemed unfit to plead, did the act or omission charged. *Section 107(4)* makes it clear that the section does not affect any existing court powers in relation to ordering an acquittal or discharging a jury.

### *Section 108 – Offences committed by defendant when a child*

387. *Section 108* deals with the admissibility of certain juvenile convictions. Subsection *(1)* repeals section 16(2) and (3) of the Children and Young Persons Act 1963. That provision precludes the use in evidence of certain juvenile convictions (those relating to offences committed under the age of 14) in a trial for an offence committed over the age of 21.

388. The admissibility of this evidence will instead fall under the general scheme for admitting evidence of bad character set out in this Part, but will also have to satisfy the two further requirements of subsection (2). The additional requirements are:

- that the offence for which the defendant is being tried and the offence for which the defendant was convicted are triable only on indictment; and
- that the court is satisfied that the interests of justice require the evidence to be admissible.

### *Section 109: **Assumption of truth in assessment of relevance or probative value***

389. *Section 109* requires a court, when considering the relevance or probative value of bad character evidence, to assume that the evidence is true. This reflects the distinction between the roles of the judge and jury: it is for the jury to form a view on matters of fact, such as the reliability of the evidence, and for the judge to rule on issues of law. However, there may be occasions where evidence is so unreliable that no reasonable jury could believe that it was true. In these circumstances, intended very much to be exceptional cases, *Section 109(2*) makes it clear that the judge does not have to assume the evidence is true. In making this decision, the court should normally make its decision based on the papers before it; however there may be exceptional circumstances in which a separate hearing on the issue (a *voir dire*) might be necessary. This reflects the current common law position as established in *R v H* [1995] 2 AC 596 which considered the admissibility of similar fact evidence in cases of alleged collusion.

### *Section 110: **Court's duty to give reason for rulings***

390. Section 110 requires a court to give reasons for its rulings under these provisions. These must be given in open court and, in the magistrates' courts, entered into the register of proceedings, ensuring that a record is kept. This applies to rulings on whether an item to evidence is evidence of bad character, rulings on questions of admissibility and exclusion and any decision to withdraw a case from the jury.

### *Section 111: **Rules of court***

391. *Section 111* makes provision for rules of court to be drawn up to require the prosecution and a co-defendant to give notice of their intention to adduce evidence of a defendant's bad character (or elicit such evidence from a witness). In relation to prosecution evidence, such rules *must* be made. Such rules may also include provision for the defendant to waive any notice requirement. (*section 111(3)*). The court is empowered to take a failure to give the required notice into account in considering the exercise of its powers in respect of costs (*section 111 (4)).*

### *Section 112: **Interpretation of** Chapter 1*

392. *Section 112* defines terms employed in this Part. *Subsection (2)* makes it clear that where the defendant is charged with two or more offences the provisions of this Part refer to each charge as separate proceedings. This means that bad character evidence that is admissible in relation to one charge in the proceedings is not automatically admissible in relation to another charge in the same proceedings, but must instead meet the provisions of this Chapter to be admissible in respect of that charge. It also means that evidence relevant on one charge is not rendered inadmissible if not also relevant to other charges. However, where the court is looking at whether the evidence should be excluded under section 101(3) then the court is to look at the effect of the admission of the evidence on the fairness of the proceedings as a whole and not just the charges for which the evidence is admissible.

393. *Section 112(3)* makes it clear that nothing in this Chapter affects the exclusion of evidence on certain other grounds. These are:

- the rule in section 3 of the Criminal Procedure Act 1865 against a party impeaching the credit of his own witness by general evidence of bad character;
- section 41 of the Youth Justice and Criminal Evidence Act 1999 which places restrictions on evidence or questions about a complainant's sexual history;
- any other power to exclude the evidence, on grounds other than it is evidence of a person's bad character, for example under section 78 of the Police and Criminal Evidence Act 1984 which provides for the exclusion of unfair evidence, or under the provisions of Chapter 2 of this Part relating to hearsay.

### *Section 113: **Armed forces***

394. *Section 113* introduces *Schedule 6*. *Schedule 6* applies the provisions of Chapter 1 to the service courts, modifying them as necessary.

### *Chapter 2: **Hearsay evidence***

### *Section 114: **Admissibility of hearsay evidence***

395. *Subsections (1)-(3)* set out the circumstances in which a statement which is not made in oral evidence during criminal proceedings can be used as evidence of the facts stated within it. For example, if B was charged with robbery of a jewellers, the prosecution might want A to testify that B told her that he was "outside the jewellers at midday on Monday" in order to prove that B was outside the jewellers at the relevant time. As these subsections remove the common law rule against the admission of such hearsay evidence, this out-of court statement will be admissible in A's testimony, *provided* it comes under one of the following heads:

- It is admissible under a statutory provision;
- It is admissible under a common law rule preserved by this Chapter of Part 11 of the Act;
- The parties agree that it can go in; or
- The court gives leave to admit the statement.

396. Before the court can grant leave to admit such a statement (under the fourth head above and found in *subsection (1)(d)*), it must be satisfied that it is in the interests of justice to admit the evidence. The intention, therefore, is that the court should be able to admit an out-of-court statement which does not fall within any of the other categories of admissibility, where it is cogent and reliable.

397. *Subsection (2)* sets out some of the factors that the court must consider when deciding whether to grant leave under the discretion in *Subsection (1)(d)*. Some of these factors are:

- the degree of relevance of the statement in proving a matter in issue in the trial (assuming the statement to be true);
- the circumstances in which it was made (if indeed it was made at all);
- the extent to which it supplies evidence which would not otherwise be available;
- the creditworthiness of the maker of the statement;
- the reason why oral evidence cannot be given;
- the extent to which the other party can challenge the statement, and the risk of unfairness.

398. The list is intended to focus attention on whether the circumstances surrounding the making of the out of court statement indicate that it can be treated as reliable enough to admit it as evidence, despite the fact that it will not be subject to cross-examination.

399. *Subsection (3)* provides that out of court statements may still be excluded even if they fulfil the requirements in this Chapter. For example, confessions must meet the additional requirements of sections 76 and 78 of the Police and Criminal Evidence Act 1984 before admission.

### *Section 115: **Statements and matters stated***

400. This section defines the type of statements which will be covered by Chapter 2. Its purpose is to overturn the ruling in *Kearley* [1992] 2 AC 228 that "implied assertions" are covered by the hearsay rule and therefore prima facie inadmissible. Under *subsection (3)*, a statement is one to which this Chapter applies if it is the purpose of the person making the statement to:

- cause the hearer to believe that the matter stated is true or to act on the basis that it is true; or
- cause a machine to operate on the basis that the matter is as stated.

401. *Section 115* therefore changes the common law position and will *not* prevent the admission of such implied assertions on the basis of the hearsay rule. Equally, where the assertion relates to a failure to record an event, sometimes known as negative hearsay, it will not be covered by Chapter 2 if it was not the purpose of the person who failed to record the event to *cause* anyone to believe that the event did not occur.

402. *Subsection (2)* preserves the present position whereby statements which are not based on human input fall outside the ambit of the hearsay rule. Tapes, films or photographs which directly record the commission of an offence and documents produced by machines which automatically record a process or event or perform calculations will not therefore be covered by Chapter 2.

### *Section 116: **Cases where a witness is unavailable***

403. This section sets out a series of categories under which first-hand hearsay evidence, whether oral or documentary, will be admissible, provided that the witness is unavailable to testify for a specified reason. The new provisions will be available to the prosecution and the defence.

404. A statement will be admissible under this section (subject to the additional conditions explained below) if the person who made it is:

- Dead (*subsection (2)(a)*);
- Ill (*subsection (2)(b)*);
- Absent abroad (*subsection (2)(c)*);
- Disappeared (*subsection (2)(d)*); or
- In fear (*subsection (2)(e)*).

405. *Subsections (2)(e) and (4)* make specific provision for the admissibility, with leave of the court, of statements of witnesses who are too frightened to testify (or to continue testifying) provided the interests of justice do not dictate otherwise. In considering the interests of justice, the court should have regard to what was said in the statement; any risk of unfairness to other parties in the case; to the fact that special measures directions may be made in relation to a witness under Part II of the Youth Justice and Criminal Evidence Act 1999; and to any other relevant circumstances (*subsection (4))*. *Subsection (3)* provides that "fear" must be widely construed.

406. There are a number of other conditions which apply to the admissibility of evidence under *Section 116.* A statement can *only* be adduced as truth of any matter stated if:

- the witness's oral evidence would have been admissible itself (*subsection (1)(a)*); and
- the person who made the statement is identified to the court's satisfaction *(subsection (1)(b))*. This will enable the opposing party to challenge the absent witness's credibility under *section 124.*

407. Additionally, even if all the relevant conditions mentioned above are satisfied, the evidence will not be allowed if a party, or someone acting on his behalf, *causes* the unavailability of the declarant (*subsection (5))*. This is intended to focus attention on cases where a party acts with the *intention* of preventing a witness from giving evidence. It is up to the party opposing admission to prove this to the court.

### *Section 117: Business and other documents*

408. This Section provides for the admissibility of statements in documentary records provided certain conditions are met. These conditions are (*subsection (2)*):

- the document was created or received by a person in the course of a trade, business, profession or as the holder of a paid or unpaid office; and
- the person who *supplied* the information in the statement had or may reasonably be supposed to have had personal knowledge of the matters dealt with in the statement; and
- each person through whom the information was supplied received the information in the course of a trade, business, profession or other occupation or as the holder of a paid or unpaid office.

409. *Subsection (2)* therefore reflects the current position relating to business and other documents in section 24 (1)(c)(ii) and section 24(2) of the Criminal Justice Act 1988, which is being repealed. However, in the case of documents prepared for the purpose of criminal investigations or proceedings, the statement will only be admissible if the *supplier* of the information is unavailable or cannot reasonably be expected to recall any of the matters dealt with in the statement.

410. Even if a statement in a documentary record meets the conditions as set out in this Section, the evidence will not be allowed if it is considered unreliable. *Subsections (6) and (7)* permit the court to direct that the statement shall not be admissible where there is reason to doubt its reliability on the basis of its contents, source of information, mode of supply and circumstances of creation or reception.

### *Section 118: Preservation of common law categories of admissibility*

411. This section preserves a number of common law exceptions to the old rule against the admission of hearsay evidence. The preservation of these rules means that in the specified circumstances, an out of court statement will be admissible as evidence of any matters stated in it. Many of these rules were also preserved under the corresponding civil evidence provisions in section 7 of the Civil Evidence Act 1995. The common law rules preserved in paragraphs (1) to (8) are as follows:

- 'Public information' will be admissible. This includes published works; public documents; records of certain courts, treaties, Crown grants, pardons and commissions; evidence relating to a person's age or date of birth;
- 'Reputation as to character' will be admissible as evidence of a person's good or bad character;

- 'Reputation or family tradition' will be admissible as evidence to prove or disprove pedigree or the existence of marriage; a public or general right; or the identity of a person or thing.
- 'Res gestae' will be admissible (this rule is explained below);
- 'Confessions' will be admissible as long as they fulfil the requirements of sections 76, 76A and 78 of the Police and Criminal Evidence Act 1984;
- 'Admissions by agents' will be admissible against the defendant as evidence of any fact stated.
- The rule of 'common enterprise' is preserved. This means that a statement made by a party to a common enterprise will be admissible against another party to the enterprise as evidence of any matter stated. For example, if it is independently proved that A and B are involved in a joint enterprise to rob a jewellers', any incriminating statements made by A will also be admissible against B.
- The rule of 'expert evidence' is preserved. This permits an expert to give evidence of any relevant matter which forms part of his professional expertise (although not acquired through personal experience) and to draw upon technical information widely used by members of the expert's profession.

412. Paragraph *(4)* preserves the common law rule known as "*res gestae*". One justification for this exception is that reported words which are very closely connected to a relevant event are reliable accounts and should therefore be admissible in certain circumstances. Such statement may be admitted if *one* of the following conditions is met:

- the statement is made by a person who was so emotionally overpowered by an event that the possibility that he was lying can be disregarded;
- the statement accompanied an act which can properly be evaluated as evidence only if considered together with the statement. For example, if the act doesn't make sense without the statement; or

the statement relates to a physical sensation or mental state, such as an intention or emotion.

### *Section 119*: ***Inconsistent statements.***

413. This section clarifies the relationship between hearsay evidence and previous inconsistent statements. It provides that if a witness admits that he has made a previous inconsistent statement or it has been proved that he made such an inconsistent statement, it is *not only* evidence which undermines his 'credibility' (as someone who makes inconsistent statements) but it is also evidence of the *truth* of its contents.

414. *Subsection (2)* envisages the following type of situation. A makes a statement to the police that she saw B 'outside the jewellers' at midday on Monday'. A does not testify at trial but her statement is admitted under *Section 116*. As explained below, *Section 124* provides that evidence can be admitted in this type of situation in relation to the credibility of A. *Subsection (2)(c)* of *Section 124* provides that evidence can be admitted to prove that A had made another statement inconsistent with this statement (for example, A had said earlier that she did not see B on Monday at all). Section*119(2)* provides that if there is such an inconsistent statement, it not only goes to the credibility of A, but it is also admissible as to the truth of its contents (that A did not see B on Monday).

### *Section 120: **Other previous statements by witnesses***

415. This section makes *other* previous statements admissible as evidence of the truth of their contents (not merely to bolster the credibility of the witness's oral evidence) in the following circumstances:

- *Subsection (2)* applies to statements which are admitted to rebut a suggestion that the witness's oral evidence is untrue;
- *Subsection (3)* applies to the situation where a witness is "refreshing his memory" from a written document. If he is cross-examined on the document and it is received in evidence, the statement will be evidence of any matter contained within it;
- *Subsections (4) - (7)* provide that a previous statement will be admissible as evidence of the facts contained within it provided the witness states that he made the statement and believes it to be true *and* one of the following conditions is met:
    - The statement describes or identifies a person, place or thing (which includes objects such as a car registration number) ; or
    - The statement was made when the incident was fresh in the witness's memory and he cannot reasonably be expected to remember the matters stated. The intention is that where a witness has to rely on another person, or a document, or both to fill in details which he or she can no longer remember, this fact should go to the *weight* of the evidence, but should not make it inadmissible; or
    - The statement consists of a complaint by a victim of the alleged offence which was made as soon as could reasonably be expected after the conduct in question, and the witness gives oral evidence in relation to the matter. There is a further requirement for such a statement to be admissible which is that the complaint must not have been made as a result of a threat or a promise.

### *Section 121: **Additional requirement for admissibility of multiple hearsay***

416. This section sets out the approach which the courts should take to multiple hearsay. "Multiple hearsay" is where information passes through more than one person before it is recorded.

417. Under the section a hearsay statement is admissible to prove the fact that another statement was made in three circumstances. These are:

- Either of the statements is admissible under sections 117 (business documents) 119 (inconsistent statements) or 120 (other previous statement of a witnesses);
- All parties to the proceedings agree; or
- The court uses its discretion to admit the statement.

418. The test for the court in deciding whether to exercise its discretion is whether it is satisfied that the value of the evidence in question, taking into account how reliable the statement appears to be, is so high that the interests of justice require the later statement to be admissible for that purpose. This discretion is intended to cover exceptional circumstances where although multiple hearsay does not fall within one of the specified categories for admissibility (in section 121 (1)(a) or (b)) it nevertheless should be admitted in the interests of justice.

### *Section 122: **Documents produced as exhibits***

419. This section provides that if a statement previously made by a witness is admitted in evidence and produced as an exhibit under *Sections 119 or 120*, the jury should not take the exhibit with them when they retire to the jury room, unless the court considers it appropriate or all the parties agree that it should accompany them.

### *Section 123: Capability to make statement*

420. This section provides that an out of court statement cannot be admitted under *sections 116, 119 or 120* if the person who made the statement did not have the "required capability" for making a statement at the time the statement was made. A statement may not be admitted under *section 117* if any person who supplied or received the information or created or received the document did not have the "required capability" or, where that person cannot be identified, cannot reasonably be assumed to have had the required capability. Under *subsection (2)* a person is deemed to have the required capability for the purposes of this section if he can understand questions put to him and give answers which can be understood. This section reflects the test for witness competence to give evidence in criminal proceedings under section 53 of the Youth Justice and Criminal Evidence Act 1999.

### *Section 124: Credibility*

421. This section makes provision for challenges to the credibility of the maker of a hearsay statement who does not give oral evidence in person in the proceedings. If such hearsay statement is admitted as evidence of a matter stated *section 124* provides certain rights for the person against whom hearsay evidence has been admitted to produce, in specified circumstances, evidence to discredit the maker of the statement or to show that he has contradicted himself. *Section 124* thus provides a replacement for the corresponding provisions in section 28(2) and paragraph 1 of Schedule 2 to the CJA 1988.

### *Section 125: Stopping the case where evidence is unconvincing*

422. *Subsection (1)* imposes a duty on the court to stop a case and either direct the jury to acquit the defendant, or discharge the jury, if the case against him or her is based wholly or partly on an out of court statement which is so unconvincing that, considering its importance to the case, a conviction would be unsafe. This issue only arises in relation to jury trials (and by virtue of paragraph 4 of Schedule 7 to service courts) because in other cases, the finders of fact would be bound to dismiss a case in these circumstances, or order a retrial if appropriate.

423. Similarly, *subsection (2)* imposes a corresponding duty on the court to direct the jury to acquit of any other offence not charged, of which they could convict by way of an alternative to the offence charged, if the judge is satisfied that a conviction would be unsafe. *Subsection (3)* extends the duty to cases under the Criminal Procedure (Insanity) Act 1964 where a jury is required to determine whether a defendant, who is deemed unfit to plead, did the act (or made the omission) charged.

### *Section 126: Court's general discretion to exclude evidence*

424. This section provides a further discretion to exclude superfluous out of court statements if the court is satisfied that the value of the evidence is substantially outweighed by the undue waste of time which its admission would cause. *Subsection (2)* preserves both the existing common law power for the court to exclude evidence where its prejudicial effect is out of proportion to its probative value and the discretion contained in section 78 of the Police and Criminal Evidence Act 1984 in relation to the admission of unfair evidence.

### *Section 127: Expert evidence: preparatory work*

425. This section seeks to address the problem which arises where information relied upon by an expert witness is outside the personal experience of the expert (for example work undertaken by an assistant) and cannot be proved by other admissible evidence. The intention is that the rules about advance notice of expert evidence will be amended so as to require advance notice of the name of any person who has prepared information on which the expert has relied. It is envisaged that any other party to the proceedings will

be able to apply for a direction that any such person must give evidence in person but a direction will only be given if the court is satisfied that it is in the interests of justice.

426. In cases where no such application is made in respect of any assistant listed, or an application is made but refused, *section 127* will enable the expert witness to base his evidence on any information supplied by that assistant on matters of which that assistant had personal knowledge. *Section 127* applies if:

- The statement was prepared for the purpose of criminal proceedings;
- The expert's assistant had or might reasonably be supposed to have had personal knowledge of the matters stated; and
- A notice has been given under the advance notice rules of the name of a person who has prepared a statement on which it is proposed that the expert witness should base any opinion or inference, and the nature of the matters stated.

427. Where *section 127(1)* applies, the expert may base an opinion or inference on the statement and any information so relied upon will be admissible as evidence of its truth.

428. *Subsections (4) and (5)* permit a party to the proceedings to apply for an order that the exception should not apply in the interests of justice. In deciding whether to make such an order, the court may take into account any of the matters mentioned in *subsection (5)*.

### *Section 128:* ***Confessions***

429. This section inserts section 76A of the Police and Criminal Evidence Act 1984. The position prior to the insertion of this new section 76A was that whilst the prosecution could not make use of a confession which was obtained in breach of sections 76 or 78 of the Police and Criminal Evidence Act 1984, a co-defendant *could* use it to undermine another co-defendant's account or to strengthen their own case. Instead, section 76A applies the same rules to confessions adduced by the co-defendant to those adduced by the prosecution under sections 76 and 78 of PACE. That is, the confession will not be allowed if obtained by oppression or is rendered unreliable. 'Oppression' is defined in identical terms to section 76(8) of PACE.

430. Unlike the requirements for the prosecution, under section 76A(2), the co-accused would only need to satisfy the court on the *balance of probabilities* that the confession was not obtained by oppression or in circumstances likely to render it unreliable.

431. *Subsection (4)* maintains the rule that the exclusion of a confession does not affect the admissibility of facts discovered as a result of that confession.

### *Section 129:* ***Representations other than by a person***

432. This section provides where a statement generated by a machine is based on information implanted into the machine by a human, the output of the device will only be admissible where it is proved that the information was accurate. *Subsection (2)* preserves the common law presumption that a mechanical device has been properly set or calibrated.

### *Section 130:* ***Depositions***

433. This repeals paragraph 5(4) of Schedule 3 of the Crime and Disorder Act 1998 which provided that a judge could overrule an objection to a deposition being read as evidence if he considered it to be in the interests of justice to do so.

### *Section 131:* ***Evidence at retrial***

434. *Section 131* provides that if a retrial is ordered by the Court of Appeal, evidence must be given orally if it was given that way at the original trial except in certain defined situations, in which case a transcript of the earlier evidence may be used. These exceptions are:

- All parties agree to the evidence being admitted;
- A witness is unavailable to give evidence in accordance with *section 116*; or
- A witness is unavailable to give evidence for a reason other than those listed in *section 116*and his evidence is admitted under the residual discretion in *section 114(1)(d)*.

### *Section 132: Rules of court*

435. *Section 132* gives a power for making rules of court about the provisions in the Act. The intention is that rules of court will govern both the notice and leave procedures under Chapter 2. *Subsection (5)(b)* provides that the court or jury can, with leave, draw an adverse inference from the failure of a party to comply with the prescribed requirements.

### *Section 133: Proof of statements in documents*

436. This section corresponds to the position under section 27 of the Criminal Justice Act 1988, whereby a statement in a document can be proved by producing either the original document or an authenticated copy. It is intended to cover all forms of copying including the use of imaging technology.

### *Sections 134-136 : Final provisions*

437. *Section 135* introduces Schedule 7 which makes provision for Chapter 2 to apply to proceedings before courts-martial, Standing Civilian Courts and the Court-Martial Appeal Court, modifying them as necessary.

*Section 136* repeals existing legislation which is spent or is superseded by this Act.

## *Chapter 3 : Miscellaneous and Supplemental*

### *Section 137: Evidence by video recording*

438. This section permits a video recording of an interview with a witness (other than the defendant), or a part of such a recording, to be admitted as evidence in chief of the witness in a wider range of circumstances than is presently the case. *Subsection (1)* provides that the court can authorise such a video recording to replace the evidence-in-chief of a witness *provided* that:

- the person claims to be an witness to the offence (or part of it) or to events closely connected to the offence;
- the video recording of the statement was made at a time when events were fresh in the witness's memory; and
- the alleged offence can only be tried in the Crown Court or is an either-way offence prescribed by Order of the Secretary of State.

439. If the recording satisfies these requirements, the court may admit the recording *provided* that:

- the witness's recollection of events is likely to be significantly better at the time he gave the recorded account than by the time of the trial; and
- it is in the interests of justice to admit the recording, having regard to whether the recording is an early and reliable account from the witness, whether the quality is adequate, and any views which the witness may have about using the recording for this purpose.

440. Under *subsection (2)* evidence given by a video recording shall be treated as if it was given orally in court in the usual way, providing the witness asserts the truth of it.

### *Section 138: Video evidence : further provisions*

441. Where a video recording (or part of one) is admitted under section 137, *section 138 (1)* states that the recording should be the final statement of any matters dealt with adequately within the recording for the purpose of the witness's evidence-in-chief.

442. *Subsection (2)* allows video recordings to be edited if the interests of justice so require. In determining whether to allow only an edited recording to be used, the court will have to consider whether the parts sought to be excluded are so prejudicial as to outweigh the desirability of using the whole recording.

### *Section 139: Use of documents to refresh memory*

443. This section creates a presumption that a witness in criminal proceedings may refresh his memory from a document whilst giving evidence providing that:

- he indicates that the document represents his recollection at the time he made it; and
- his recollection was likely to be significantly better at the time the document was made (or verified).

The fact that the witness has read the statement before coming into the witness box will not affect this presumption.

444. In view of the practical difficulties associated with memory refreshing in the witness box from an audio or video recording, *subsection (2)* makes provision for a witness to refresh his memory from a transcript of such a recording.

## Part 12 - Sentencing

### *Chapter 1: General provisions about sentencing*

### *Section 142: Purposes of sentencing*

445. For the first time, the purposes of adult sentencing will be set out in statute. *Subsection (1)* sets out what these are: punishment, crime reduction, the reform and rehabilitation of offenders, public protection, and reparation. There are exceptions where these purposes will not be applicable, specified in *subsection (2)*. These exceptions are where an offender is under 18 (there are separate purposes for the aims of the youth justice system which can be found in the Crime and Disorder Act 1998), where the sentence is fixed by law (i.e. a mandatory life sentence imposed for murder), where offences require certain custodial sentences (Sections 225 to 228 of this Act and sections 110 and 111 of the Powers of Criminal Courts (Sentencing) Act 2000, and section 51A of the Firearms Act 1968), and where various provisions under the Mental Health Act 1983 apply.

### *Section 143: Determining the seriousness of an offence*

446. This section sets out certain principles the court must follow when determining the seriousness of an offence. The court must consider the offender's culpability in committing the offence and any harm which the offence caused, was intended to cause or might foreseeably have caused. Any previous convictions, where they are recent and relevant, should be regarded as an aggravating factor which should increase the severity of the sentence. A previous conviction is defined by subsection (4) to mean a previous conviction by a court in the United Kingdom or a finding of guilt in service disciplinary proceedings. The term "service disciplinary proceedings" is defined in section 305(1). This is a strengthening of the existing principle in section 151(1) of the Powers of Criminal Courts (Sentencing) Act 2000. *Subsection (3)* re-enacts section 151(2) of that Act and provides that the fact that an offence was committed while the offender was on bail should also be regarded as an aggravating factor.

### *Section 144: **Reduction in sentence for guilty pleas***

447. This section re-enacts section 152(1) and (3) of the Powers of Criminal Courts (Sentencing) Act and makes provision for the reduction of sentences for early guilty pleas, in order to encourage those defendants who are guilty not to take up valuable court time and trouble victims and witnesses unnecessarily. *Subsection (1)* requires the court to take into account exactly when in the course of proceedings the guilty plea was made and the circumstances in which it was given. For those sentences falling to be imposed under sections 110(2) or 111(2) of Powers of Criminal Courts (Sentencing) Act the court can reduce the sentence by up to 20 per cent.

### *Section 145: **Increase in sentence for racial or religious aggravation***

448. This section re-enacts section 153 of the Powers of Criminal Courts (Sentencing) Act 2000 and provides that, except in the case of offences under sections 29 to 32 of the Crime and Disorder Act 1998, the court must treat the fact that the offence was religiously or racially aggravated as increasing the seriousness of the offence, and must state in open court it was so aggravated. The definition of "racially or religiously aggravated" can be found in section 28 of the 1998 Act.

### *Section 146: **Increase in sentences for aggravation related to disability or sexual orientation***

449. This is a new provision, which is based upon the preceding section, and provides that the seriousness of an offence (and thus the severity of the resulting sentence) should be increased if the offender demonstrates hostility based on the victim's sexual orientation or disability or if the offence was motivated by hostility by reason of a person's sexual orientation or disability. The court must state in open court if the offence is aggravated for these reasons.

### *Section 147: **Meaning of "community sentence" etc.***

450. This section defines "community sentence" for the purposes of Part 12 of the Act and also defines "youth community order" for the purposes of Chapter 1 of that Part.

### *Section 148: **Restrictions on imposing a community sentence***

451. *Subsection (1)* re-enacts section 35(1) of the Powers of Criminal Courts (Sentencing) Act. *Subsection (2)* re-enacts with a few minor changes section 35(3) of that Act. *Subsection (3)* sets out the same principles for youth community orders which remain in the Powers of Criminal Courts (Sentencing) Act. The section makes provision as to when it is appropriate to impose a community sentence. If an offence is not serious enough for a community sentence, a fine, conditional discharge or absolute discharge would be appropriate. For a community sentence to be passed, an offence should be serious enough to warrant one. Further, the requirements which will form part of the (new) community sentence should be the most suitable ones for the offender and the restrictions on the liberty of the offender (such as a curfew requirement) must be in line with the seriousness of the offence. There is an exception, where an offence itself does not warrant a community sentence but where the offender has committed several similar offences in the past. This case is dealt with in section 151.

### *Section 149: **Passing of community sentence on offender remanded in custody***

452. If an offender has been remanded in custody, and then receives a custodial sentence, his time on remand counts towards his sentence. This is covered in section 240. Section 149 enables the court to have regard to any time spent on remand when putting together the requirements of a community sentence, and deciding upon what restrictions on liberty ought to be imposed.

### *Section 150: **Community sentence not available where sentence fixed by law, etc.***

453. This section re-enacts section 34 of the Powers of Criminal Courts (Sentencing) Act, but now refers to the new sentences for dangerous offenders. A community sentence is not available in respect of offences for which the sentence is fixed by law, or where sentences for dangerous offenders (in *Sections 225 to 228*) or under sections 110 and 111 of the Powers of Criminal Courts (Sentencing) Act, or under section 51A of the Firearms Act 1968 apply.

### *Section 151: **Community order for persistent offender previously fined***

454. This section replaces existing provisions in section 59 of the Powers of Criminal Courts (Sentencing) Act. In addition to the general principle set out in section 143 for dealing with persistent offenders, this section provides the court with an additional discretionary power for dealing with persistent petty offenders. Where an offender aged 16 or over has been sentenced to a fine on at least three previous occasions, the court may impose a community sentence even if the current offence is one which would on its own warrant a fine. *Subsection (3)* directs the court to consider the nature of the previous offences, and how recent and relevant they are to the current offence. *Subsection (6)* provides that, for the purposes of determining whether the criteria are met, it does not matter whether the offender has on previous sentencing occasions received community or custodial sentences. *Subsection (7)* makes it clear that this Section does not interfere with the court's wider power to treat previous convictions as increasing the seriousness of the offence (see section 143).

### *Section 152: **General restrictions on imposing discretionary custodial sentences***

455. As with community sentences, a court cannot impose a custodial sentence except where the offence, taken in combination with any past offences, merits it. This section, which largely re-enacts section 79 of the Powers of Criminal Courts (Sentencing) Act, sets out this principle. *Subsection (1)* excludes from this consideration those offences which fall to be punished under the scheme for sentencing dangerous offenders (sections 225 to 228) and those which fall to be sentenced under sections 110 and 111 of the Powers of Criminal Courts (Sentencing) Act and section 51A of the Firearms Act 1968. *Subsection (2)*, which is based on section 79(2)(a) of the Powers of Criminal Courts (Sentencing) Act, states that a custodial sentence must only be imposed if the offence(s) is so serious that neither a fine nor a community sentence would be adequate punishment for it. *Subsection (3)* re-enacts section 79(3) of the Powers of Criminal Courts (Sentencing) Act. It provides that *subsection (2)* does not prevent a court from passing a custodial sentence on an offender who fails to consent to requirements imposed as part of a community sentence, where such consent is required) or if he refuses to comply with an order under section 161(2) to provide samples for the purposes of drug testing.

### *Section 153: **Length of discretionary custodial sentences: general provision***

456. This section re-enacts section 80 of the Powers of Criminal Courts (Sentencing) Act but modifies that provision to direct the court to impose the shortest term that is commensurate with the seriousness of the offence(s), subject to mandatory minimum sentences (in sections 110 and 111 of the Powers of Criminal Courts (Sentencing) Act and 51A of the Firearms Act 1968) and the provisions of the extended sentence in Sections 227 and 228. *Subsection (1)* provides an exception to the rule for the case where the sentence is fixed by law (i.e. as a mandatory life sentence), and in the case of a discretionary life sentence or a new sentence of imprisonment or detention for public protection (sections 225 and 226).

### *Section 154: **General limits on magistrates' court's power to impose imprisonment***

457. This section re-enacts section 78 Powers of Criminal Courts (Sentencing) Act but with a significant amendment. This is an increase in magistrates' sentencing powers so as to

enable them to impose custodial sentences of up to and including 12 months in respect of any one offence. These powers are, by virtue of *subsection (4)* without prejudice to any term of imprisonment which may be imposed for non-payment of a fine.

### *Section 155: **Consecutive terms of imprisonment***

458. This section amends the Magistrates Courts Act 1980, adding to the powers in section 154, by giving magistrates the power to impose a custodial term of 65 weeks in respect of two or more offences to be served consecutively.

### *Section 156: **Pre-sentence reports and other requirements***

459. This section re-enacts with amendments the existing provisions in sections 36 and 81 of the Powers of Criminal Courts (Sentencing) Act which cover pre-sentence reports for community and custodial sentences. When a court is considering whether to impose a discretionary custodial sentence and how long it should be, or whether to impose a community sentence and what restrictions to put on the offender's liberty as part of that sentence (*Sections 148, 152 and 153*) the court must take into account all the information available to it, including information about the offence and about the offender.

460. Before imposing such a sentence, the Court must obtain a pre-sentence report. Pre-sentence reports are written in the case of adults by the probation service based on an interview and analysis of the offender and his offending history and needs. The pre-sentence report contains advice about what punishment might be appropriate and what rehabilitative work would be likely to prove effective with the offender in order to reduce the risk that he will re-offend.

461. However, *subsection (4)* provides that the court need not obtain a pre-sentence report if it considers it unnecessary to do so in any individual case. *Subsection (5)* provides further protection for juvenile offenders and exempts them from subsection (4). As a result, for offenders under the age of 18, the court must not dispense with the requirement to obtain a pre-sentence report, unless there already is one that relates to the offender and the court has access to it. Under *subsection (6)*, no sentence is invalidated by the failure of a court to obtain and consider a pre-sentence report, even if a pre-sentence report is required under *subsection (3)*.

462. If the offender appeals against sentence, and the lower court did not obtain a pre-sentence report, a pre-sentence report must be obtained and considered unless the appellate court believes the original court was justified in not obtaining a pre-sentence report or the current circumstances are such that a pre-sentence report is not necessary. The situation in relation to appeals for offenders under the age of 18 is slightly different. Unless there is a previous pre-sentence report about the offender and the court has access to it (*subsection (8)*) the court may not decide the original court was justified in not requiring a pre-sentence report or deciding that current circumstances are such that a pre-sentence report is not necessary.

### *Section 157: **Additional requirements in case of mentally disordered offender***

463. This section re-enacts section 82 of the Powers of Criminal Courts (Sentencing) Act. Special provision is made for mentally disordered offenders: qualified medical practitioners must be consulted before a custodial sentence is imposed (unless the sentence is one that is fixed by law). The court can also decide not to request a medical report if it considers it unnecessary in a particular case. The court must consider any information before it relating to the offender's mental condition and the likely effect of a custodial sentence on the offender and on any treatment which might be available to him. If the court does not obtain a medical report this does not invalidate any sentence passed, but on appeal the court must obtain and consider a medical report. *Subsection (6)* defines a medical report, which is different from a pre-sentence report,

and *subsection (7)* says that provisions under this Section do not limit the provisions for pre-sentence reports in section 156.

### *Section 158: **Meaning of "pre-sentence reports"***

464. This section re-enacts section 162 of the Powers of Criminal Courts (Sentencing) Act and provides a definition for a pre-sentence report described in the preceding Sections. Such a report must be prepared by an "appropriate officer", defined in *subsection (2)* as an officer of the local probation board where the offender is over 18, or where the offender is under 18 a probation officer, social worker or member of a youth offending team.

### *Section 159: **Disclosure of pre-sentence reports***

465. This section re-enacts section 156 of the Powers of Criminal Courts (Sentencing) Act with changes in respect of the disclosure of pre-sentence reports to juveniles. Where the court does obtain a written pre-sentence report, copies of it must be provided to the persons specified in this section. Normally this should be the offender or his legal representative, the parent or guardian of an offender who is under 18, and the prosecutor. If however, the prosecutor is not of a description prescribed by the Secretary of State, the requirement to give the prosecutor a copy may be dispensed with if the court considers it inappropriate that he should receive one (*subsection (4)). Subsection (5)* provides that the prosecutor is only able to use the information in the pre-sentence report either for determining whether to make representations to the court or for making representations to the court about the content of the report. Where the offender is under 18 and it appears to the Court that the disclosure of a report to the offender or his parent or guardian would cause harm to the offender, the court is not obliged to give a copy to the offender or his parent or guardian if present in court (*subsection (3)*).

### *Section 160: **Other reports of local probation boards and members of youth offending teams***

466. This section re-enacts section 157 of the Powers of Criminal Courts (Sentencing) Act. It applies where a report (other than a pre-sentence report) is made by a probation officer or a member of a youth offending team with a view to assisting the court in deciding how best to deal with a person in respect of an offence (*subsection (1))*. Where the court does obtain a written report other than a pre-sentence report, copies of it must be provided to the persons specified in this section. Normally this should be the offender or his legal representative and the parent or guardian of an offender who is under 18. Where the offender is under 18 and it appears to the court that the disclosure of a report to the offender or his parent or guardian would cause harm to the offender, the court is not obliged to give a copy to the offender or his parent or guardian if present in court (*subsection (3)*).

### *Section 161: **Pre-sentence drug testing***

467. Pre-sentence drug testing is available to assist the court when it is considering imposing a community sentence. This section re-enacts, with some modifications, section 36A of the Powers of Criminal Courts (Sentencing) Act 2000(which provides for the pre-sentence drug testing of persons aged 18 and over). It enables the court to make an order, in the case of convicted offenders who are at least 14 years old, to be tested for any specified Class A drug. Where the offender is under the age of 17 years, provision must be made for an appropriate adult (as defined in subsection (8)) to be present when the sample is taken. Failure to provide a sample without a reasonable excuse is punishable by a fine. This power is only exercisable in the areas where the court has been notified by the Secretary of State that the power to make such orders is exercisable by the court. The power is extended under this section additionally to apply where the court is considering imposing a suspended sentence.

### *Section 162*: ***Powers to order statement as to offender's financial circumstances***

468. This section re-enacts section 126 of the Powers of Criminal Courts (Sentencing) Act. In some cases the court might wish to know the financial circumstances of the offender. The court can make a "financial circumstances order" in respect of an offender on conviction before sentencing him or if he pleads guilty without appearing before the court. The offender must report his financial circumstances to the court. If the offender fails to comply he commits an offence and is liable to a fine. If the offender falsifies or omits relevant information from a statement of his financial circumstances he also commits an offence and is liable to a fine. *Subsection (6)* enables proceedings for an offence under subsection (5) to be begun within two years from the date of the offence or within 6 months from its discovery.

### *Section 163*: ***General power of the Crown Court to fine offender convicted on indictment***

469. This section re-enacts section 127 of the Powers of Criminal Courts (Sentencing) Act. In general, the Crown Court can impose a fine on the offender either instead of, or in addition to, dealing with the offender in any other way. This section does not apply in relation to an offence for which the sentence is fixed by law or which falls to be imposed under sections 110 and 111 of the Powers of Criminal Courts (Sentencing) Act or the provisions for dangerous offenders in sections 225 to 228 of the Act.

### *Section 164*: ***Fixing of fines***

470. This section re-enacts section 128 of the Powers of Criminal Courts (Sentencing) Act with some modifications. The court must inquire into the financial circumstances of an offender before fixing the amount of a fine on an offender (*subsection (1)*). When determining the amount of a fine, the court must take the financial circumstances of the offender, the seriousness of the offence and the circumstances of the case into account. In certain cases where the information is not available, such as where the offender has not furnished a statement of his financial circumstances, and the court has been unable to assess the offender's financial circumstances, the court may go ahead and fix the amount it thinks appropriate (*subsection (5)).*

### *Section 165*: ***Remission of fines***

471. This section re-enacts section 129 of the Powers of Criminal Courts (Sentencing) Act. If an offender's financial circumstances are made clear to the court after it has fixed a fine, it can reduce the fine or withdraw it completely. If the offender is in prison for failing to pay the fine when such a decision is made, his term is to be reduced accordingly.

### *Section 166*: ***Savings for powers to mitigate sentences and deal appropriately with mentally disordered offenders.***

472. This section re-enacts and modifies section 158 of the Powers of Criminal Courts (Sentencing) Act and allows the court to take into account any relevant matters in mitigation of the sentence, irrespective of the obligations imposed by section 148 of this Act in respect of community sentences, by sections 152, 153 and 157 of this Act in respect of custodial sentences, by section 156 of this Act in respect of pre–sentence reports and other requirements and by section 163 or this Act in respect of fines. None of the sections mentioned in *subsection (1)* are to prevent the court from passing any sentence it considers appropriate. *Subsection (2)* additionally makes clear that the Court can impose a community sentence, providing there are relevant mitigating factors, even where the offence(s) would normally have justified a custodial sentence. The court can reduce the sentence by considering other penalties given to the offender at the same time and where an offender is convicted of two or more offences by applying the totality principle, which is that the total punitive weight of the sentence must be commensurate with the offences committed (*subsection (3)*).

### *Section 167: **The Sentencing Guidelines Council***

473. *Subsection (1)* provides for the membership of the Sentencing Guidelines Council, which exists to promulgate guidelines to enable all courts dealing with criminal cases to approach the sentencing of offenders from a common starting point. It stipulates that there will be 7 judicial members and 4 non-judicial members, and provides that the Lord Chief Justice is to be the Chairman of the Council.

474. *Subsection (2)* sets out those persons eligible to be judicial members. *Subsection (3)* is designed to ensure that membership reflects those courts regularly dealing with criminal cases. The Lord Chief Justice is required to appoint a Deputy Chairman from amongst the Council members under *subsection (7)*.

475. Under *subsection (4)* the non-judicial members must have experience in one or more of the following fields: policing, criminal prosecution, criminal defence, and the promotion of the welfare of victims of crime. Under *subsection (9),* the Secretary of State may appoint as an observer a person with experience of sentencing policy and the administration of sentences. This person may attend and speak at meetings of the Council. *Subsection (6)* ensures that each area of experience is represented on the Council.

476. *Subsection (8)* enables the Lord Chief Justice to nominate another judge to attend in his stead if he is unable to attend a Council meeting.

### *Section 168: **Sentencing Guidelines Council supplementary provisions***

477. This section enables the Lord Chancellor to deal with matters of appointment and removal of members, and Council proceedings by order. It also enables payment of remuneration and expenses to Council members. Lay justices can be remunerated for the time given to membership of the Council. All other judicial members will be salaried, full time members of the judiciary and no further remuneration is necessary. However, provision is made for appropriate expenses to be reimbursed, as determined by the Lord Chancellor under *subsection (4)(b)*. Similarly, by virtue of *subsection (5)* the Home Secretary may determine what payment by way of either remuneration or expenses is appropriate, for the non-judicial members.

### *Section 169: **The Sentencing Advisory Panel***

478. This section provides for the continuation of the Sentencing Advisory Panel, constituted, as at present, by the Lord Chancellor after consultation with the Secretary of State and the Lord Chief Justice. Subsection (2) contains the requirement that the Lord Chancellor must appoint a Chairman of the Panel after consultation with the Home Secretary and the Lord Chief Justice. Subsection (3) re-enacts provision authorising the Lord Chancellor to remunerate members of the Panel or provide expenses.

### *Section 170: **Guidelines relating to sentencing and allocation***

479. This section sets out the responsibility for issuing guidelines and sets out the matters to be taken into account in the process of creating them.

480. *Subsection (1)* defines "sentencing guidelines" and "allocation guidelines" as meaning guidelines relating to the sentencing of offenders and guidelines as to the allocation of cases between courts.

481. *Subsection (2)* allows the Secretary of State to ask the Council to frame or revise guidelines relating to allocation, a general matter affecting sentencing (for example, relating to the credit to be given for a guilty plea), to a particular category of offender (such as those with previous convictions), or relating to a particular offence. The Council itself can decide to frame guidelines, under *subsection (3)*, and must consider whether to do so where it receives a proposal from the Sentencing Advisory Panel or the Secretary of State (as described above). *Subsection (4)* obliges the Council to keep

its guidelines under review (where they have been formally issued) and revise them if appropriate.

482. *Subsection (5)* sets out the factors to be taken into account by the Sentencing Guidelines Council when creating or revising sentencing guidelines. The list (which reproduces the existing list in section 80(3) of the Crime and Disorder Act 1998) is not intended to be exhaustive.

483. *Subsection (6)* sets out certain factors to be taken into account by the Sentencing Guidelines Council when creating or revising allocation guidelines. These are the importance of promoting consistency in decisions under section 19 of the Magistrates' Courts Act 1980 (which relates to determining mode of trial) and the views of the Sentencing Advisory Panel.

484. *Subsection (7)* requires the Council to include in its guidelines criteria to determine the seriousness of the offence being dealt with. Where appropriate those criteria need to include criteria for determining the significance of any previous convictions of the offender.

485. *Subsection (8)* requires the Council to publish proposed guidelines in draft for consultation with the Secretary of State, any other person the Lord Chancellor after consultation with the Secretary of State directs and any other person the Council considers to be appropriate. It is anticipated that the second of these categories will include the House of Commons Home Affairs Committee. This consultation will follow that undertaken by the Sentencing Advisory Panel (see *Section 171(3))* and will reflect the need to avoid duplication of effort.

486. *Subsection (9)* provides for the Council, after making such amendments as it considers appropriate, to issue the guidelines as definitive guidelines.

### *Section 171: Functions of Sentencing Advisory Panel in relation to guidelines*

487. This Section makes provision for the functions of the Sentencing Advisory Panel. The Council is obliged to notify the Sentencing Advisory Panel when it decides to frame new guidelines or to revise existing guidelines. This will enable the Panel to prepare advice to assist the Council. However, under subsection (2) the Panel is also able to propose to the Council that guidelines are framed or revised by the Council.

488. *Subsection (3)* provides that where guidelines are under consideration (either as a result of the Panel's own initiative or that of the Council), the Panel must consult with those that the Council stipulates. The Council will make that decision after consultation with the Secretary of State and Lord Chancellor. The Panel must prepare advice where guidelines are proposed and submit it to the Council. *Subsection (4)* allows the Council to authorise the Panel to dispense with the consultation required under *subsection (3)* if the urgency of a case makes this impractical.

### *Section 172: Duty of court to have regard to sentencing guidelines*

489. This Section places a duty on courts to have regard to any sentencing guidelines issued by the Council.

### *Section 173: Annual report by Council*

490. The Council must prepare an annual report on the exercise of its functions, which it must present to Ministers, who in turn must lay a copy of the report before each House of Parliament. The Council must then publish the report. Some leeway is allowed for the publication of the first report which can be published at the end of the financial year following the one in which section 167 comes into force *(subsection* (2)).

### *Section 174: Duty to give reasons for, and explain effect of, sentence*

491. This section imposes a general statutory duty on courts to give reasons for, and explain the effect of, the sentence passed. In doing so, it seeks to bring together in a single provision many of the obligations on a Court to give reasons when passing sentence which are currently scattered across sentencing legislation.

492. *Subsection (1)* requires a Court to explain its reasons for deciding on the sentence to be passed but to do so in non-technical terms. The aim is to enable the offender and other interested parties to understand why this particular sentence was chosen. The Court will also be under an obligation to explain to the offender how the sentence is structured, what the sentence requires him to do, what will happen if it is not done and any power that exists to vary or review the sentence.

493. *Subsection (2)* extends the obligation to give reasons stated in subsection (1) by setting out certain matters that have to be dealt with. Where the Sentencing Guidelines Council has issued definitive guidelines relevant to the sentence, and the Court departs from them it must give reasons for doing so. In the case of a custodial sentence or a community sentence, the court must explain why it regards the offence as being sufficiently serious to warrant such a sentence. Where the Court reduces a sentence on account of a guilty plea, that fact must be included in the reasons, as must any other aggravating or mitigating factors relevant to the sentencing decision which the Court regarded as being of particular importance.

494. *Subsection (3)* excludes from the obligation to give reasons those cases where the sentence is fixed by law (a separate duty to give reasons in relation to such sentences being made by section 270) or falls to be imposed under the provisions of sections 110 and 111 of the Powers of Criminal Courts (Sentencing) Act, and section 51A of the Firearms Act.

495. *Subsection (4)*provides the Secretary of State with an order-making power to confer exemptions from the duty to give reasons for and explain the effect of the sentence passed. He may also prescribe cases in which the reasons or explanation may be given in the absence of the offender. *Subsection (5)* requires a magistrates' court which passes a custodial sentence to ensure that the reason required under *subsection (1)* should be recorded on the warrant authorising the commitment of the offender and also entered in the court register.

### *Section 175: Duty to publish information about sentencing*

496. This section amends section 95 of the Criminal Justice Act 1991, so as to require the Secretary of State publish information each year on the effectiveness of sentencing in preventing re-offending and in promoting confidence in the criminal justice system. He is already required to publish information on race, gender and costs in the criminal justice system.

### *Section 176: Interpretation of Chapter 1*

497. This section defines various terms used in the Chapter.

### *Chapter 2 : Community Sentences for offenders aged 16 or over*

### *Section 177: Community orders*

498. *Subsection (1)* provides that a community order may impose on the offender one or more of the following requirements:

- an unpaid work requirement;
- an activity requirement;

- a programme requirement;
- a prohibited activity requirement;
- a curfew requirement;
- an exclusion requirement;
- a residence requirement;
- a mental health treatment requirement;
- a drug rehabilitation requirement;
- an alcohol treatment requirement;
- a supervision requirement;
- if an offender is under 25, an attendance centre requirement.

499. Certain of the requirements are subject to restrictions, identified in *subsection (2). Subsection (3)* provides that if the court makes a community order that includes a curfew requirement or an exclusion requirement, it must also impose an electronic monitoring requirement (as defined in *Section 215)* unless electronic monitoring is not available in the local area or if someone else whose consent is required (e.g. a landlord) withholds that consent. The court may also decide electronic monitoring is inappropriate in the particular case. Subject to the same provisos, under *subsection (4),* the court may impose electronic monitoring in conjunction with any of the other requirements listed above. *Subsection (5)* states that community orders cannot exceed three years in length, and the court can specify the duration of requirements within a community order. *Subsection (6)* requires the court to consider the compatibility of the various requirements it proposes to include.

### *Section 178: **Power to provide for court review of community orders***

500. This section enables the Secretary of State to make an order allowing or requiring a court to review the progress of an offender under a community order. The Secretary of State can also allow a court to attach or remove a review provision from a community order, and regulate the timing of reviews. Such an order may in particular contain provisions similar to those applying to reviews of suspended sentences, as provided in sections 191 and 192. It is intended that the decision to extend reviews to community orders would be based on consultation with the courts.

### *Section 179: **Breach, revocation or amendment of community order***

501. This section introduces Schedule 8 which sets out procedures relating to the enforcement, revocation or amendment of community orders.

### *Section 180: **Transfer of community orders to Scotland or Northern Ireland***

502. This section introduces Schedule 9 which sets out the procedures for community sentences transferred to Scotland and Northern Ireland.

## *Chapter 3 : **Prison sentences of less than 12 months***

### *Section 181: **Prison sentences of less than 12 months***

503. This section ensures that in general all prison sentences of less than 12 months will consist of a short period of custody followed by a longer period on licence, during which the offender has to comply with requirements fixed by the courts as part of his sentence. *Subsection (2)* sets out the minimum and maximum lengths of the sentence. *Subsection (3)* requires the court to specify both the 'custodial period' and the 'licence

period'. During the licence period the offender is to be subject to conditions specified in the "custody plus order". *Subsection (5)* makes provision for the length of the custodial period, which must be between 2 and 13 weeks. *Subsection (6)* requires the licence period to be at least 26 weeks. *Subsection (7)* makes provision for consecutive sentences and limits the total term of imprisonment for two or more offences to 15 months, with a maximum of 6 months in custody. *Subsection (9)* provides that, in the case of a suspended sentence, the court need not when passing sentence specify the licence conditions that would apply should the sentence take effect.

### *Section 182:* ***Licence conditions***

504. This section lists the requirements which the court may attach to the licence period under the custody plus order provided for in section 181. *Subsection (2)* sets out restrictions which apply when attaching certain requirements

505. *Subsections (3 and (4)* make provision for the imposition of an electronic monitoring requirement. Depending upon the other requirements which are imposed the court is either under a duty or has a discretion whether to impose this requirement. *Subsection (5)* requires the court to consider whether the requirements attached to the licence period are compatible.

### *Section 183:* ***Intermittent custody***

506. *Subsection (1)* enables a court passing a sentence of imprisonment of under 12 months to specify the number of days the offender must serve in prison, and at the same time provide for his release on licence, subject to specified conditions, at set intervals throughout his sentence. *Subsections (2) and (3)* are interpretative provisions. *Subsection (4)* makes provision for the minimum and maximum length of the sentence, which like a custody plus sentence under section 165 must always be at least 28 weeks but no more than 51 in respect of any one offence. *Subsection (5)* provides for the minimum and maximum amount of time the offender must spend in prison. *Subsection (6)* prohibits a court from imposing a sentence of this nature unless the offender consents. *Subsection (7)* makes provision for consecutive sentences and limits the total term to 65 weeks, with a maximum of 180 days in custody. *Subsection (8)* enables the Secretary of State by order to make provision about licence periods that the court may specify. He may make provision about the length of licence periods (such as 86 or 120 hours) which enables the custodial days to be served during the week or at the weekend); particular days of the week on which licence periods may begin or end (to restrict custodial periods to weekends, for example); and periods including or not including specified parts of the week (for example 'not Fridays'). *Subsection (9)* enables the court to require different requirements to be fulfilled within different time limits.

### *Section 184:* ***Restrictions on power to make intermittent custody order***

507. Intermittent custody may not be available in all parts of the country. *Subsection (1)* provides that a court must not make an intermittent custody order unless it has been notified by the Secretary of State that suitable arrangements are available in the relevant area. *Subsection (2)* requires the court to ensure that suitable prison accommodation is available for the custodial periods and that the offender has somewhere suitable to live during the licence periods. The court must consult an officer of the local probation board before making an intermittent custody order in respect of an offender. This is intended to assist the court in assessing whether the offender is suitable for intermittent custody.

### *Section 185* ***Intermittent custody: licence conditions***

508. *Subsection (1)* sets out the restrictions on licence conditions available for intermittent custody. *Subsection (2)* provides that subsections (3) to (5) of section 182 (which relate to electronic monitoring of licence conditions and compatibility of licence conditions in the context of custody plus orders) apply to intermittent custody orders.

### *Section 186: Further provisions relating to intermittent custody*

509. *Subsection (1)* provides that payments under section 21 of the Prison Act 1952 (expenses of conveyance to prison) are not available in relation to intermittent release. *Subsection (2)* gives the Prison Service discretion to pay expenses for transport. *Subsection (3)* stipulates that a person who has been temporarily released under an intermittent custody order shall be deemed to be unlawfully at large if he fails to return at the end of his temporary licence period. *Subsection (5)* creates an offence of remaining at large after temporary release in pursuance of an intermittent custody order.

### *Section 187: Revocation or amendment of order*

510. This section introduces Schedule 10, which deals with the revocation or amendment of custody plus orders and the amendment of intermittent custody orders. The Schedule is explained below.

### *Section 188: Transfer of custody plus order or intermittent custody order to Scotland or Northern Ireland*

511. This section introduces Schedule 11 which sets out the procedure for transferring custody plus orders and intermittent custody orders to Scotland or Northern Ireland.

### *Section 189: Suspended sentences of imprisonment*

512. This section deals with suspended sentences of imprisonment. *Subsection (1)* enables a court which passes a prison sentence of less than 12 months to suspend that sentence for a period of between six months and two years while ordering the offender to undertake certain requirements in the community. The custodial part of the sentence will not take effect unless the offender fails to comply with those requirements or commits another offence within the period of suspension. The period during which the offender undertakes requirements is called "the supervision period" and the entire length of suspension is called "the operational period". *Subsection (2)* makes provision for consecutive sentences and limits the total term to 65 weeks. Under *subsection (3)* the length of time the offender undertakes requirements may be less (but not more) than the entire period of suspension, but each of the two periods must last between six months and two years. *Subsection (4)* provides that the supervision period must not exceed the operational period. *Subsection (5)* prohibits the court from imposing a community sentence alongside a suspended sentence (though a fine or compensation order could be imposed). *Subsection (6)* provides that a suspended sentence is to be treated as a sentence of imprisonment.

### *Section 190: Imposition of requirements by suspended sentence order*

513. This section specifies the requirements that can be attached to a suspended sentence order. Subsection (1) lists those requirements. Subsection (2) sets out certain restrictions on imposing particular requirements. Subsection (3) states that where the court imposes a curfew requirement or an exclusion requirement, it must also impose an electronic monitoring requirement (as defined in Section 215) unless electronic monitoring is not available in the local area or someone else whose consent is required (e.g. a landlord) withholds that consent. Subsection (4) provides for the court to add an electronic monitoring requirement to ensure compliance with certain other requirements. Subsection (5) requires the court to consider the compatibility of the requirements before imposing them.

### *Section 191: Power to provide for review of suspended sentence order*

514. *Subsection (1)* confers a discretion on courts to provide that a suspended sentence order passed under section 189(1) be subject to periodic review at a review hearing. *Subsection (2)* excludes cases where the offender is subject to an order that imposes a drug rehabilitation requirement that is subject to court review, as those orders will

already be subject to review. A review hearing is conducted by the court responsible for the order. *Subsections (3) to (5)* specify which court is responsible for the order in particular situations.

### *Section 192: **Periodic reviews of suspended sentence order***

515. This section makes provision for what is to happen at a review hearing. *Subsection (1)* confers on the court a power to amend any community requirement of the suspended sentence order, following consideration of the responsible officer's report. *Subsection (2)* limits the power of amendment. In particular, the court cannot impose a new requirement unless the offender consents, but it can impose a requirement of the same kind (this is explained in subsection (3)). An offender's consent is also required before amending a drug, alcohol or mental health treatment requirement. The court may extend the supervision period, but not so that it lasts longer than two years or ends later than the operational period. The court may not amend the operational period. Unless the offender consents, the court may not amend the order if an appeal against it is pending. *Subsection (3)* provides that a requirement of the same kind as another paragraph if it falls within section 190(1). It also has the effect of allowing the court to add an electronic monitoring requirement to an existing requirement.

516. Under *subsection (4),* where on the basis of the responsible officer's report, the court is of the opinion that the offender is making satisfactory progress, it can dispense with a review hearing. It may also amend the order to provide that subsequent reviews can be held on the papers, and without a hearing. *Subsection (5)* provides the court with the power to require the offender to attend a review hearing where the court is of the opinion his progress is no longer satisfactory. Under *subsection (6)* the court may adjourn a review hearing where it wishes to deal with the offender in respect of a breach of a requirement under formal breach proceedings. *Subsection (7)* enables the court to adjust the intervals between review hearings. *Subsection (8)* is an interpretation provision.

### *Section 193: **Breach, revocation or amendment of suspended sentence order, and effect of further conviction***

517. This section introduces Schedule 12.

### *Section 194: **Transfer of suspended sentence orders to Scotland or Northern Ireland***

518. This section introduces Schedule 13 which sets out the procedure for transferring suspended sentence orders to Scotland or Northern Ireland.

### *Section 195: **Interpretation of** Chapter 3*

519. This section defines various terms used in the Chapter.

### *Chapter 4 : **Further provisions about orders under** Chapters 2 **and** 3*

### *Section 196: **Meaning of "relevant order"***

520. This section defines "relevant order" for the purposes of this Chapter as meaning a community order, a suspended sentence order, a custody plus order or an intermittent custody order.

### *Section 197: **Meaning of "the responsible officer"***

521. This Section defines who the responsible officer is. Under *subsection (1)(a),* if an order imposes a curfew or exclusion requirement but no other requirement, and if that curfew or exclusion order is electronically monitored, the responsible officer is the person responsible for the electronic monitoring (currently the private sector providers under contract to the Home Office). If an offender is 18 or over and under 25, he may be

given an attendance centre requirement. If this is as the only requirement of the order, *subsection (1)(b)* provides that the responsible officer is the officer in charge of the attendance centre. In all other cases, under *subsections (1)(c) and (2),* the responsible officer is either an officer of the local probation board, or for offenders under 18 at the time of the order, the responsible officer can be either an officer of the local probation board or a member of a youth offending team. *Subsection (3)* confers a power on the Secretary of State to amend subsections (1) and (2) by order subject to affirmative procedure, and *subsection (4)* provides that such an order may provide for the court to decide in individual cases which description of 'relevant officer' is to apply.

### *Section 198:* ***Duties of responsible officer***

522. The statutory duties of the responsible officer are set out in *subsection (1).* Where the responsible officer is an officer of a local probation board or a youth offending team member, he or she must make any necessary arrangements for the offender to fulfil the requirements of the order, promote the offender's compliance with the requirements, and take enforcement action in the case of non-compliance. *Subsection (2)* makes an exception for responsible officers who are electronic monitoring providers.

### *Section 199:* ***Unpaid work requirement***

523. This section re-enacts, with some modification, section 46 of the Powers of Criminal Courts (Sentencing) Act (which deals with "community punishment", previously called "community service"). Unpaid work is done on projects set up by the probation service in consultation with sentencers and the local community. These can include environmental projects such as clearing canals, removing graffiti, painting and decorating community facilities, and working in homes for the elderly. Under *subsection (2)* no offender can be required to do more than 300 hours of unpaid work or less than 40. The Act increases the current upper limit from 240 hours. By *subsection (3)*, the court must not impose an unpaid work requirement unless it is satisfied that the offender is a suitable person to perform work under such a requirement. If the court thinks that it is necessary to do so, it will first hear from an appropriate officer (as defined in *subsection (4)*). *Subsection (5)* provides that where the court is sentencing an offender for two or more offences, and imposes unpaid work requirements in respect of each of them, it can decide whether the hours of unpaid work should be served concurrently or consecutively. However, the total number of hours must not exceed 300.

### *Section 200:* ***Obligations of person subject to unpaid work requirement***

524. Under *subsection (1)* the offender must perform work as and when required by his responsible officer. *Subsection (2)* applies where an unpaid work requirement is imposed as part of a community order or a suspended sentence order. In these cases, the work must generally be completed within twelve months. *Subsections (3) and (4)* deal with the situation where an offender fails to complete the unpaid work within that period of time.

### *Section 201:* ***Activity requirement***

525. These provisions are based on the requirements as to activities at paragraph 2 of Schedule 2 of the Powers of Criminal Courts (Sentencing) Act 2000. *Subsection (1)* defines an activity requirement as a requirement that the offender must either present himself to a specified person, at a specified place, for a certain number of days, and/or take part in specified activities for a certain number of days. An activity requirement may include such tasks as receiving help with employment, or group work on social problems. Reparative activities are a particular aim of this requirement. *Subsection (3)* also requires the court to consult before making such an order. If the offender is aged 18 or over, the court must consult an officer of a local probation board. If the offender is under 18, the court must consult either an officer of a local probation board or a member of a youth offending team. By virtue of *subsection (4)*, the court must not

impose an activity requirement on an offender before obtaining the consent of any other person whose co-operation is needed. *Subsection (5)* sets the maximum number of days of activity at 60. *Subsection (6)* sets out the duties of a person subject to an activity requirement. The offender is required to present himself at a place or places specified by his responsible officer on the number of days specified in the order, and to comply with instructions given by or under the authority of the person in charge of that place. The responsible officer will tell the offender where he needs to go and for how many hours, and that he must comply with the instructions of the person in charge of the place. *Subsection (7)* describes where activities must take place. If the place is a community rehabilitation centre, *subsection (8)* requires an offender to present himself elsewhere if the person in charge of the community rehabilitation centre instructs him to. *Subsection (9)* makes further provision as to the obligations of the offender when he is required to participate in activities. *Subsection (10)* defines the terms used in the section.

### *Section 202: **Programme requirement***

526. *Subsection (1)* defines a "programme requirement" as a requirement that the offender must participate in an accredited programme on a certain number of days. Programmes are courses which address offending behaviour, covering such topics as anger management, sex offending, substance misuse, etc. *Subsections (2) and (3)* define "accredited programme", "programme" and "the accreditation body". The Secretary of State may by order designate what the accreditation body is. This is left to delegated legislation as changes in the list of accredited bodies will be required from time to time. Under *subsection (4)* an officer of a local probation board (an officer of a local probation board or youth offending team member if the offender is under 18) must recommend that the specified programme is suitable for the offender before the court imposes a programme requirement. The court must also be satisfied that a place on the programme is available for the offender. *Subsection (5)* provides that the court must not impose a programme requirement on an offender before obtaining the consent of any person (other than the offender or responsible officer) whose co-operation is needed. *Subsection (6)* sets out the obligations of an offender who is subject to a programme requirement. The offender is required to participate in the programme as specified in the order in accordance with instructions given by his responsible officer. The offender must also comply with any instructions given by, or under the authority of, the person in charge of the programme. By virtue of *subsection (7)*, a place must not be specified in an order unless it has been approved by the local probation board.

### *Section 203: **Prohibited activity requirement***

527. *Subsection (1)* defines a prohibited activity requirement. The court can require an offender to refrain from participating in certain activities. For example, it might forbid him to contact a certain person. The offender may be prohibited from participating in specified activities on a certain day or on a number of days or during a period of time. Under *subsection (2),* before setting such a requirement the court must consult an officer of the local probation board, or, in the case of an offender who is under 18, an officer of the local probation board or a member of a youth offending team. *Subsection (3)* makes it clear that the court can make a prohibited activity requirement which prohibits a defendant from possessing, using or carrying a firearm.

### *Section 204: **Curfew requirement***

528. This section re-enacts, with some modification, section 37 of the Powers of Criminal Courts (Sentencing) Act *Subsection (1)* defines a curfew requirement as a requirement that the offender must remain at a place specified by the court for certain periods of time. By *subsection (2)*, the periods of time must not be less than two hours or more than twelve hours in any given day. The order might, for example, require the offender to stay at home during the evening and night hours. *Subsections (3) to (5)* limit the curfew period(s) for community orders, custody plus orders and intermittent custody orders respectively. Under *subsection (6)* the court must obtain and consider information about

the place specified in the order and the attitude of persons likely to be affected by the presence of the offender.

### *Section 205: **Exclusion requirement***

529. This section re-enacts, with some modification, section 40A of the Powers of Criminal Courts (Sentencing) Act (inserted by section 46 of the Criminal Justice and Court Services Act 2000). That provision has not yet been brought into force. *Subsection (1)*defines an exclusion requirement as a requirement prohibiting the offender from entering a place during a period specified in the order. *Subsection (3)* makes it clear that the order may stipulate that the prohibition operates only for certain periods of time and may specify different places for different periods. By *subsection (2)* an exclusion requirement cannot last longer than two years. Under *subsection (4)* the order can specify an area rather than a specific place. For example, an offender might be required to stay away from a specified town centre at night.

### *Section 206: **Residence requirement***

530. The residence requirement is based on the existing requirements as to residence that can be included in a community rehabilitation order (see paragraph 1 of Schedule 2 to the Powers of Criminal Courts (Sentencing) Act 2000). *Subsection (1)* defines residence requirement as a requirement that the offender must reside at a place specified in the order for a specified period. Under *subsection (2)* the court can allow the offender to live at an alternative address, with the approval of his responsible officer. Under *subsection (3),* before making a residence requirement the court must consider the situation at the offender's accommodation. *Subsection (4)* provides that the court must only place the offender in a hostel or similar accommodation with the recommendation of an officer of the local probation board.

### *Section 207: **Mental health treatment requirement***

531. The mental health treatment requirement is based on the requirements as to treatment as part of a community rehabilitation order (paragraph 5 of Schedule 2 of the Powers of Criminal Courts (Sentencing) Act 2000). *Subsection (1)* provides for the court to direct an offender to undergo mental health treatment for certain period(s) as part of a community sentence or suspended sentence order, under the treatment of registered medical practitioner or chartered psychologist. *Subsection (2)* provides that treatment may be provided in an independent hospital or care home (within the meaning of the Care Standards Act 2000) or a hospital (within the meaning of the Mental Health Act 1983), or as a non-resident patient at a place specified in the order, or as treatment under the direction of such registered medical practitioner or chartered psychologist as specified in the order. Under *subsection (3),* before including a mental health treatment requirement, the court must be satisfied that the mental condition of the offender requires treatment and may be helped by treatment, but is not such that it warrants making a hospital or guardianship order (within the meaning of the Mental Health Act 1983). The court must also be satisfied that arrangements can be made for the offender to receive treatment as specified in the order, and the offender's consent must be obtained before imposing the requirement.

532. Under *subsection (4),* the offender's responsible officer will supervise him only to the extent necessary for revoking or amending the order. *Subsection (5)* applies section 54(2) and (3) of the Mental Health Act 1983 for the purposes of the section. *Subsection (6)* defines "chartered psychologist".

### *Section 208: **Mental health treatment at place other than that specified in order***

533. *Subsection (1)* allows the medical practitioner or chartered psychologist to decide that treatment would be better or more convenient in a different place from that specified in the order and make arrangements to change the place of treatment. The change cannot

be made without the consent of the offender. Under *subsection (2)* the offender can be placed in residential treatment, even if the institution was not one that could have been specified for that purpose in the original order. Arrangements for informing appropriate people are set out in *subsection (3)*.

### *Section 209:* ***Drug rehabilitation requirement***

534. As part of a community sentence or suspended sentence the court may impose a drug rehabilitation requirement, which includes drug treatment and testing. In order to impose such a requirement, the court must be satisfied that the offender is dependent on or has a propensity to misuse any controlled drug and as such requires and would benefit from treatment. In addition, the court must be satisfied that the necessary arrangements are or can be made for the treatment and that the offender has expressed a willingness to comply with the drug rehabilitation requirement. The treatment provided may not be for a period of less than six months. A suitably qualified or experienced individual supervises the treatment. It is for the court to decide whether treatment should be residential or non-residential. The Secretary of State may provide guidance as to the arrangements for testing.

### *Section 210:* ***Drug rehabilitation requirement: provision for review by court***

535. *Subsection (1)* provides that the court may provide for the review of any drug treatment and testing requirement, and it must provide for the review of any drug treatment and testing requirement lasting more than 12 months. The reviews cannot take place more frequently than once a month. The review occurs at a review hearing, at which the offender is present. The responsible officer is to provide a written report on the offender's progress before each hearing, which is to include the results of the offender's drug tests. A review hearing takes place before the court responsible for the order. *Subsections (2)* to *(3)* provide that the court responsible for a drug treatment and testing requirement is the court which made the order, unless it specifies a different court in the case where an offender does not live in the area of the court which convicts him. Where the drug treatment and testing requirement was made on appeal from the Crown Court, under *subsection (4)* the Crown Court will be the responsible court.

### *Section 211:* ***Periodic review of drug rehabilitation requirement***

536. This section sets out what happens at a review of a drug rehabilitation requirement. *Subsection (1)* provides for the court to amend the order as respects that requirement after considering the responsible officer's report. *Subsection (2)* prevents the court from amending the requirement unless the offender consents. It cannot reduce the term of treatment and testing below the minimum specified in section 209(3) (i.e. six months). Unless the offender's consent is obtained the court cannot amend a requirement while an appeal against the order is pending. Under *subsection (3),* if the offender does not consent to amending the order, the court may revoke the order and re-sentence the offender as if he had just been convicted. If it does so, under *subsection (4)* it must take into account the extent to which the offender has complied with the requirements of the order. If the court wishes, it may sentence the offender to a custodial sentence, providing the offence was punishable with imprisonment. *Subsection (5)* relates to the powers of a magistrates' court in a case where the offender was under 18 when the order was made, the offence would have been triable only on indictment had it been committed by an adult and the offender has attained the age of 18 by the time of the review hearing. In these circumstances, subsection (5) extends the court's powers where a person has failed to consent to an amendment proposed by the court.

537. If the offender's progress is satisfactory, under *subsection (6)* the court can state that for future reviews the offender need not be present. *Subsection (7)* provides that, if an offender's progress is unsatisfactory and he is not present, the court can require the offender to attend a future hearing. Under *subsection (8)* at that hearing the court may exercise the powers that it has in the case of a review hearing. It may also amend the

order to provide for future review hearings. *Subsection (9)* explains what is meant by "court" in this section.

### *Section 212*: ***Alcohol treatment requirement***

538. Alcohol treatment is currently available as part of a community rehabilitation order, under paragraph 6 of Schedule 2 of the Powers of Criminal Courts (Sentencing) Act. Under *subsection (1)* the court can require the offender to undergo alcohol treatment. The treatment must be by or under the direction of a person who is qualified or experienced to reduce or eliminate the offender's dependency on alcohol. This person is to be identified in the order. *Subsection (2)* requires that the court be satisfied that the offender is dependent on alcohol, that his dependency requires and is susceptible to treatment, and that arrangements can be made for treatment. *Subsection (3)* requires the court to obtain the offender's consent before imposing an alcohol treatment requirement. *Subsection (4)* states that an alcohol treatment requirement must last at least six months. Under *subsection (5)* the treatment itself must consist of either residential or non-residential treatment in a place the court decides, or by or under a qualified or experienced person whom the court identifies in the order.

### *Section 213*: ***Supervision requirement***

539. Supervision is a central part of community rehabilitation orders imposed under section 41 of the Powers of Criminal Courts (Sentencing) Act. The responsible officer might review with the offender his supervision plan, challenge his offending behaviour, hold him to account on the requirements, monitor his progress, and assist him with various problems, such as accommodation, employment, or finance. *Subsection (1)* provides that the court can oblige the offender to meet with his responsible officer, or someone else specified by the responsible officer, or attend a community rehabilitation centre as required. *Subsection (2)* states that a supervision requirement is for the purpose of rehabilitation. *Subsection (3)* sets the length of the supervision requirement for the different orders.

### *Section 214*: ***Attendance centre requirement***

540. Attendance centre orders are currently free-standing orders for certain young offenders, under Chapter 4 of Part 4 of the Powers of Criminal Courts (Sentencing) Act. At an attendance centre, practical activities, including sport, can be run to occupy offenders for a certain number of hours to keep them out of trouble. This is often on Saturdays as attendance centres were originally set up for football-related offenders.*Subsection (1)*enables the court to require an offender to attend an attendance centre for a specified number of hours. *Subsection (2)* requires the total number of hours an order may specify to be between 12 and 36. Under *subsection (3)* the court must be satisfied that the offender can get to the centre and must consider the circumstances of the offender when making the appointments. *Subsection (4)* provides that the first appointment is to be set by the responsible officer, and under *subsection (5)* any subsequent appointments are to be made by the person in charge of the centre. *Subsection (6)* provides that the offender cannot be required to attend more than once a day or for more than three hours on any one day.

### *Section 215*: ***Electronic monitoring requirement***

541. The court can order the electronic monitoring of the compliance of an offender with any of the other requirements set out in the order. Electronic monitoring has been available throughout England and Wales since 1999, following a series of pilot projects which operated in selected areas during the previous ten years.

542. In almost all cases of electronic monitoring, the technical equipment uses radio frequency transmissions. It consists of a transmitter (the "tag"), which is usually worn round the ankle, and a receiver unit which is either connected to a landline telephone or

incorporates mobile phone technology. The receiver unit communicates with a central computer system at a monitoring centre. The transmitter sends signals to the receiver at regular intervals and these are sent on to the central computer. The signal strength of the transmitter is calibrated to the receiver so that if the subject goes out of range (generally this means outside the building where the receiver is located), there is a break in signal and this is also registered by the central computer which generates follow-up action. The transmitter can be removed only by breaking its strap. This interferes with the fibre-optic circuitry inside the strap and is immediately registered as a tamper, also generating follow-up action.

543. Under the existing law electronic monitoring can be used as part of home detention curfew (see *Section 246*), curfew orders (which will be replaced for adults by community orders with curfew requirements), bail (12-16 year olds throughout England and Wales, and 17 year olds in specified areas), and detention and training orders (under 18s).

544. *Subsection (1)* enables the court to set an electronic monitoring requirement to ensure an offender's compliance with other requirements in the order. The period(s) of electronic monitoring can be set by the court or the responsible officer. Under *subsection (2),* if another person's compliance is needed to effect the electronic monitoring, that person's consent must be obtained before the order is made. This person might include a landlord. *Subsections (3) and (4)* set out administrative arrangements surrounding electronic monitoring, and in particular deal with the notification of the requirement by the responsible officer to the relevant parties. *Subsection (3)* gives the Secretary of State an order making power to specify a description of a person responsible for electronic monitoring. This is left to delegated legislation as changes in the description of electronic monitoring providers will be required from time to time. For example new types of electronic monitoring technologies are being developed which may necessitate changes in the description of providers.

### *Section 216: Petty sessions area to be specified in relevant order*

545. This section provides that a petty sessions area in which the offender will live must be specified in the case of community orders and suspended sentence orders, and for the supervision periods of short custodial sentences and intermittent custody. This means that where an offender is sentenced in an area in which he does not reside, his home area will have to be specified in the order.

### *Section 217: Requirement to avoid conflict with religious beliefs, etc.*

546. *Subsection (1)* requires the court to try to avoid, as far as practicable, making any order which clashes with an offender's religious beliefs, or with the times of his education or employment. *Subsection (2)* applies the same requirement to any instructions the responsible officer is to give during the course of the order. Under *subsection (3)* the Secretary of State has the power to add further restrictions by order. Additional restrictions may be required in the light of the experience of operating the new sentencing framework. For example, it might become necessary to introduce additional restrictions on the making of orders for offenders with particular domestic responsibilities if it were found that the new sentences were interfering with their caring responsibilities.

### *Section 218: Availability of arrangements in local area*

547. This section obliges the court to ensure that certain requirements are available in the local area before imposing them. Under *subsection (1)* unpaid work is one such requirement. *Subsection (2)* applies the obligation to an activity requirement, and *subsection (3)* to an attendance centre requirement. *Subsections (4) to (8)* prevent a court from imposing an electronic monitoring requirement unless the Secretary of State

has notified the court that electronic monitoring is available and can be provided in the relevant areas.

### *Section 219*: ***Provision of copies of relevant orders***

548. The court has to provide copies of the order it makes to certain people who are relevant to the carrying out of the order. *Subsection (1)* requires the court to provide copies to the offender, an officer of a local probation board assigned to the court (if an offender is over 18) or an officer of a local probation board assigned to the court or a youth offending team member if the offender is 16 or 17. Where the order specifies another petty sessions area the court must send a copy to the local probation board in that area. *Subsection (2)* introduces Schedule 14, which contains a list of persons to whom copies of the order must be given depending on what requirements are included in the order. Under *subsection (3)* if an offender will be carrying out the order in a different area, the court will have to send a copy of the order to the magistrates' court in that area as well as to the local probation board in that area. Any other documents and information relating to the case that the court thinks the second court would find necessary it must send to that court.

### *Section 220*: ***Duty of offender to keep in touch with responsible officer***

549. An offender must keep in touch with his responsible officer, in accordance with any instructions in that regard from the responsible officer. The offender must also notify the responsible officer of any change of residence. Under *subsection (2),* if the offender does not keep in touch as required, or if he changes his residence without notifying the responsible officer, he is liable to breach proceedings.

### *Section 221*: ***Provision of attendance centres***

550. This section re-enacts section 62 of the Powers of Criminal Courts (Sentencing) Act 2000, which enables the Secretary of State to provide attendance centres and make arrangements with local authorities and police authorities regarding premises to be used. *Subsection (2)* defines "attendance centres".

### *Section 222*: ***Rules***

551. This section gives the Secretary of State the power to regulate a number of aspects of the different requirements. These are: the supervision of offenders subject to relevant orders; the functions of responsible officers; arrangements for unpaid work; providing and managing attendance centres and community rehabilitation centres; the attendance of offenders (including attendance records) at activity requirements; attendance centre requirements or supervision requirements; electronic monitoring; the duties of the people responsible for delivering electronic monitoring. *Subsection (2)* specifies that in particular, these rules might limit the number of hours of unpaid work to be done on any one day, the reckoning of hours worked and the payment of expenses involved in unpaid work.

552. This is left to delegated legislation given the need for flexibility and the level of detail that is likely to be required. It is intended that any rules under this section will be made after consultation with practitioners.

### *Section 223*: ***Power to amend limits***

553. Various of the requirements described in the previous paragraphs have limits attached to them. A person cannot be required to do more than 300 hours of unpaid work, for example. This section gives the Secretary of State the power to amend certain limits by order. This is left to delegated legislation as amendments may be desirable in the light of experience. The Secretary of State currently has this power relating to community sentences.

## *Chapter 5: **Dangerous offenders***

### *Section 224: **Meaning of "specified offence" etc***

554. This Section defines 'specified offence' and 'serious offence' for the purposes of this Chapter. Specified offences are those sexual or violent offences listed in Schedule 15 (all of which carry a maximum penalty of 2 years or more). A serious offence is defined as a specified sexual or violent offence which carries a maximum penalty of ten years or more (including life). This section also defines various other terms for the purposes of this Chapter.

### *Section 225: **Life sentence or imprisonment for public protection for serious offences***

555. *Section 225* provides for a new sentence of imprisonment for public protection, which is an indeterminate sentence. This sentence may only be passed by a court if the offender is convicted of a specified sexual or violent offence (listed in Schedule 15) carrying a maximum sentence of ten years or more and the court considers that the offender poses a significant risk of serious harm as defined in *subsection (1)(b). Subsection (2)* sets out that where the offence carries a maximum sentence of life imprisonment, the court must pass a discretionary life sentence if the seriousness of the offence justifies it. In all other cases to which the section applies, *subsection (3)* requires the court to impose a sentence of imprisonment for public protection. When passing sentence the court must set the relevant part of the sentence that will be served in custody for the purposes of punishment and deterrence. After the offender has served this relevant part then their release will be dependent upon the recommendation of the Parole Board. This sentence therefore provides for the indeterminate detention of those dangerous offenders who continue to pose a significant risk of harm to the public. Release provisions for this sentence are set out in more detail in section 230 and Schedule 18.

### *Section 226: **Detention for life or detention for public protection for serious offences committed by those under 18***

556. *Section 226* applies the sentence of public protection to those aged under 18 although for juveniles it is a sentence of detention rather than imprisonment. As in the case of adults, the sentence may be passed by a court if the offender is convicted of a specified sexual or violent offence carrying a maximum sentence of ten years or more and the court considers that the offender poses a significant risk of serious harm as defined in *subsection (1)(b). Subsection (2)* sets out that, where the offence carries a maximum sentence of detention for life under section 91 of the Sentencing Act, the court must pass such a sentence, if the seriousness of the offence justifies it. In other cases, *subsection (3)* requires the court to choose between a sentence of detention for public protection or an extended sentence under section 228. It will impose a sentence of detention for public protection if it thinks that an extended sentence is not adequate to protect the public.

### *Section 227: **Extended sentence for certain violent and sexual offences: persons 18 or over***

557. This section replaces and extends the current provisions for extended supervision for sexual and violent offenders contained in section 85 of the Powers of Criminal Courts (Sentencing) Act 2000. The Section makes provision for the extended sentence for certain violent and sexual offences and sets out the conditions which must be met in order for this sentence to be passed. These conditions require that the offender is over 18, has committed a specified sexual or violent offence (listed in Schedule 15) carrying a maximum penalty of between two and ten years and is judged by the court to pose a significant risk of serious harm to the public as defined in *subsection (1)(b).* If these conditions are met then *subsection (2)* requires the court to pass an extended sentence. *Subsection (2)* also provides that the extended sentence is made up of the "appropriate

custodial term" and an "extension period". The appropriate custodial term is defined in *subsection (3)* as the period that the court considers to reflect the seriousness of the offence committed (subject to a minimum of 12 months). During the second half of the appropriate custodial term the offender may be released on the recommendation of the Parole Board (see section 247). The court must also specify an extended period of supervision on licence to be added to the sentence for the purpose of public protection. The court may add an extension period of up to five years for violent offenders and eight years for sexual offenders (see *subsection (4))*. The total term of the extended sentence must not be more than the maximum penalty available for the offence in question (*subsection (5))*.

### *Section 228*: ***Extended sentence for certain violent or sexual offenders: persons under 18***

558. *Section 228* applies the extended sentence to those aged under 18 whom the court considers to pose a significant risk of serious harm as defined in *subsection (1)(b)*. Where the offender has been convicted of a specified offence the court must impose an extended sentence, unless the offence is a serious offence and the case is one in which a sentence under section 226 is appropriate. The sentence operates in the same way as it does for adults, but is a sentence of detention rather than imprisonment.

### *Section 229*: ***The assessment of dangerousness***

559. This section deals with the assessment of dangerousness required for the court to establish whether the offender poses a 'significant risk to members of the public of serious harm occasioned by the commission by him of further specified offences' and therefore whether they are eligible for one of the new sentences for dangerous offenders. The risk criteria are based on the existing provisions at section 161(4) of the Powers of Criminal Courts (Sentencing) Act 2000. When making this assessment the court must take into account all the information available to it about the nature and circumstances of the offence and it may also take into account any information about the pattern of behaviour of which the offence forms a part and any information about the offender. *Subsection (3)*sets out that in cases where an offender is aged 18 or over and has a previous conviction for a relevant offences (as defined by *subsection (4)* the offender will be assumed to be dangerous, unless the court considers on the basis of the evidence before it this assumption to be unreasonable. For the purposes of the provision in *subsection* (3), *subsection (4)*provides the definition of a relevant offence. This includes any specified offence in Schedule 15 and equivalent sexual or violent offences committed in Scotland or Northern Ireland, listed in Schedules 16 and 17, which are introduced by this section.

### *Section 230*: ***Imprisonment or detention for public protection: release on licence***

560. This section introduces Schedule 18 which sets out the release provisions for the sentences for public protection.

### *Section 231*: ***Appeals where previous convictions set aside***

561. This section applies to cases where an offender has been sentenced under the provisions relating to the commission of a second relevant offence (contained within *Section 229(3))*. If subsequently, the first conviction is overturned on appeal, Section 231 enables notice of appeal against the new sentence to be given at any time within 28 days from the date which the previous conviction was set aside.

### *Section 232*: ***Certificates of convictions for the purposes of*** *section 229*

562. This section provides for a court in England and Wales to certify that it has convicted a person of a relevant offence.

### *Section 233: Offences under service law*

563. This section provides for equivalent convictions under service law to be taken into account for the purpose of Section 229, which relates to the assumption of dangerousness.

### *Section 234: Determination of day when offence committed*

564. Where an offence has been committed over several days, this section treats it as having been committed on the last of those days.

### *Section 235: Detention under Sections 226 and 228*

565. This section provides that a juvenile sentenced to a sentence of detention for public protection or an extended sentence may be detained in such place as may be determined by the Secretary of State or by such other person as may be authorised by him.

### *Section 236: Conversion of sentences of detention into sentences of imprisonment*

566. This section amends section 99 of the Powers of Criminal Courts (Sentencing) Act 2000. This enables the Secretary of State to direct that an offender sentenced to a sentence of detention may be treated as if he had been sentenced to a term of imprisonment if he has reached the age of 21 or, if he has reached the age of 18, if he has been reported by the board of visitors as exercising a detrimental influence on the other inmates. This section extends this power to the new sentence of detention for public protection and the new extended sentence.

## *Chapter 6: Release of Prisoners on Licence*

### *Section 237: Meaning of "fixed-term prisoner"*

567. This section is an interpretation provision. In particular it defines "fixed-term prisoner" for the purposes of this Chapter.

### *Section 238: Power of the court to recommend licence conditions for certain prisoner*

568. This section gives the court the power to recommend, when passing a custodial sentence of 12 months or more, particular conditions that in its view should be included in the licence to which the offender is subject on release. It also places a duty upon the Secretary of State, when setting the conditions of the licence, to have regard to any recommendations which the court may have made.

### *Section 239: The Parole Board*

569. This section re-enacts section 32 of the Criminal Justice Act 1991. Its effect is to continue in being, and make provision for the constitution of, the Parole Board. The statutory duty of the Parole Board as set out in *subsection (2)* is to advise the Secretary of State on the release and recall of prisoners. In undertaking this function the Board must consider any evidence which the Secretary of State puts before it and any other evidence which it obtains (see *subsection (3)*). *Subsections (5) and (6)*give the Secretary of State the power to make rules concerning the proceedings of the Board and to give directions to the Board with regard to protecting the public and preventing further offences being committed. *Subsection (7)* introduces Schedule 19.

### *Section 240: Crediting of periods of remand in custody: terms of imprisonment and detention*

570. This Section re-enacts with amendments section 87 of the Powers of Criminal Courts (Sentencing) Act 2000, which makes provision for the crediting of time spent on remand

(and which is not yet in force). It allows for time spent in custody on remand to count as time served by the offender as part of his sentence (see *subsection (3)*). These provisions are only relevant where a custodial sentence is passed and the remand was in connection with the same offence, or a related offence. When crediting periods of remand in custody the Court is required by *subsection (5)* to state in open court the number of days spent on remand in connection with the offence and the number of days which count towards time served under the sentence as a result of this. *Subsection (4)*allows the court not to give a direction should this be in the interests of justice in a particular case. Where the court does not exercise its full powers in relation to the crediting of time spent on remand, *subsection (6)* requires that it must state a reason for this decision.

### *Section 241*: *Effect of direction under section 240 on release on licence*

571. *Section 241* ensures that time spent on remand counts towards time served under the sentence for the purpose of calculating whether or not an offender has served a particular proportion or period of his sentence. The application of these provisions to a sentence of intermittent custody is dealt with in *subsection (2)*.

### *Section 242*: *Interpretation of sections 240 and 241*

572. This section defines the sentences to which the crediting of remand time applies, and provides definitions of the term 'remanded in custody' used within sections 240 and 241. Time spent in police detention will not count as time spent on remand for the purposes of section 240. This is because there is a qualitative difference between time spent on remand and time spent in police custody, the former being preventative and imposed by the courts whereas the latter is an unavoidable feature of the investigation of crime.

### *Section 243*: *Persons extradited to the United Kingdom*

573. This section re-enacts (with some modification) section 47 of the Criminal Justice Act 1991. *Subsection (2)* ensures that in the case of an extradited prisoner (as defined by *subsections (1)*), days spent in custody awaiting extradition may subsequently be subtracted from any custodial sentence passed by the court.

### *Section 244*: *Duty to release prisoners*

574. The release provisions for all prisoners (excluding those subject to a life sentence or one of the new sentences for dangerous offenders under Chapter 5) are dealt with in this section. All prisoners must spend a "requisite custodial period" in custody before the Secretary of State is required to release them on licence. This requisite period is calculated according to the particular sentence as described in *subsection (3)*. For all prisoners serving a sentence of twelve months or more (excluding dangerous offenders and life sentence prisoners) the Secretary of State is required to release them on licence at the halfway point of their sentence. For prisoners serving a sentence of less than twelve months, release will be at the end of the specified 'custodial period'. For those serving a sentence of intermittent custody release will take place at the end of each custodial period as defined by *section 183*. These provisions are subject to the arrangements for prisoners who have been returned to custody following a period of being unlawfully at large, as provided in section 245.

### *Section 245*: *Restrictions on operation of section 244(1) in relation to intermittent custody Prisoners*

575. *Subsections (1) and (2)* provide that an offender who has been returned to custody following a period unlawfully at large does not have to be released under section 244(1). He can be held while an application is made to the court to alter the pattern of intermittence under paragraph 6(1)(b) of Schedule 10. The Secretary of State has to

make such an application within 72 hours, or release the offender to continue serving his sentence on an intermittent basis. If while being held, the offender's custodial days expire, he is to be released under *subsection (1)(b)*. *Subsection (3)* provides that an intermittent custody prisoner who has been recalled to prison does not fall to be released for his next licence period under section 244.

### *Section 246: **Power to release prisoners on licence before required to do so***

576. This section relates to home detention curfew (HDC). The Crime and Disorder Act 1998 amended the Criminal Justice Act 1991 so that certain categories of prisoner, after being risk assessed, could spend the last part of their custodial sentence on HDC. HDC operates as a transitional phase immediately after leaving prison. Under the existing law in section 34A of the Criminal Justice Act 1991, an offender can be released up to 135 days early if he is assessed as suitable for HDC by the Prison Service. A curfew is imposed and the offender is monitored electronically to ensure he keeps to the terms of the curfew. If he violates the curfew or any standard condition of his licence (such as being of good behaviour) he is recalled to prison. HDC came into operation in 1999. Since that time there have been over 80,000 participants (around 3500 at any one time). The successful completion rate of HDC is 90%. The curfew condition is dealt with in section 253.

577. *Subsection (1)* maintains the maximum period available for HDC at 135 days. *Subsection (6)*also gives the Secretary of State the power to amend by order the period available for HDC. Not all prisoners are eligible for release under the HDC scheme. Those ineligible include prisoners serving one of the sentences applicable to dangerous offenders, and prisoners who are liable to deportation. Also, prisoners who have less than 14 days to serve of their required custodial period following sentence (e.g. due to remand time being deducted from the required custodial period) are not eligible for HDC. Ineligible categories are specified in *subsection (4)*. *Subsections (1), (2) and (3)* have the effect of providing for the period spent on HDC to be tapered according to the length of sentence. Subsection (1)(b) provides for prisoners serving a sentence of intermittent custody. As with normal prison sentences, on intermittent custody the offender will spend a number of days on HDC equal to the days he would have spent in custody had he not received HDC.

### *Section 247: **Release on licence of prisoner serving extended sentence under** section 227 **or** 228*

578. This section sets out the release provisions for the extended sentences covered in sections 227 and 228. *Subsection (2)* provides that once an offender has served one half of the "appropriate custodial term", then subject to the recommendation of the Parole Board the prisoner may be released on licence. Once the prisoner has served the full 'appropriate custodial term' he must be released and will then remain on licence until he has served his full extended supervision period.

### *Section 248: **Power to release prisoners on compassionate grounds***

579. This section re-enacts section 36 of the Criminal Justice Act 1991, and sets out the procedure for releasing fixed-term prisoners on compassionate grounds. The Secretary of State may only release prisoners on these grounds if exceptional circumstances exist (for example where the prisoner is suffering from a terminal illness). In such cases *subsection (2)* requires the Parole Board is to be consulted prior to release wherever possible.

### *Section 249: **Duration of licence***

580. *Subsection (1)* provides that, after release, all prisoners serving determinate sentences remain on licence following release for the remainder of the sentence. Particular provision is made in *subsection (2)* for intermittent custody, reflecting the fact that the

offender must return to prison at the end of each intermittent licence period before being subject to final release. In either case, the provisions as to the duration of licence are subject to the fact that the offender may be recalled into custody in the event of breach of a licence condition.

### *Section 250*: *Licence conditions*

581. This section makes provision in relation to the conditions which may be attached to a licence following a prisoner's release. All licences must include "the standard conditions" as defined insofar as they are compatible with the other licence conditions. An example of a "standard condition" that could be prescribed is a requirement that the offender be of good behaviour. Other than the standard conditions, the content of the licence will vary according to the sentence being served. For prisoners serving one or more sentences of less than twelve months the conditions of the licence are set by the court at the point of sentence (see *section 189*). These conditions apply in conjunction with the standard conditions and with any condition prescribed for this purpose by the Secretary of State for the purpose of public protection (see *subsection (2)(b)(ii)*). *Subsection (3)* provides that court-ordered licence conditions apply where a prisoner is released on licence for compassionate reasons or on Home Detention Curfew. For prisoners serving one or more sentence of more than 12 months the conditions of the licence are set by Prison and Probation Service prior to the prisoners' release. In this case, *subsection (4)* provides that the standard conditions will apply, together with any other condition prescribed for this purpose by the Secretary of State and specified in the licence. Conditions as to electronic monitoring and drug testing may also be applied under section 62 or 64 of the Criminal Justice and Court Services Act 2000. *Subsection (5)* ensures every Home Detention Curfew licence has a curfew condition. *Subsection (6)* provides that if a court-ordered licence in a sentence of less than 12 months has a curfew condition, it is not to operate at the same time as an HDC curfew. *Subsection (7)* applies the arrangements on consecutive and concurrent terms to the section. *Subsection (8)* requires the Secretary of State to have regard to several factors including the protection of the public and the prevention of re-offending when creating standard conditions.

### *Section 251*: *Licence conditions on re-release of prisoner serving sentence of less than 12 months*

582. If an offender serving a sentence of less than 12 months is recalled to prison, it is likely that his court-ordered licence conditions will be disrupted. This section provides that after recall, the Secretary of State has the power to re-set licence conditions upon the re-release of the offender. These must include standard conditions and may include drug testing or electronic monitoring, or conditions prescribed by the Secretary of State in an order. In other words, following recall, licence conditions in a sentence of less than 12 months will be imposed as they are for sentences of 12 months or more.

### *Section 252*: *Duty to comply with licence conditions*

583. This section requires the offender to comply with any conditions attached to their licence.

### *Section 253*: *Curfew condition to be included in licence under section 246*

584. *Subsection (1)* defines the curfew condition to be attached to early release on Home Detention Curfew (HDC), as provided in *section 246*. The curfew condition specifies periods during which the offender must remain in a specified place, and includes a requirement that the curfew is electronically monitored. Under *subsection (2)*the curfew condition can specify more than one place and/or more than one period. There are time limits; except for the first and last days, a curfew cannot last for less than 9 hours in any one day. Under *subsection (3)* the curfew condition is to last until the date the offender would have been released from prison if he had not received early

release. *Subsection (4)* provides for the curfew condition in sentences of intermittent custody. *Subsections (5) and (6)* set out administrative arrangements for the provision of electronic monitoring.

### *Section 254: **Recall of prisoners while on licence***

585. *Subsection (1)* enables the Secretary of State to revoke the licence of an offender and recall him to prison. Under *subsection (2)* a person recalled has to be informed of the reasons for his recall and can make written representations about it. *Subsection (3)* provides for the Parole Board to consider all recalls. Under *subsection (4),* if the Board decides that the person should be released, the Secretary of State must release him. *Subsection (5)* provides that if the Parole Board immediately re-releases an intermittent custody prisoner who has been recalled he is to continue his sentence on an intermittent basis. *Subsection (6)* provides that if a person on licence is recalled he can be detained and if at large he will be treated as unlawfully at large. *Subsection (7)* provides that this section does not apply to offenders recalled from Home Detention Curfew, who are dealt with in *Section 255*.

### *Section 255: **Recall of prisoners released under s.246***

586. *Subsection (1)* enables the Secretary of State to revoke the licence of an offender on Home Detention Curfew and recall him to prison if he has failed to comply with a licence condition or if his whereabouts can no longer be electronically monitored. Under *subsection (2)* if a person on HDC has his licence revoked, he must be informed of the reason when he returns to prison, and he is able to make written representations about the revocation. *Subsection (3)* enables the Secretary of State to cancel a revocation of an HDC licence after considering such representations. Under *subsection (4)* such a cancellation has the effect that the licence is taken not to have been revoked. *Subsection (5)* provides that an offender whose HDC licence is revoked may be detained, is to be considered unlawfully at large, and is subject to arrest.

### *Section 256: **Further release after recall***

587. When an offender has been recalled to prison, arrangements are made with a view to his further release. Under *subsection (1)* the Parole Board must either set a date for future release or set a date for it to review the offender's case. Under *subsection (2),* the date fixed must be within one calendar year. *Subsection (3)* provides that a future date need not be fixed if the offender was due for release within 12 months. Under *subsection (4)* if the Board decides upon a future release date the offender must be released on that date.*Subsection (5)* provides that at a review the Board can either recommend immediate release or fix a date for future release or for future review.

### *Section 257: **Additional days for disciplinary offences***

588. This Section re-enacts section 42 of the Criminal Justice Act 1991, which enables rules under the Prison Act 1952 to provide for additional days to be added to prisoners' sentences if they are found to be guilty of disciplinary offences whilst in custody.

### *Section 258: **Early release of fine defaulters and contemnors***

589. This Section re-enacts, with appropriate modifications, section 45 of the Criminal Justice Act 1991 (as amended), which sets out the release provisions for persons committed to custody in default of payment of a fine or for contempt of court, which are not sentences of imprisonment and therefore are not covered by the normal release provisions.

590. *Subsection (2)* provides for unconditional release at the half-way point of the term. This would cover those serving terms of both under and over 12 months. *Subsection (3)* makes provision for offenders who are also serving a sentence of

imprisonment. *Subsection (4)* provides a power to release these persons unconditionally on compassionate grounds.

### *Section 259: **Persons liable to removal from the United Kingdom***

591. Section 259 is an interpretative provision, defining what 'persons liable to removal from the United Kingdom' for the purposes of Chapter 6 of Part 12 of the Act.

### *Section 260: **Early removal of prisoners liable to removal from United Kingdom***

592. Under the Criminal Justice Act 1991 any short-term foreign national prisoners (those serving a sentence of less than 4 years) who are liable to removal from the UK are automatically released from prison and liable to be removed from the UK at the half-way point in their sentence. They are statutorily excluded from early release under the Home Detention Curfew scheme (section 34A(e) of the 1991 Act as amended by the Crime and Disorder Act 1998).

593. Long-term foreign national prisoners (those serving a determinate sentence of 4 years or more) are considered for early release at the halfway point of their sentence (their Parole Eligibility Date). The decision whether to release is based upon a careful risk assessment. Those who are not considered an acceptable risk for release on parole remain in custody until their automatic release date at the two-thirds point of sentence.

594. Both short and long term foreign national prisoners released from prison are liable to be detained under immigration law until they are finally removed from the UK.

595. *Section 260* introduces a new scheme for early removal from prison for foreign national prisoners liable to removal as defined in section 259. Eligible prisoners may be removed from prison up to 135 days earlier than their normal release date.

596. *Subsections (1) and (2)* set out the minimum requisite custodial period to which the scheme will apply and the period of time to be served before removal from prison will be possible.

597. Certain prisoners will be excluded from the scheme. These statutory exclusions are set out in *subsection (3).*

598. *Subsections (4) and (5)* will ensure that prisoners remain liable to be detained in pursuance of their sentences whilst remaining in the UK so that if, for example, the prisoner makes an application for asylum, after being removed under the scheme, the prisoner will be returned to prison to continue to serve the sentence until the normal release date, at which point the prisoner will become subject to immigration law.

599. *Subsection (6)* gives the Secretary of State the power to amend by order the eligibility requirements of the minimum sentence and custodial period to be served for early removal under the scheme

### *Section 261: **Re-entry into United Kingdom of offender removed from prison early***

600. *Section 261* sets out the provisions for dealing with a prisoner who returns to the UK following early removal under section 261. Prisoners who return before their sentences expire will be liable to be detained in pursuance of their sentence for a period equal to the outstanding custodial period to be served or until the sentence expiry date, whichever is the earlier.

### *Section 262: **Prisoners liable to removal from United Kingdom: modifications of Criminal Justice Act 1991***

601. *Section 262* introduces Schedule 20, which makes provision for a similar scheme to apply under the 1991 Act prior to the commencement of the Act.

### *Section 263: **Concurrent terms***

602. This section deals with release in the case of an offender serving two or more terms of imprisonment at the same time (concurrently). In such cases the offender must serve the longest custodial period of the sentences which have been passed before being released on licence. He will then remain on licence until the expiry of the longest sentence. *Subsection (3)* states that in cases where a sentence of more than and a sentence of less than 12 months are ordered to be served concurrently, the Secretary of State (in practice the Prison and Probation Services) may set the licence conditions without having regard to any conditions which the court set when passing the shorter sentence.

### *Section 264: **Consecutive terms***

603. This section deals with release in the case of offenders serving two or more terms of imprisonment to be served one after the other (consecutively). In such cases the offender must serve a period equal to the aggregate of the custodial periods of the sentences which have been passed before being released on licence. Where sentences of less than 12 months and more than 12 months (including the extended sentence) are passed at the same time, or where more than one sentence of more than 12 months is passed, following release the offender will remain on licence for a period equal in length to the aggregate of the lengths of the individual licence periods for each sentence. *Subsection (4)* provides that where sentences of less than 12 months are to be served consecutively the offender will remain on licence until he has served a term equal in length to the longest licence period for any one of his sentences. Therefore the term to be served will be the aggregate of the custodial periods plus the longest licence period.

### *Section 265: **Restriction on consecutive sentences for released prisoners***

604. This section re-enacts with changes provisions in section 84 of the Powers of Criminal Courts (Sentencing) Act 2000. The section provides that if an offender is sentenced to imprisonment for an offence while he is on licence in connection with a sentence for another offence, the prison term for the new offence is to start immediately, and not wait until the first term expires.

### *Section 266: **Release on licence, etc: drug testing requirements***

605. This section amends section 64 of the Criminal Justice and Court Services Act 2000. It provides that should a responsible officer, as defined in subsection (6), be of the opinion that the offender has a propensity to misuse any specified Class A drugs and that such misuse has caused or contributed to any offence of which he was convicted or is likely to cause or contribute to him committing further offences, the offender must provide, when requested, a sample to ascertain whether he has a specified Class A drug in his system. The requirement that a trigger offence has been committed is removed. The minimum age of persons to whom drug testing under this provision applies is lowered to 14 years. A sentence of detention under section 226 or 228 of this Act will be included for the purposes of this section. The presence of an appropriate adult, as defined in subsection (6), is required for the taking of a sample in the case of an offender who is under the age of 17 years.

### *Section 267: **Alteration by order of relevant proportion of sentence***

606. This section gives the Secretary of State the power to amend by order the proportion of a custodial sentence of 12 months or more which must be served in prison before the release. It also enables the Secretary of State to amend by order the proportion of an extended sentence for certain sexual and violent offences (see sections 227 and 228) which must be served before a prisoner is eligible for release on the recommendation of the Parole Board.

### *Section 268: **Interpretation of** Chapter 6*

607. This section explains various terms used in the Chapter.

## *Chapter 7: **Effect of Life Sentence***

### *Section 269: **Determination of minimum term in relation to mandatory life sentence***

608. This section relates to mandatory life sentences (that is, life sentences fixed by law). The only offences carrying a mandatory life sentence are murder and certain offences involving murder.

609. This Section requires a court passing a mandatory life sentence to make an order specifying a period of time the prisoner must serve before the Parole Board can consider release on licence under the provisions of section 28 of the Crime (Sentences) Act 1997 (i.e. the "minimum term"). The exception is that if the offender was 21 or over at the time of the offence, and the court takes the view that the murder is so grave that the offender ought to spend the rest of his life in prison, the order is that those early release provisions are not to apply to the offender (See subsection (4)).

610. A life sentence is defined (by section 277) as meaning a sentence of imprisonment for life, which is imposed on those convicted of murder who are 21 or more years of age, a sentence of custody for life, which is for those aged 18, 19 or 20 years of age, and a sentence of detention during Her Majesty's Pleasure, which is for those under 18 years of age.

611. The "whole life", 30 year, and 15 year starting points set out in Schedule 21 do not apply to juveniles: all juveniles who receive a mandatory life sentence are subject to a starting point of 12 years.

612. *Subsection (3)* requires the court to set the minimum term by reference to the seriousness of the offence, and also to take into account time spent on remand.

613. *Subsection (5)* makes further provision in relation to the assessment of the seriousness of the offence. It requires the court to have regard to the principles set out in Schedule 21, and to any guidelines issued by the Sentencing Guidelines Council (provided they are compatible with the provisions of Schedule 21). Schedule 21 is explained in detail below.

614. *Subsection (6)* enables the Secretary of State to amend Schedule 21 by order (subject to affirmative resolution procedure). The Secretary of State has a duty to consult the Sentencing Guidelines Council before making such an order.

### *Section 270: **Duty to give reasons***

615. *Section 270* is designed to ensure that everyone concerned is afforded a clear and readily understood explanation of the reasoning of the court in arriving at the minimum term imposed. (The court is also required by section 174(1)(b) to explain the effect of the sentence.)

### *Section 271: **Appeals***

616. *Subsection (1)* ensures that the opportunity to apply to the Court of Appeal, and thereafter to House of Lords, in order to appeal against a minimum term is open to prisoners in respect of whom an order under section 269 is made following sentence in the Crown Court. *Subsection (2)* contains similar provisions in relation to sentences passed by courts-martial.

### *Section 272: Review of minimum term on reference by Attorney General*

617. Section 36 of the Criminal Justice Act 1988 provides for the Attorney General to refer a case concerning certain offences to the Court of Appeal for review if he is of the opinion that the sentence imposed is unduly lenient. As a matter of sentencing practice the Court of Appeal, when increasing a sentence which in its view is unduly lenient, operates a "double jeopardy" discount in favour of the offender to take account of the fact that he or she is being sentenced for a second time. A person convicted of murder is in any event subject to a life sentence and has no certain prospect of a particular release date. The amendment to section 36 of the Criminal Justice Act 1988 will prevent the Court of Appeal from applying a discount of this kind in referred cases relating to minimum term orders under section 269(2). (Equivalent amendments are made to relevant legislation covering the different armed forces.)

### *Section 273: Life prisoners transferred to England and Wales & Section 274: Further provisions about references relating to transferred life prisoners*

618. The need to provide for judicial determination of minimum terms in mandatory life sentences affects not only those convicted here but also the small number of prisoners who have been convicted in jurisdictions outside the British Islands (i.e. the United Kingdom, the Channel Islands and the Isle of Man) and who consent to be transferred to England and Wales in order to serve their sentence here. Section 273 provides for the cases of these transferred life sentence prisoners to be referred to the High Court for a minimum term to be fixed. section 274 contains further provisions about references under section 273, including provision for appeals.

### *Section 275: Duty to release certain life prisoners*

619. *Section 275* deals with the release of mandatory life prisoners. In accordance with the ruling of the European Court of Human Rights in the case of *Stafford* this provision brings the arrangements for the release of mandatory life prisoners into line with those for discretionary life prisoners under section 28 of the Crime (Sentences) Act 1997. The amendments ensure that, like discretionary life sentence prisoners, a mandatory life sentence prisoner will be able to require the Secretary of State to refer his case to the Parole Board once he has served his minimum term. Once a case is referred to it the Parole Board decides whether a prisoner is to be released and may direct his release only if it is satisfied that the prisoner's continued detention is no longer necessary for the protection of the public. The Secretary of State is then under a duty to release the prisoner on a life licence.

### *Section 276: Mandatory life sentences : transitional cases*

620. This section introduces Schedule 22 dealing with existing life sentence prisoners. This Schedule is explained below.

### *Chapter 8: Other Provisions about sentencing*

### *Section 278: Deferment of Sentence*

621. This section introduces Schedule 23, which deals with deferred sentences.

### *Section 279: Drug treatment and testing requirement in action plan order or supervision order*

622. This section introduces Schedule 24, which enables a requirement as to drug treatment and testing to be included in an action plan order or a supervision order.

623. The action plan order is a community sentence, which is available where a child or young person aged between 10 and 17 years old is convicted of any offence for which the sentence is not fixed by law. The order lasts for a period of three months and provides

a short but intensive and individually tailored programme of intervention designed to address the young person's offending behaviour and associated risk factors. The court may attach a range of requirements such as offending behaviour work, education and reparation.

624. The supervision order is a community sentence available for a child or young person aged between 10 and 17 years old. The duration of the order may range from a minimum of six months to a maximum of three years. A range of requirements may be attached to the supervision order such as residence, reparation, night restrictions and activities specified by a youth offending team.

### *Section 280*: ***Alteration of penalties for summary offences***

625. This section is consequential on the changes in the structure of short sentences which this Act introduces and the corresponding increase in magistrates' sentencing powers. It introduces Schedules 25 and 26, which make changes to the maximum penalties for summary only offences that previously carried a maximum penalty of less than 12 months. These offences are either to have the maximum penalty lowered so that they are no longer punishable with imprisonment (see Schedule 25) or raised to 51 weeks imprisonment so that they may be punishable with a new sentence of imprisonment of less than 12 months, custody plus (see Schedule 26).

### *Section 281*: ***Alteration of penalties for other summary offences***

626. This section provides for the alteration of penalties for certain summary offences. *Subsections (1) to (3)* enable the Secretary of State to amend by order the maximum penalties for summary only offences currently carrying a maximum custodial penalty of five months or less. Under *subsection (1)* such amendments may be made only in relation to offences which are not listed in Schedule 25 or 26 and are contained either in an Act passed before or in the same Session as this Act, or any subordinate legislation made before the passing of this Act. In such cases the Secretary of State may (by order) either remove imprisonment as a penalty for the offence or raise the maximum penalty for the offence to 51 weeks imprisonment. *Subsections (4) and (5)* provide for all summary offences contained in Acts passed before or in the same Session as this Act with a maximum penalty of six months imprisonment to have this maximum penalty raised automatically to 51 weeks. *Subsection (6)*ensures that any alteration of penalties made under this section does not affect the penalty for any offence committed before the commencement of this section.

### *Section 282*: ***Increase in maximum term that may be imposed on summary conviction of offence triable either way***

627. This section provides for an increase in the maximum sentence available on the summary conviction of a triable either way offence following commencement of this section so that it corresponds with the extent of the magistrates' sentencing powers. S*ubsection (4)* provides for the maximum penalties for offences falling within subsection (3) to be increased to 12 months imprisonment on summary conviction. This section also makes consequential amendments to the Magistrates' Courts Act 1980 in so far as it deals with penalties on summary conviction of triable either way offences.

### *Section 283*: ***Enabling powers: alteration of maximum penalties***

628. *Section 283* makes the necessary provisions for offences created under enabling powers to have their maximum penalties altered so that they may be compatible with the new sentencing framework. *Subsection (1)* gives the Secretary of State the power to amend by order any enabling powers within any Act (passed before or in the same Session as this Act) which allow for making offences punishable with imprisonment on summary conviction, excluding those listed in Schedule 27. *Subsection (2)* provides that an order under this power may amend the relevant enactment containing an enabling power so as

either to remove its ability (through subordinate legislation) to make a summary offence punishable with imprisonment or to increase the maximum term of imprisonment to 51 weeks. *Subsection (3)* also enables an order under *subsection (1)* to amend enabling powers which make a triable either way offence punishable with imprisonment on summary conviction. *Subsection (4)* introduces Schedule 27.

### *Section 284: **Increase in penalties for drug related offences***

629. This section introduces Schedule 28, which increases the maximum penalty for trafficking Class C drugs from 5 years' to 14 years'imprisonment.

### *Section 285: **Increase in penalties for certain driving-related offences causing deaths***

630. This section increases to 14 years' imprisonment the maximum penalty for the three offences of causing death by dangerous driving, causing death by careless driving under the influence of drink or drugs and aggravated vehicle-taking where the aggravating feature is that, owing to the driving of the vehicle, an accident occurs and death results. These increases in maximum penalties also apply to similar driving offences in Northern Ireland.

### *Section 286: **Increase in penalties for offences under section 174 of Road Traffic Act 1988***

631. This section increases the maximum penalties for the offences of giving false statements and withholding material information in relation to road traffic documentation/offences. For those offences, when tried on indictment the maximum penalty is increased to 2 years or a fine or both; and when tried summarily the maximum penalty is increased to 6 months or the statutory maximum or both.

### *Section 287: **Minimum sentence for certain firearms offences***

632. This section inserts a new section 51A into the Firearms Act 1968 ("the 1968 Act") to provide a new minimum custodial sentence for unauthorised possession of certain types of firearm.

633. *Subsection(1)* of the new section 51A sets out the particular offences which will attract the new minimum sentence, and applies it to persons aged 16 or over when the offence was committed. Under subsection (5) the minimum is fixed at five years for persons aged 18 or over (in England and Wales) or aged 21 or over (in Scotland) when the offence was committed, and three years for persons aged under 18 (in England and Wales) or aged under 21 (in Scotland).

634. Under*subsection (2)* courts will be required to impose the minimum sentence, unless there are exceptional circumstances relating to the offence or offender which justify not doing so. Examples of exceptional circumstances might be where the holder of a firearms certificate inadvertently forgets to renew his authority or where a war trophy is discovered among a deceased person's effects.

### *Section 288: **Certain firearms offences to be triable only on indictment***

635. This Section amends Part 1 of Schedule 6 to the 1968 Act and makes all offences to which the minimum sentence applies triable on indictment only. At present, these offences are triable either way. However, the minimum sentence is beyond the sentencing powers of magistrates and (but for this section) magistrates would have to make a preliminary assessment of whether any exceptional circumstances were involved before determining whether a case should go to the Crown Court.

### *Section 289: Power to sentence young offender to detention in respect of certain firearms offences: England and Wales*

636. This section amends section 91 of the Powers of Criminal Courts (Sentencing) Act 2000 to ensure that persons aged 16 or 17 can be sentenced to the term of detention required by the new section 51A of the 1968 Act.

### *Section 290: Power to sentence young offender to detention in respect of certain firearms offences: Scotland*

637. This section amends the Criminal Procedure (Scotland) Act 1995 to ensure that where offenders aged 16 or 17 are convicted on indictment under section 5 of the 1968 Act, the court itself retains the power to order detention and to dispose of the case.

### *Section 291: Power by order to exclude application of minimum sentence to those under 18*

638. This section enables the Secretary of State by order to prevent the minimum sentence applying to those aged 16 or 17. There is also power to make consequential amendments of other legislation. An order under this power is subject to affirmative resolution procedure.

### *Section 292: Sentencing for firearms offences in Northern Ireland*

639. Section 292 introduces Schedule 29, which makes provision for Northern Ireland similar to that made for England and Wales found in sections 287 and 288 of the Act. In particular the Schedule applies the minimum sentence provision to handguns, which are currently not prohibited in Northern Ireland.

### *Section 293: Increase in penalty for offences relating to importation or exportation of certain firearms*

640. This section amends the Customs and Excise Management Act 1979 to increase from 7 years' imprisonment to 10 years' imprisonment the maximum penalty for smuggling prohibited weapons covered by the minimum sentence provisions. The offences concerned are: improper importation of goods (section 50), exportation of prohibited or restricted goods (section 68) and fraudulent evasion of duty etc (section 170).

### *Section 294: Duration of directions under Mental Health Act 1983 in relation to offenders*

641. *Section 294* makes amendments to section 50 of the Mental Health Act 1983 dealing with arrangements for the release, or return to prison, of serving prisoners who have been transferred to hospital for medical treatment. It replaces references to the expiration of a prisoner's sentence with references to his release date. This means that the Secretary of State can only treat the patient as a restricted patient until the time when the prisoner would have been released from prison. On the release date the Secretary of State ceases to be able to send the patient back to prison or control decisions on leave, transfer or discharge from hospital under the 1983 Act. New section 50(3) of the 1983 Act provides that the release date means the date on which the prisoner would be entitled to be released if he had not been transferred to hospital, disregarding any powers that the Parole Board would have if he were still detained in prison, or any discretionary powers of early release exercisable by the Secretary of State. This means that schemes for early release such as the home detention curfew scheme are not taken into account and that (subject to the changes made in section 295 of the Act) life prisoners have to return to prison and to apply to the Parole Board in order to be released.

### *Section 295: **Access to Parole Board for certain patients serving prison sentences***

642. *Section 295* makes amends section 74 of the Mental Health Act 1983. The inserted subsection (5A) relates to transferred prisoners detained in hospital beyond their release date whose detention in hospital has been found by the mental health review tribunal to be no longer justified by their mental disorder, but who the tribunal has recommended should remain in hospital, rather than return to prison, in the event that the Secretary of State does not agree to discharge them from hospital. It provides that the fact that restrictions under the Mental Health Act remain in force does not prevent an application or reference to the Parole Board for release. It further provides that if the Parole Board directs or recommends release, the restrictions cease to have effect at the time he is entitled to release. The effect of this is that the transferred prisoner is assured access to the Parole Board, and the possibility of release on licence, once he has reached his release date and the mental health review tribunal find he is no longer appropriately detained in hospital for medical treatment.

### *Section 296: **Duration of directions under Mental Health (Northern Ireland) Order 1986 in relation to offenders***

643. *Section 296* makes amendments to Article 56 of the Mental Health (Northern Ireland) Order 1986 dealing with the arrangements in Northern Ireland for the release or return to prison of serving prisoners who have been transferred to hospital for medical treatment. It substitutes references to the expiration of a prisoner's sentence with references to his release date. This ensures that the Secretary of State can only treat the patient as a restricted patient until the time when the prisoner would have been released from prison. New article 56(3) provides that the release date means the date on which the prisoner would be entitled to release if he had not been transferred to hospital, (regardless of any powers of the Sentence Review Commissioners or the Life Sentence Review Commissioners), if he was still detained in prison.

### *Section 297: **Access to Sentence Review Commissioners and Life Sentence Review Commissioners for certain Northern Ireland patients***

644. *Section 297* makes an insertion into Article 79 of the Mental Health (Northern Ireland) Order 1986. It relates to transferred prisoners detained in hospital beyond their release date whose detention in hospital has been found by the mental health review tribunal for Northern Ireland to be no longer justified by their mental disorder but who the tribunal has recommended should remain in hospital rather than return to prison in the event that the Secretary of State does not agree to their discharge from hospital. It provides that the fact that restrictions under the Mental Health Order remain in force does not prevent an application or reference to the Sentence Review Commissioners or the Life Sentence Review Commissioners for release. It further provides that if the Commissioners direct release, the restrictions cease to have effect at the time he is entitled to release. The effect of this is that the transferred prisoner is assured access to the Review Commissioners, and the possibility of release on licence once he has reached his release date and the mental health review tribunal find that he is no longer detained in hospital for medical treatment.

### *Section 298: **Term of a detention and training order***

645. This section is related to the increase in the maximum sentence for some summary-only offences from 6 months to 51 weeks. The Section provides that the maximum sentence for such offences in the case of those under 18 will remain as a 6-month detention and training order.

### *Section 299: **Disqualification from working with children***

646. This section introduces Schedule 30, which is explained below.

### *Section 300: Power to impose unpaid work requirement or curfew requirement on fine defaulter*

647. This section re-enacts, with appropriate modifications to make them applicable for the new sentencing framework, the fine default provisions in section 35 of the Crime Sentences Act 1997.

648. Where a court has the power to commit an offender to prison in default of payment of a fine, *subsection (2)* provides the court with an alternative power to order the offender to comply with an unpaid work or curfew requirement. Such an order is named a "default order" by *subsection (3)*. *Subsection (4)* allows these requirements to be subject to electronic monitoring. *Subsection (5)* provides the Court with a power to postpone the making of a default order until such time as thinks fit. *Subsection (6)* applies the breach provisions in Schedule 8, the transfer of community order provisions in Schedule 9 and the provisions of Chapter 4, subject to set out the modifications outline in Schedule 31, to the making of default orders.

649. Should the offender pay the whole or part of the sum of the fine originally defaulted, *Subsection (7)* provides for the number of hours of unpaid work or days of curfew to be reduced by a proportion corresponding to the amount repaid, or for the order to cease to have effect altogether.

### *Section 301: Fine defaulters: driving disqualification*

650. This section re-enacts the provisions of section 40 of the Crime Sentences Act 1997. As an alternative to committing an offender to custody in default of payment of a sum, it provides the Court in subsection (2) with a power to disqualify an offender from driving for a period of up to 12 months.

651. Under *subsection (3)* if the fine is repaid the order ceases to have effect, or if it is repaid in part, the total number of weeks or months is reduced by a corresponding proportion. *Subsection (5)* provides the Secretary of State with an order-making power to alter the period of disqualification (currently 12 months) specified in *subsection (2)*.

## *Chapter 9 : Supplementary*

### *Section 302: Execution of process between England and Wales and Scotland*

652. This section enables summonses and warrants issued to persons under the sentencing provisions of the Act to be served in Scotland. The section lists the relevant sentencing provisions which involve summonses and warrants. This section applies only applies to the magistrates' court, as nothing is needed to allow summonses and warrants issued by the Crown Court to be served in Scotland.

### *Section 303: Sentencing: repeals*

653. This section lists the main provisions superseded by this Part of the Act. Full details of all repeals are found in Schedule 37.

### *Section 304: Amendments relating to sentencing*

654. This Section introduces Schedule 32.

### *Section 305: Interpretation of Part 12*

655. This Section defines various terms used in this Part of the Act. It also outlines how to determine the age of an offender for sentencing purposes and how to construe "imprisonment" in relation to young offenders.

## Part 13 : Miscellaneous

### Section: 306: Limit on period of detention without charge of suspected terrorists

656. *Section 306* relates to detention under Schedule 8 to the Terrorism Act 2000. This relates to persons arrested under section 41 of that Act as suspected terrorists.

657. *Section 306* gives the "judicial authority" as defined in paragraph 29 of Schedule 8 to the Terrorism Act, power to extend the period of detention for up to a total of fourteen days from the existing starting times set out in paragraphs 29(3) and 36(3) provided the conditions in paragraph 32 are met. These conditions are that there must be reasonable grounds for believing that the further detention of the person concerned is necessary to obtain relevant evidence, and the investigation in connection with which the person is detained is being conducted diligently and expeditiously. Paragraph 37 provides that the detainee must be released immediately if the grounds for his detention no longer apply.

658. The judicial authority is only able to extend the period in the warrant for more than seven days if the warrant already authorises detention for the maximum seven days currently permitted. For example, the section does not allow the police to ask for ten more days' detention if the warrant only authorises detention for four days. At that stage the judicial authority would only be able extend the warrant for three more days. The section only permits an extension of detention for longer than seven days if the warrant already permits detention for the current maximum of seven days. Nevertheless, the Section does not prevent an application for an extension of the warrant for longer than seven days being made before the seven day period has expired so long as the warrant already authorises detention for seven days. Accordingly, it is not possible for the fourteen days to be granted in one block no matter how compelling the reason.

659. The procedural requirements for making an application for extension to detention as stipulated in paragraphs 30(3) and 31 to 34 apply to extensions for up to 14 days just as they apply to other extensions of detention under paragraph 36.

### *Section 307: Enforcement of regulations implementing Community legislation on endangered species:*

660. This section provides for the maximum prison sentences for offences arising from EC Regulations 338/97 and 1808/2001 on the protection of wild fauna and flora by regulating trade therein (the 'Wildlife Trade Regulations') to be increased. Subsection (1) provides definitions for the purposes of this Section. Subsection (2) disapplies the provisions of the European Communities Act 1972, which would otherwise limit the maximum penalties for offences arising from these Regulations, and tried on indictment, to two years, imprisonment and a fine. This ensures that for offences created in new secondary legislation implementing the Wildlife Trade Regulations (currently implemented by the Control of Trade in Endangered Species (Enforcement) Regulations 1997; (SI 1997 No. 1372) and predominantly triable either way), the possibility of a maximum penalty of up to five years imprisonment for offences tried on indictment can be introduced. *Subsection (3)* disapplies the provisions of the 1972 Act for new offences under the Wildlife Trade Regulations tried summarily in Scotland and Northern Ireland, so allowing the possibility of a maximum prison sentence of six months (currently a maximum sentence of only three months is permissible).

661. *Subsection (5)* modifies subsection (3), by providing that the provisions of the 1972 Act are also disapplied, until the sentencing provisions in Part 12 of the Act are commenced, in relation to: Wildlife Trade Regulations offences in England and Wales; and offences arising from Council Directive 92/43/EEC on the conservation of natural habitats and wild fauna and flora ('Habitats Directivethe ") in England and Wales. The subsection supersedes and repeals sections 81(2) and (3) of the Countryside and Rights of Way Act 2000, which are repealed by the Act.

662. *Subsection (4)* confers a power of arrest without warrant for a constable in Scotland, for wildlife trade offences. Section 24 of the Police and Criminal Evidence Act 1984 and Article 26(1) of the Police and Criminal Evidence Order (NI) 1983, already provide that in other parts of the UK, offences which attract a maximum prison sentence of five years are automatically 'arrestable'. This subsection ensures that the arrest powers available to police officers throughout the UK are broadly consistent for these offences. *Subsection (6)* ensures that if any of the "relevant Community instruments" are amended, repealed or re-enacted, that the provisions of the section will still apply to them.

### *Section 308: Non-appearance of defendant: plea of guilty*

663. This section extends the cases in which a defendant in the magistrates' court can plead guilty and be dealt with in his absence. At present this is not possible where the offence is punishable with imprisonment for a term exceeding 3 months, but it will be possible in the future by virtue of this section.

### *Section 309: Preparatory hearings for serious offences not involving fraud*

664. This section amends section 29 of the Criminal Procedure and Investigations Act 1996 which sets out the circumstances in which a statutory preparatory hearing may be held in cases not involving fraud. At present, preparatory hearings may be held in non-fraud cases where it appears to the judge that the case is of such complexity or length that holding a preparatory hearing is likely to bring substantial benefits. This section adds "seriousness" to these criteria.

### *Section 310: Preparatory hearings to deal with severance and joinder of charges*

665. This section amends sections 7(1), 9(3) and 9(11) of the Criminal Justice Act 1987 and sections 29(2) and 31(3) of the Criminal Procedure and Investigations Act 1996. It adds issues of severance and joinder to the purposes for which preparatory hearings may be held under these Acts and also provides that the judge may make rulings on severance and joinder in preparatory hearings. These rulings will be appealable under the 1987 Act or the 1996 Act by both the prosecution and the defence, subject to the leave of the judge or the Court of Appeal.

### *Section 311: Reporting restrictions for preparatory hearings*

666. This section extends to Northern Ireland the reporting restrictions that apply to preparatory hearings held in long or complex fraud cases under the Criminal Justice Act 1987 and those held in long or complex non-fraud cases held under the Criminal Procedure and Investigations Act 1996. At present these restrictions extend only to Great Britain. *Subsections (3) and (7)* provide that the consent of the Attorney General for Northern Ireland is required before proceedings for these offences can be instituted in Northern Ireland.

### *Section 312: Award of costs*

667. This section remedies a gap in existing legislation by means of an amendment to the Prosecution of Offences Act 1985. It provides that the Court of Appeal may award defence costs from central funds or award costs against the defendant following an appeal from a preparatory hearing in a non-fraud case under the Criminal Procedure and Investigations Act 1996. The amendment will bring appeals under the 1996 Act in line with equivalent appeals under the Criminal Justice Act 1987.

### *Section 313: Extension of investigations by Criminal Cases Review Commission in England and Wales*

668. Section 23A of the Criminal Appeal Act 1968 empowers the Court of Appeal, where a defendant has been given leave to appeal against conviction, to direct the Criminal

Cases Review Commission to investigate and report to the Court on any matter relevant to the determination of the case and likely to assist in resolving it. The Court of Appeal has no equivalent power to direct the Commission to investigate and report to it on any matter where the defendant is still applying for leave to appeal.

669. *Section 313* amends the Criminal Appeal Act 1968 to permit the Court of Appeal to direct the Commission to investigate and report on any matter where the defendant is applying for leave to appeal against conviction, as well as on an appeal against conviction.

670. *Section 313* also adds a new subsection (1A) to section 23A of the 1968 Act. The new subsection makes it clear that a direction to the Criminal Cases Review Commission to investigate may not be given by a single judge. The purpose of the stipulation is to require the full court to consider such directions before they are made, and thus ensure that they are used sparingly.

### *Section 314:* ***Extension of investigations by Criminal Cases Review Commission in Northern Ireland***

671. *Section 314* makes similar amendments to the Criminal Appeal (Northern Ireland) Act 1980 as *section 313* makes to the Criminal Appeal Act 1968.

### *Section 315:* ***Appeals following reference by Criminal Cases Review Commission***

672. *Section 315* adds a new section 14(4A) to the Criminal Appeal Act 1995. Under section 14(5) of the 1995 Act, an appellant whose case is referred to the Court of Appeal by the Criminal Cases Review Commission may introduce an unlimited number of additional grounds of appeal, including grounds which bear no relation to the Commission's reasons for referring the case. New section 14(4A) of the 1995 Act introduces a leave requirement before such an appellant can add grounds of appeal unrelated to the reasons the Commission had for making the reference. The change applies to both England and Wales and Northern Ireland.

### *Section 316:* ***Power to substitute conviction of alternative offence on appeal in England and Wales.***

673. Where a defendant is found guilty by a jury and appeals against conviction, the Court of Appeal has the power under section 3 of the Criminal Appeal Act 1968, instead of allowing or dismissing the appeal, to substitute a conviction of an alternative offence on the same facts. However, it has no power to do this where the defendant appeals against conviction after pleading guilty. *Section 316* inserts a new section 3A into the Criminal Appeal Act 1968 allowing the Court of Appeal to substitute a conviction of an alternative offence, where the facts admitted by the appellant by virtue of the guilty plea justify a conviction of that other offence.

### *Section 317:* ***Power to substitute conviction of alternative offence on appeal in Northern Ireland***

674. *Section 317* makes similar amendments to the Criminal Appeal (Northern Ireland) Act 1980 as *section 316* makes to the Criminal Appeal Act 1968.

### *Section 318:* ***Power to substitute conviction of alternative offence on appeal from court-martial***

675. *Section 318* makes similar amendments to the Court-Martial (Appeals) Act 1968 as *sections 316 and 317* make to the Criminal Appeal Act 1968 and the Criminal Appeal (Northern Ireland) Act 1980.

### *Section 319*: ***Appeals against sentences in England and Wales***

676. Section 10(2) of the Criminal Appeal Act 1968 gives certain defendants who have not been tried in the Crown Court, but are sentenced there, a right of appeal to the Court of Appeal against the Crown Court's sentence. By virtue of section 10(3) of the 1968 Act, however, no appeal lies under section 10(2) where the offender is sentenced to less than six months imprisonment, unless he receives certain specified kinds of sentence described in section 10(3)(b), 10(3)(c) or 10(3)(cc) of the 1968 Act (for example, an order banning him from holding or obtaining a driving licence).

677. *Section 319* simplifies section 10 of the 1968 Act by amending it to remove the six month limitation and various exceptions to that limitation. The overall effect of *section 319* is that anybody committed to the Crown Court for sentence in future, or dealt with by the Crown Court under the other circumstances set out in section 10(2) of the 1968 Act, will have a right of appeal to the Court of Appeal against the Crown Court's sentence.

### *Section 320*: ***Offence of outraging public decency triable either way***

678. This section makes the offence of outraging public decency triable summarily in a magistrates' court as well as on indictment. The maximum penalties on summary conviction for this offence are to be those provided for by section 32(1) of the Magistrates' Courts Act 1980. These are currently six months' imprisonment or a fine of £5000 or both.

### *Section 321*: ***Jury service***

679. This section introduces Schedule 33.

### *Section 322*: ***Individual support orders***

680. Section 1 of the Crime and Disorder Act 1998 permits the police, the British Transport police, local authorities and registered social landlords to apply for anti-social behaviour orders (ASBOs) in the Magistrates' court. Orders can be issued to persons over 10 years who have acted in an anti-social manner and where the order is necessary to protect the public from further anti-social acts. Section 1 defines an anti-social manner as that which causes or is likely to cause harassment, alarm and distress to one or more persons not of the same household. Anti-social behaviour includes harassment, noise nuisance, writing graffiti and verbal abuse. An ASBO prohibits the person under the order from doing anything described in the order. Section 292 inserts sections 1AA (Individual support orders) and 1AB (explanation, breach, amendment etc.) after section 1A of the Crime and Disorder Act 1998. These sections allow for a new order aimed at preventing further anti-social behaviour to be available where an anti-social behaviour order has already been granted against a person under 18.

681. *Subsection (1)* of section 1AA (Individual support orders) obliges the court to consider the question of making an ISO after an anti-social behaviour order is made against a child or young person (that is a person aged 10-17). *Subsection (2)* states that the court must make an ISO if it is satisfied that the ISO conditions in *subsection (3)* are satisfied. *Subsection (2)(a)* ensures that requirements under the order cannot exceed a period of 6 months. *Subsection (2)(b)* allows the order to require the defendant to comply with directions given by a 'responsible officer' who can be one of the persons set out in subsection (10).

682. All three conditions set out in *subsection (3)* have to be satisfied for an ISO to be made. If the conditions are not met and an ISO is not made, subsection (4) requires the court to state in open court why it considers that the conditions are not met.

683. *Subsection (5)* sets out the nature of the requirements which a court can make in an ISO, namely any requirement that the court considers desirable in the interests of preventing a repetition of the anti-social behaviour which led to the ASBO.

684. *Subsection (6)* sets out certain things which an ISO may require the defendant to do or which a responsible officer may direct the defendant to do. *Subsection (7)* ensures that the person subject to the order cannot be required to attend any place (or different places) under the order on more than two occasions in any given week. *Subsection (8)* obliges the court, when imposing requirements, to avoid conflict with religious beliefs and avoid interference with other educational attendance requirements as far as this is practicable.

685. *Subsection (9)* allows the court to obtain whatever information it considers necessary in order to determine whether the individual support conditions set out in subsection (3) are fulfilled and in order to determine the requirements that should be included in an order. The court is empowered to obtain this information from a social worker of a local authority social services department or a member of youth offending team.

686. *Subsection (1)* of section 1AB (Individual Support Orders: explanation, breach, amendment etc) sets out the court's obligation to explain to the defendant in open court the effect of the order, the consequences of breach and the power to review the order on application.

687. *Subsection (2)* allows for the Secretary of State to prescribe cases where: the requirement to explain to the defendant in open court will not apply; where the explanation can be made in writing; or the explanation can be given in the absence of the defendant.

688. *Subsection* (3) sets the maximum fines available for non-compliance with an ISO. In the magistrates courts where these breaches would be heard there is a cap imposed by the section 135 of the Powers of Criminal Courts (Sentencing) Act 2000. For under 18 it is £1,000; for under 14 it is £250. *Subsection (4)* proscribes the use of referral orders for non-compliance with an ISO.

689. *Subsection (5)* requires an ISO to cease if the ASBO to which it is linked ceases. Subsection (6) allows the person who is subject to the order or the responsible officer to apply to the court for the order to be varied or discharged. *Subsection (7)* allows a court to vary or discharge an ISO if it is varying the ASBO to which the ISO is linked.

### *Section 323*: ***Individual support orders: consequential amendments***

690. *Section 323* makes changes consequential to the introduction of the ISO to sections 4, 18 and 38 of the Crime and Disorder Act 1998 and to section 143 of the Magistrates Courts Act 1980.

691. *Subsection (2)* amends section 4 of the Crime and Disorder Act 1998, which sets out the provision for appeals against orders. This subsection allows for section 4 to apply to ISOs and allows for any ISO amended or made by the Crown Court to be treated as if it were an order of the magistrates' court.

692. *Subsection* (3) inserts definitions of individual support orders and responsible officers into the Crime and Disorder Act 1998.

693. *Subsection (4)* amends s18(4) of the Crime and Disorder Act to ensure that the correct responsible officer is identified for the ISO.

694. *Subsection (5)*, by inserting provision of responsible officers into the definition of local provision of youth services, ensures that there are obligations on the local authority to provide, and the bodies set out in 38(2) of the Crime and Disorder Act 1998 to co-operate in the provision of, responsible officers for ISOs.

695. *Subsection (6)* inserts ISOs into section 143(2) of the Magistrates' Courts Act 1980 and allows the Secretary of State to amend the level of fines for ISOs if there has been a substantial change in the value of money.

### *Section 324: Parenting orders and referral orders*

696. *Section 324* introduces Schedule 34, which makes provision about the interaction of parenting orders, made under sections 8 to 10 Crime and Disorder Act 1998, and referral orders made under Part 3 of the Powers of Criminal Courts (Sentencing) Act 2000.

697. *Paragraph 1: Removal of restriction in Crime and Disorder Act 1998*. This together with the amendment made in paragraph 3 of the Schedule removes from section 8 of the Crime and Disorder Act 1998 the restriction currently on a court for the making of a Parenting Order alongside a Referral Order.

698. *Paragraph 2: Supplemental provisions relating to Parenting Orders.* This amends section 9 of the Crime and Disorder Act 1998 (which makes supplemental provision relating to Parenting Orders).

699. *Subparagraph (2)* substitutes a new subsection (1A) into section 9. The old subsection was one of the provisions ensuring that a parenting order and a referral order could not be made in respect of the same offence. The new subsection provides that the normal duty on the court to make a parenting order (or explain why it would not help to prevent the offender from committing another offence) where a person under the age of 16 is convicted of an offence does not apply where the court makes a referral order in respect of the offence.

700. *Subparagraph (3)* inserts a new subsection (2A) and (2B) into section 9. This provides that where the court does decide to make a Parenting Order with a Referral Order, the court must obtain and consider a report by a probation officer, a local authority social worker, or a member of a youth offending team. The report should indicate what the requirements of the Parenting Order might include, the reasons why it would be desirable, and also, if the offender is under age 16 years, information about the family's circumstances and the likely effect of the Order on those circumstances.

701. *Subparagraph (4)* inserts a new subsection (7A) which defines a Referral Order as an order imposed under section 16(2) or (3) of the Powers of Criminal Courts (Sentencing) Act 2000.

702. *Paragraph 3: Removal of Restriction in Powers of Criminal Courts (Sentencing) Act 2000.* This removes the restriction in section 19(5) of the Powers of Criminal Courts (Sentencing) Act 2000 preventing the court from imposing a parenting order and a referral order in respect of the same offence.

703. *Paragraph 4: Panel to refer case back to Youth Court where parent or guardian fails to comply.* This inserts a new subsection (2A) into section 22 of the Powers of Criminal Courts (Sentencing) Act 2000. A court making a referral order may require a parent or guardian to attend the meetings of the youth offender panel under section 20 of the Powers of Criminal Courts (Sentencing) Act 2000. Where the parent or guardian fails to comply with such an order, the new subsection provides the power to the panel to refer the case back to the offender's youth court. This would then allow the court the opportunity to decide whether it should impose a Parenting Order.

704. *Paragraphs 5 and 6: Arrangements when a panel refers a parent or guardian to the youth court.* These insert new provisions into section 28 of and Schedule 1 to the Powers of Criminal Courts (Sentencing) Act 2000. These provisions set out the arrangements when a youth offender panel refers a parent or guardian to the appropriate youth court using the power set out in the new section 22(2A). The panel must make a report to the court explaining why the parent is being referred to it and the court can require the parent to appear before it by means of the issue of a summons, or a warrant for arrest. Where the parent then appears before the youth court, the court may make a Parenting

Order if both of two conditions are satisfied. The first is that the court is satisfied that the parent has failed without reasonable excuse to comply with an order made by the court under section 20 to attend the youth offender panel. The second is that the court believes that it is desirable in the interests of preventing further offences being committed by the offender. The provisions also set out that a Parenting Order means an order requiring the parent to comply for up to twelve months with requirements the court considers to be desirable in the interests of preventing further offences by the offender and to attend a counselling or guidance programme for up to three months. The counselling or guidance programme can include or consist of a residential course provided the court is satisfied that this is likely to be more effective than a non-residential course and that any interference with family life is proportionate. The provisions also state which of the provisions of the Crime and Disorder Act relating to parenting orders apply to a parenting order made in these circumstances and provide for a right of appeal to the Crown Court against the making of a parenting order in these circumstances.

### *Section 325: **Arrangements for assessing etc. risks posed by certain offenders***

705. This Section re-enacts with amendments section 67 of the Criminal Justice and Courts Services 2000. It places a duty on the "responsibility authority" (the chief officer of police, the local probation board for each area and the Prison Service) to establish and keep under review arrangements for assessing and managing the risks posed by "relevant sexual and violent offenders" or other offenders who may cause serious harm to the public (see *subsection* (2)). The arrangements which have been established at area level to undertake this duty take the form of "multi-agency public protection arrangements".

706. Under *subsection (3),* the responsible authority and those bodies listed in *subsection (6)* must co-operate with each other, in order to enable the responsible authority to perform its duty. *Subsection (5)* states that a memorandum outlining this process must be produced. The Secretary of State is given the power in *subsection (7)* to amend the list of specified bodies which must co-operate with the responsible authority, so as to add or remove an entry.

### *Section 326: **Review of arrangements***

707. This section requires the responsible authority to keep the effectiveness of the arrangements it has established under review and to change them where necessary. This review must be conducted in consultation with two lay advisers to be appointed for each area by the Secretary of State. This Section also requires the responsible authority to publish an annual report detailing how it has discharged its functions.

### *Section 327: Section 325 – **interpretation***

708. This Section defines "relevant sexual or violent offender" for the purposes of section 325. It therefore clarifies to which offenders multi-agency protection arrangements should apply.

### *Section 328: **Criminal record certificates: amendments of Part 5 of Police Act 1997***

709. *Section 328* introduces Schedule 35 which makes a number of amendments to Part 5 of the Police Act 1997 ('the 1997 Act') which governs the disclosure of criminal and other records by the Criminal Records Bureau (CRB) for employment vetting purposes. The CRB's higher level disclosure service was launched in March 2002. This is intended for employers and voluntary organisations seeking to appoint persons to work with children or vulnerable adults or involving other sensitive positions of trust.

710. *The CRB* experienced some initial difficulties in meeting its published performance standards; as a result, in September 2002, the Home Secretary appointed an Independent Review Team to take a fundamental look at the operations of the CRB. The Home Secretary announced the Government's response to the Review

Team's recommendations on 27th February 2003 (Official Report, col: 32WS-36WS). The amendments to the 1997 Act implement a number of the Review Team's recommendations.

711. *Paragraphs 2, 3(2)(b) and 4(2)(b)* of Schedule 35 amend sections 112(1)(a), 113(1)(a) and 115(1)(a) of the 1997 Act respectively to enable regulations to be made prescribing the manner in which an application for a disclosure must be made. In the case of standard and enhanced disclosures, the intention is to require applications to be submitted to the CRB via a registered body (which is already the current practice) and, in due course, to require applications to be submitted electronically. Paragraphs 3(2)(c) and 4(2)(c) amend sections 113(1)(b) and 115(1)(b) respectively so that regulations may also be made prescribing the manner in which the fee for a standard or enhanced disclosure application is to be payable. Again, it is the intention to require the fee to be routed to the CRB via the registered body countersigning the application, although liability for payment will remain with the individual applicant.

712. *Paragraph 3(3) and 4(5)* insert a new subsection into sections 113 and 115 respectively. The purpose is to enable the CRB to issue a standard disclosure where an enhanced disclosure has been applied for but the application does not satisfy the requirements for such a disclosure, and vice versa. The CRB will first and foremost seek to educate and support registered bodies to ensure that they correctly apply the criteria for each type of disclosure; accordingly it is intended that this reserve power will only be used in exceptional circumstances.

713. *Paragraph 4(3) and (4)* repeal the existing subsections in section 115 which determine who qualifies for an enhanced disclosure. The intention is that, henceforth, the criteria will be specified in regulations so that there is the flexibility to alter them as circumstances require, for example, because of a change to the risk assessment in relation to a given occupational group. *Paragraph 5* makes a similar change to section 116 of the 1997 Act which relates to applications for enhanced disclosures for judicial appointments and Crown employment.

714. *Paragraphs 6 to 9* enable the CRB to set clear standards for registered bodies, particularly in respect of validating the identity of applicants for disclosures, and confers powers on the CRB to suspend or revoke registration where such standards are not complied with.

715. *Paragraph 6* amends section 120 of the 1997 Act which relates to registered persons. Section 120(2) of the 1997 Act requires the Secretary of State to register any person who satisfies the requirements for registration. These requirements are set down either in regulations (hitherto made under section 120(3), but in future made under new section 120ZA(2) as inserted by paragraph 6 of the Schedule) or in section 120(4) to (6) of the 1997 Act which relate to the legal status of the person applying for registration and whether that person can ask (on his own or another person's behalf) an exempted question under the provisions of the Rehabilitation of Offenders Act 1974. The revised section 120(2) sets down an additional requirement, namely that the applicant has not had his registration cancelled in the past two years.

716. *Paragraph 7* inserts new section 120ZA into the 1997 Act. This new section replaces and extends the existing power to make regulations about registration. In particular, the new power enables regulations to make provision for the registration of any registered body to be subject to conditions. It is envisaged that such conditions would require a registered body to take specified steps to verify the identity of any applicant for disclosure, to ensure that disclosure applications are properly completed and to ensure that adequate security measures are in place to control the use of, access to and security of disclosures. Registered bodies will also be required to pay disclosure application fees monthly in arrears rather than submitting a separate fee with each individual application. A condition might also be imposed requiring applications for disclosure to be submitted to the CRB by electronic means. It would be open to a registered body to delegate the identity validation function to one or more agents (e.g. a Local Education Authority may

delegate the function to headteachers of maintained schools), but would retain overall responsibility for ensuring that identity checks were properly carried out.

717. *Paragraph 8* makes a consequential amendment to the heading of section 120A of the 1997 Act (refusal and cancellation of registration).

718. *Paragraph 9* inserts new sections 120AA and 120AB into the 1997 Act. New section 120AA sets out further grounds on which a registration may be refused, suspended or cancelled, while new section 120AB sets out the procedure to apply in the event of a suspension or cancellation. Under new section 120AA(1) registration may be refused where an applicant is likely to countersign fewer than a prescribed minimum number of disclosure applications per year. A registration may be suspended or cancelled where a registered body is no longer likely to wish to countersign disclosure applications (this ground for cancellation may currently be found in regulations); has not countersigned the prescribed minimum number of applications in the past 12 months; or has failed to comply with any condition attached to registration. Before a decision to suspend or cancel a registration takes effect, a registered body must be given an opportunity to submit representations. If, following consideration of the representations, the decision is confirmed the registered body has a 6 week period of grace before the suspension or cancellation takes effect to allow time for alternative arrangements for counter-signing disclosure applications to be put in place. Regulations may be made to extend (or reduce) the 6 week period of grace.

719. *Paragraph 10* inserts new section 122A into the 1997 Act. This enables the Secretary of State to delegate his functions under Part 5 of the 1997. Act to another person (e.g. to a Public Private Partnership provider or Managed Service provider). The Home Secretary is precluded from delegating his powers to make regulations or to publish or revise a code of practice.

720. *Paragraph 11* inserts a new section 124A into the 1997 Act. This new section makes it an offence for any person to whom the Secretary of State has delegated functions under new section 122A (e.g. a PPP provider or his employees) to disclose any personal information obtained in connection with those functions. There are certain exceptions, including where the disclosure is made in the course of the person's duties.

### *Section 329:* ***Civil proceedings for trespass to the person brought by an offender***

721. *Section 329* makes new provision about cases where a person who has been convicted of an imprisonable criminal offence takes civil action for damages for trespass to the person against the victim of the offence or against a third party who has intervened, for example to protect the victim or to protect or recover property.

722. *Subsection (1)* set out the circumstances in which the section will apply. These are where the person bringing the civil action (the claimant) claims that the defendant did an act amounting to trespass to his or her person; and where the claimant has been convicted in the United Kingdom of an imprisonable offence committed on the same occasion as that on which the defendant's act is alleged to have been done.

723. *Subsection (2)* provides that in these circumstances proceedings may only be brought with the permission of the court.

724. *Subsection (3)* sets out the only circumstances in which the court may give permission for the proceedings to be brought. These are if there is evidence that the condition set out in subsection (5) is not met, or if there is evidence that in all the circumstances the defendant's act was grossly disproportionate.

725. *Subsection (4)* provides that if the court does give permission and the proceedings are brought, the defendant will not be liable if he can prove that the condition set out in subsection (5) is met, and that in all the circumstances his act was not grossly disproportionate.

726. *Subsection (5)* sets out the condition referred to in subsections (3) and (4). This is that the defendant only did the act amounting to trespass to the claimant's person because he believed that (a) the claimant was either about to commit an offence, in the course of committing an offence, or had committed an offence immediately beforehand; and (b) the act was necessary to defend himself or another person; protect or recover property; prevent the commission or continuation of an offence; apprehend or secure the conviction of the claimant after he had committed the offence; or that the act was necessary to assist in achieving any of those things.

727. *Subsection (6)* ensures that the defence available to the defendant under subsection (4) does not prejudice his ability to rely on any other defence.

728. *Subsection (7)* ensures that the provisions of the section apply where members of the armed forces are found guilty of equivalent offences under the terms of the services Acts.

729. *Subsection (8)* defines various terms used in the section. Paragraph (a) provides that "trespass to the person" comprises assault, battery, or false imprisonment; paragraph (b) provides that references to the defendant's belief are to his honest belief, whether or not it was also reasonable; paragraph (c) provides that "court" in proceedings under this Section means the High Court or a county court; and paragraph (d) defines "imprisonable offence" as an offence which in the case of a person aged 18 or over is punishable by imprisonment.

## Part 14 : General

### *Section 330: Orders and rules*

730. This Section provides that where the Act confers power on a Minister to make an order or rules, the power is exercisable by statutory instrument.

731. *Subsection (4)* specifies that this power may also include the power to make transitional and consequential provisions and savings, whenever a provision in the Act is commenced by order under Section 330.

732. *Subsection (5)* lists statutory instruments that are to be subject to affirmative resolution procedure. All other instruments made under powers to which the Section applies, apart from those excluded by *subsection (7)*, are subject to negative resolution procedure. An instrument made under any of the provisions mentioned in subsection (7) is not subject to any parliamentary procedure.

### *Section 331: Further minor and consequential amendments*

733. This Section introduces Schedule 36.

### *Section 332: Repeals*

734. This Section introduces Schedule 37.

### *Section 333: Supplementary and consequential provision etc*

735. This section enables the Secretary of State to make supplementary, incidental or consequential provision, and transitory, transitional or saving provision. An order made under this power will be subject to negative resolution procedure (see section 330(6)), other than where primary legislation is being amended in which case it is subject to the affirmative resolution procedure (see section 330(5)(b)).

736. Where one provision of the Act is brought into force before another, the power includes power to modify the provision brought into force so as to take account of the fact that the other provision is not yet in force. The power also includes a general power to make consequential amendment of other Acts.

737. *Section 333* is different from the power provided in Section 330(4) in that it is exercisable independently of the commencement power in Section 336 and creates in effect a new, free-standing power to make transitional or consequential provisions at any time, including a power to amend primary legislation. It was considered necessary, particularly in respect of the sentencing provisions, to pick up any consequential amendments not identified before the Act's introduction or during its passage; and also to deal with long-term transitional arrangements created by the introduction of a new system which will gradually replace the existing arrangements.

### *Section 334:**Provisions for Northern Ireland***

738. *Subsections (1)*to *(3)* of this section provide that an Order in Council under section 85 of the Northern Ireland Act 1998 (c. 47) (or during direct rule, paragraph 1 of the Schedule to the Northern Ireland Act 2000 (c. 1)), is to be subject to the negative resolution rather than the affirmative resolution procedure if it contains a statement that it is made only for purposes corresponding to those in Part 1, sections 1, 3(3), 4, 7 to 10 and 12 (amendments of Police and Criminal Evidence Act 1984), paragraphs 1, 2, 5 to 10 and 20 of Schedule 1 (amendments related to Part 1), Part 8 (live links), Part 9 (prosecution appeals) and Part 11 (evidence).

739. Section 41(2) of the Justice (Northern Ireland) Act 2002 (c. 26) provides that once a local Attorney General for Northern Ireland has been appointed under section 22(2) of that Act the functions of the Attorney General for Northern Ireland to consent to prosecutions shall transfer to the Director of Public Prosecutions for Northern Ireland (subject to certain exceptions in Schedule 7 of that Act). *Subsection (4)* ensures that any function of the Attorney General for Northern Ireland of consenting to the institution of criminal proceedings conferred by an amendment made by the Act will be included in the transfer of functions provided for in section 41(2).

740. *Subsection (5)* provides that any reference in the Access to Justice (Northern Ireland) Order 2003 (S.I. 2003/435 (N.I. 10)) to any provision in the Criminal Appeal (Northern Ireland) Act 1980 (c. 47) is to be read as a reference to the provision, as amended by the Act.

### *Section 336:* ***Commencement***

741. The provisions listed in *subsection (1)* came into force (i.e. on 20th November 2003) on Royal Assent (i.e. on 18th December 2003). The life sentence provisions listed in subsection (2) come into force 4 weeks later. The remaining provisions in the Act will be brought into force by order. A commencement order may make different provision for different purposes or different areas.

### *Section 337:* ***Extent***

742. This section provides that in general the Act extends to England and Wales only, subject to the exceptions mentioned.

### *Section 338:* ***Channel Islands and Isle of Man***

743. This section enables the provisions of the Act to be extended to the Channel Islands and Isle of Man, with modifications as necessary, by Order in Council

## SCHEDULES

### *Schedule 1:* ***Amendments related to** Part 1*

744. *Paragraphs 1 to 10* make various amendments which are consequential on the specific modifications and extensions to powers set out in Part 1.

745. *Paragraph 11* amends section 2 of the Criminal Justice Act 1987 to allow "appropriate persons" to exercise the powers of a constable executing a warrant under that section. "Appropriate persons" are either members of the Serious Fraud Office or authorised by the Director of that Office to accompany a constable executing a warrant under that section. This amendment is similar to that made by Section 2 of the Act. "Appropriate persons" may exercise those powers only in the company and under the supervision of a constable. *Paragraphs 12 and 13* make related amendments of section 2.

746. *Paragraph 14* extends the meaning of property seized by a constable, for the purposes of section 56(1) of the Criminal Justice and Police Act 2001, to include property seized by persons accompanying constables executing warrants (as allowed for by Section 2 of, and paragraph 11 of Schedule 1 to, the Act). This amendment is required for those cases in which a person accompanying a constable executing a warrant has (because of the changes made by the Act) a power of seizure to which section 50, 53, 54 or 55 of the Criminal Justice and Police Act 2001 applies. Section 50 confers extended powers of seizure and sections 53 to 55 impose obligations to return certain seized items. Section 56 is relevant in determining whether items must be returned under sections 53 to 55 or whether they may be retained. Its effect is to authorise the retention of certain items.

747. *Paragraph 15* extends stop and search powers under section 2 of the Armed Forces Act 2001 to articles made, adapted or intended for use in causing criminal damage. This amendment is similar to that made by Section 1 of the Act.

748. *Paragraphs 16 to 20* amend Schedule 4 to the Police Reform Act 2002 which allows certain police powers to be exercised by designated civilian members of staff. The amendments are necessary to ensure that those provisions are consistent with the amendments to PACE powers set out in the Act.

### *Schedule 8* – ***Breach, revocation and amendment of community order***

749. This Schedule largely reproduces with some amendments the provisions of Schedule 3 to the Powers of Criminal Courts (Sentencing) Act 2000 (which will continue to apply to certain orders for young offenders). *Part 1* deals with interpretation and other matters. *Part 2* deals with breaches of requirements of a community order.

750. Under *paragraph 5*, if an offender's responsible officer is of the view that he has failed to comply with any of the requirements of a community order without reasonable excuse, he either must give the offender a written warning or start enforcement proceedings. Under *paragraph 6*, if the offender fails again to comply, within a 12 month period and without reasonable excuse, the responsible officer must start enforcement proceedings. The responsible officer institutes proceedings by laying an information before a magistrates' court or the Crown Court, depending on the order.

751. Under *paragraph 7*, the magistrates' court may issue a summons requiring the attendance of the offender (or a warrant for his arrest) if it appears that he has failed to comply with any of the requirements of either of the following: a community order made by a magistrates' court; a community order made by the Crown Court which includes a direction that any failure to comply with the requirements of the order is to be dealt with by a magistrates' court. In the case of a community order which includes a drug rehabilitation requirement which is subject to review, the summons or warrant must direct the offender to appear or be brought before the magistrates' court responsible for the order.

752. *Paragraph 8* confers similar powers on the Crown Court where it has made a community order which does not include a direction that a failure to comply with the requirements be dealt with by the magistrates' court.

753. *Paragraph 9* provides that if a magistrates' court is satisfied that the offender has failed to comply with the community order it must deal with him in one of the ways specified. It can amend the order to make the requirements more onerous on the offender

(for example by extending the duration of a particular requirement, but not beyond the limits that apply to that certain requirement nor beyond the three year limit of a community order). It can revoke the order and re-sentence the offender as if he had just been convicted. If the original offence was not punishable with imprisonment but the offender has wilfully and persistently failed to comply with the order the court can revoke the order and sentence him to a custodial sentence of not exceeding 51 weeks. When choosing any of these options the court must take into account the extent to which the offender has complied with the order. If the court takes the second or third option, it must revoke the community order if it is still in force. If the offender is re-sentenced, he can appeal against the new sentence. Where the order was made by the Crown Court (and that court directed that failures to comply should be dealt with by the magistrates' court) the magistrates' court dealing with the breach can remand the offender in custody or release him on bail to appear before the Crown Court. In this instance, it must send various details to the Crown Court regarding the breach.

754. *Paragraph 10* sets out how the Crown Court must deal with failure to comply with a community order whether dealt with directly under paragraph 8 or on committal from a magistrates' court under paragraph 9. The Crown Court's powers are similar to the magistrates' courts', except that the Crown Court will be able to exercise its own wider sentencing powers when re-sentencing. The court determines whether a breach has occurred, not a jury.

755. Under *paragraph 11,* if an offender has refused to comply with a mental health, drug or alcohol treatment requirement, and the refusal is believed by the court to be reasonable under the circumstances, it is not to count as a breach of the order.

756. *Paragraph 12* deals with the powers of a magistrates' court in a case where the offender was under 18 when the order was made, the offence would have been triable only on indictment had it been committed by an adult and the offender has attained 18 by the time the court deals with the enforcement proceedings.

757. *Part 3* of the Schedule deals with the revocation of community orders. Under *paragraph 13* either the offender or the responsible officer can apply to have the order revoked, due to circumstances that have arisen since the order was made. An example might be if the offender has become very ill and is unable to complete the requirements. The court can also revoke the order and re-sentence the offender as if he had just been convicted. This might occur if the offender or his responsible officer wanted to apply for a community order with different requirements, for example due to the good progress of the offender. If the court re-sentences, it must take into account the extent to which the offender complied with the original order. The offender can appeal against the second sentence. If the offender has not made the application to revoke, the court must summon him to appear in order to revoke or revoke and re-sentence. An offender cannot apply to revoke the order if an appeal against it is pending.

758. *Paragraph 14* gives similar powers to the Crown Court in the case of orders it has made which do not contain a direction that failure to comply is to be dealt with by the magistrates' court.

759. Under *paragraph 15*, if the offender was under 18 when the community order was made, and the offence was triable only on indictment had it been committed by an adult, as part of revocation and re-sentencing after he attains 18 the court can impose a fine up to £5000 or re-sentence him as if he had just been convicted of an offence punishable with imprisonment for a term not exceeding 51 weeks.

760. *Part 4* of the Schedule deals with amendment of community orders. *Paragraph 16* deals with amendments by reason of the offender changing residence. A change of residence may necessitate amendment of the order to refer to an alternative petty sessions area. In this case, the change may be made on application by either the offender or his responsible officer. The appropriate court may (and if the application was made by the responsible officer, must) cancel or change any requirements of the order that are not

available in the area to which the offender wishes to move. This is especially important in the case of a programme requirement. The appropriate court is the Crown Court where the order was made by the Crown Court and the order does not include a direction that any failure to comply should be dealt with by the magistrates' court or, in any other case, a magistrates' court in the petty sessions area concerned.

761. Under *paragraph 17* an offender or his responsible officer can also apply to have the requirements of an order amended, even if he is not planning to move. The court cannot add a wholly new requirement or substitute a different requirement for one that was originally specified in the order. The appropriate court can cancel a requirement or adjust it, for example to alter the hours of a curfew or substitute one activity for another. It can also impose electronic monitoring onto any requirement of the order. Any amendment is subject to the same restrictions as would be in place if the order were being made at that point. The court cannot amend a drug rehabilitation, alcohol treatment or mental health treatment requirement without the offender's consent. If the offender fails to consent, the court can revoke the order and re-sentence him. If it re-sentences him it must take into account the extent to which the offender has complied with the requirements of the community order. It can impose a custodial sentence if the original offence was punishable with imprisonment. If the offender was under 18 when the community order was made, and the offence would have been triable only on indictment had it been committed by an adult, as part of re-sentencing the court can impose a fine up to £5000 or re-sentence him as if he had just been convicted of an offence punishable with imprisonment for a term not exceeding 51 weeks.

762. *Paragraph 18* provides that, where a community order includes a drug rehabilitation, alcohol treatment or mental health treatment requirement, and the medical practitioner or other person responsible for the treatment is of the opinion that the treatment should be extended beyond the period specified in the order, that the offender should receive different treatment, that the offender is not susceptible to treatment or that the offender does not require further treatment he must make a report to the responsible officer. He can also report that he is unwilling to continue to treat (or direct the treatment) of the offender for any reason. The responsible officer must then apply to the court to have the requirement amended or cancelled.

763. Under *paragraph 19*, where a community order includes a drug rehabilitation requirement with provision for review, the responsible officer can apply to the court to amend the order to provide for future reviews to take place with or without hearings.

764. *Paragraph 20* provides that, on the application of the offender or the responsible officer, the court may extend an unpaid work requirement beyond the 12 months limit specified in section 193, if it believes it to be in the interests of justice to do so having regard to circumstances which have arisen since the order was made.

765. *Part 5* deals with the powers of the court in relation to a community order where the offender is subsequently convicted for another offence. *Paragraph 21* sets out what the magistrates' court can do in this situation. It may, if it appears to the court to be in the interests of justice, revoke the order, or revoke the order and re-sentence the offender for the original offence as if he had just been convicted of it. If it re-sentences him, the court must take into account the extent to which the offender complied with the order. If it re-sentences, the offender has the right of appeal. If the magistrates' court is dealing with the new offence but the community order was made in the Crown Court it can commit the offender to custody or release him on bail to appear at the Crown Court.

766. *Paragraph 23* makes similar provision in relation to the powers of a Crown Court following conviction of a subsequent offence.

767. *Part 6* of the Schedule contains supplementary provisions. The court cannot amend an order while an appeal against the order is pending. Where a court is amending an order or dealing with a breach, and the application is not by the offender, the court must summon the offender to appear before the court and may issue a warrant if he does not

appear. This does not apply if the court is cancelling a requirement, reducing the period of a requirement or substituting a new petty sessions area or place in the order. When amending a requirement any restrictions on the requirement still apply. The rest of this Part sets out arrangements for sending copies of the order to relevant parties.

### *Schedule 9 – Transfer of community orders to Scotland or Northern Ireland*

768. This Schedule is based on Schedule 4 to the Powers of Criminal Courts (Sentencing) Act 2000, and provides for community orders made in England and Wales to transfer to Scotland or Northern Ireland. An order can transfer either at the point of sentence or once the sentence has begun.

769. *Paragraphs 1 and 2* concern arrangements to transfer community orders to Scotland, while *paragraphs 3 to 4* do the same for Northern Ireland. *Paragraphs 5 to 15* are general provisions that apply to transfers to either place.

770. If the court is considering making or amending a community order so that the offender can move to Scotland or Northern Ireland, it must check whether provision can be made for the offender to comply with the requirements and that arrangements for his supervision can be made in the locality in Scotland or Northern Ireland where he proposes to live. If the court is amending an existing order to allow it to transfer, and any requirement cannot be complied with in the locality of Scotland or Northern Ireland (for whatever reason) it must be removed from the order. Otherwise, the court can decline to amend the order and require it to be carried out in England and Wales.

771. When an order transfers, it will be treated as a Scottish or Northern Ireland community order, so the court must specify which corresponding order the community order will transfer as. For example, if the community order requiring unpaid work, it will transfer as a Scottish or Northern Ireland community service order.

772. *Paragraph 5* defines various terms used in the Schedule. *Paragraph 6* provides for the sentencing court to send copies of the order and other information to the court that will have jurisdiction in Scotland or Northern Ireland. *Paragraph 7* describes how the 'responsible officer' provisions are to be interpreted in the case of a transferred community order.

773. *Paragraph 8* provides for the order to be treated as a corresponding order in Scotland and Northern Ireland. *Paragraph 9* requires the court to explain how the order will function once transferred. *Paragraph 10* describes what powers the Scottish or Northern Ireland court will have in relation to the order.

774. Under *paragraph 11* the Scottish and Northern Ireland courts may summons the offender to the court which made the order if he fails to comply with the requirements of the order (they can also deal with the breach themselves if they wish, as currently)). *Paragraph 12* provides that if the offender fails to appear, the court can issue a warrant, and can exercise any power in respect of the community order as if the court were in England and Wales. *Paragraph 13* prevents the court from amending a community order unless arrangements can be made for the offender to comply with the amended requirements.

775. *Paragraph 14* provides that if a Scottish or Northern Ireland court amends a community order in response to breach, this Schedule continues to apply to that order. *Paragraph 15* concerns sending documents to the court which made the order, if the offender is summonsed to appear before that court due to a failure to comply with the requirements.

### *Schedule 10: Revocation or amendment of custody plus orders and amendment of intermittent custody orders*

776. This Schedule makes provision for revoking custody plus orders, and amending custody plus and intermittent custody orders. In both cases the prison sentence itself will not be revoked or amended. *Paragraph 3* provides for the court to revoke custody plus orders

and remove requirements as to licence conditions from intermittent custody orders on application of the offender or responsible officer and where it deems it to be in the interests of justice to do so. *Paragraph 4* provides for the court to amend the order to refer to another petty sessions area if the offender proposes to change, or has changed, his residence, or if the responsible officers or Secretary of States requires him to. If a requirement is not available in the new area the court may cancel that requirement or substitute it for another which can be complied with in the new area. Specifically, a programme requirement cannot be imposed on amendment unless it is available in the new area.

777. Under *paragraph 5*, the court may, on application of the offender, the responsible officer or the Secretary of State, amend a custody plus or intermittent custody order by cancelling a requirement or replacing it with another of the same kind (that is, if it is in the same paragraph of section 177(1)). New requirements are subject to the same restrictions as they would have been if the order was being made. *Paragraph 6* provides that the court may, on application of the offender, the responsible officer or the Secretary of State, amend the licence periods of an intermittent custody order, if suitable prison accommodation is available. The court may also amend the order such that the intermittence of the licence periods is removed. This provision could be used if the offender, for example, loses his job, which had provided the reason for intermittence. He might want to serve his sentence in the normal manner in order to get the custodial days over with as soon as possible. Another example might be if the offender turned out to be unsuitable for intermittent custody. The responsible officer could apply to have the intermittence removed from the sentence, so that the custodial periods are served consecutively, followed by a single licence period.

778. *Paragraphs 7 to 9* contain supplementary provisions. No application under this Schedule can be made if an appeal against the order is pending. Where a court is amending an order, and the application is not by the offender, the court must summon the offender to appear before the court and may issue a warrant if he does not appear. This does not apply if the court is cancelling a requirement. Paragraph 9 sets out arrangements for sending copies of the order to relevant parties.

### *Schedule 11 – **Transfer of custody plus orders or intermittent custody orders to Scotland or Northern Ireland***

779. *Schedule 11* provides for the transfer of custody plus and intermittent custody orders to Scotland and Northern Ireland.

780. Part 1 is an interpretative provision. Parts 2 and 3 relate to Scotland and Northern Ireland, respectively, Part 4 contains general provisions applicable to both and Part 5 contains supplementary provisions.

#### Parts 2 and 3

781. *Paragraphs 2(1) and 9(1)* allow the court to set requirements that can be complied with in Scotland and Northern Ireland, respectively. Paragraphs 2(2) and 9(2) ensure that arrangements can be made for the offender to comply with the requirements in the locality in Scotland or Northern Ireland in which he will live, and that supervision can be arranged.

782. *Paragraphs 2(3) and 9(3)* do not set out a complete list of requirements available for transfer. They list those which have arrangements associated with them that the court has to confirm are available. These arrangements involve third parties, whose co-operation must be obtained before imposing them. For example, supervision does not need further arrangements because it only concerns the offender and the probation officer. A programme requirement, however, requires a place to be available on a suitable course.

783. *Paragraphs 2(4) and 9(4)* provide for the eventuality that the Secretary of State declines to transfer the prisoner after the court has set requirements that can be complied with in Scotland or Northern Ireland. It is the Secretary of State who takes the decision on all prisoner transfers. If he declines, an application has to be made to the court to change the requirements so that they can be complied with in England and Wales.

784. *Paragraphs 3 and 10* allow custody plus orders and intermittent custody orders to transfer once they have begun (the latter will only transfer once all of the custodial periods have been served). It gives the court the power to amend the order such that it requires the requirements to be complied with in Scotland and Northern Ireland, respectively. The court must be satisfied that the offender lives there, the Secretary of State must have made, or indicated his willingness, to transfer the offender, and arrangements must be made so that the offender can comply with the requirements in Scotland or Northern Ireland.

785. *Paragraph 4* prevents the court from including an attendance centre requirement in an order to be transferred to Scotland, as they do not have them there.

786. *Paragraphs 5 and 11* require the order to specify the local authority area in Scotland and the petty sessions district in Northern Ireland where the offender will be living. A supervising officer will also be assigned.

787. *Paragraphs 6 and 12* provide for a copy of the order to be sent to the local authority in Scotland or the Probation Board in Northern Ireland, along with any other relevant information. The provision regarding who would receive the order if it were not transferring are disapplied.

788. *Paragraphs 7 and 13* modify Chapter 4 of Part 12, which provides the requirements available under relevant orders, so that it can apply in Scotland or Northern Ireland, for the purpose of transferred orders. *Sub-paragraph (3)* of *paragraphs 7 and 13* omits all of the provisions which state that the provider of a certain requirement have to be specified by the Secretary of State. This needs to be omitted because it would not include providers in Scotland and Northern Ireland, and thus those requirements would not be able to form part of a transferred order.

## Part 4

789. Part 4 contains general provisions applying to custody plus and intermittent custody orders transferred to either Scotland or Northern Ireland. Under *paragraph 17(1)* the home court (the local court in Scotland or Northern Ireland) can amend a transferred order as regards the residence of the offender, or as regards the requirements, exactly as a court in England and Wales can for an ordinary custody plus or intermittent custody order. *Sub-paragraphs (2) and (3)* set out procedural requirements for ensuring that the offender is present for any amendment not applied for by the offender, except when the court cancels a requirement, as it is assumed an offender would not object to that. *Sub-paragraph (4)* ensures that where an amendment is being considered to a requirement which can only be made on recommendation of an officer of the local probation board, "officer of the local probation board" refers to the supervising officer in the case of transferred orders.

790. *Paragraph 18* gives the Scottish or Northern Ireland court the option to decline to amend the order and send it back to the original court to deal with.

791. *Paragraph 19* requires the court to ensure that any amendments to a transferred suspended sentence order can be complied with in the area of Scotland or Northern Ireland in which the offender lives.

792. *Paragraph 20* applies the Schedule to any amended order as it applies to an unamended order. *Paragraph 21* provides for the distribution of copies of the amended order.

793. *Paragraph 22* applies to cases where orders have been made or amended such that they can be complied with in Scotland and Northern Ireland, but the offender will in fact be serving his sentence in England and Wales, either because the Secretary of State has declined to transfer him or because he wants to transfer back to England and Wales. *Sub-paragraph (1)(a)* concerns the case indicated in paragraphs 2(4) and 9(4) where the Secretary of State declines to transfer a prisoner who has already had his order amended so as to be able to be complied with in Scotland or Northern Ireland. In this case the court must amend the order so that it can be complied with in England and Wales.

794. *Sub-paragraph (1)(b)* provides for the home court to amend the requirements of a custody provides for custody plus and intermittent custody orders transferred to Scotland or Northern Ireland to be transferred back to England and Wales. Before the court amends the requirements so that they can be complied with in England and Wales the Secretary of State must have agreed to the transfer, or indicated his willingness to agree to it.

795. *Sub-paragraph (3)* indicates that the court must amend the order in the case where the Secretary of State has declined to transfer the prisoner. *Sub-paragraph (4)* requires the court to substitute or cancel any requirement which cannot be complied with in England and Wales. *Sub-paragraph (5)* requires the court to ensure that an appropriate programme is available in the new area. *Sub-paragraph (6)* ensures that the petty sessions area is specified on the order when it is transferred back. *Sub-paragraph (7)* concerns distributing copies of the amended order and *sub-paragraph (8)* disapplies this Schedule to orders transferred back to England and Wales.

796. *Part 5* of this Schedule ensures that the Scottish legislation in relation to electronic monitoring reports being submitted in court will apply to transferred suspended sentence orders, and that summonses, citations and warrants can be executed on offenders in different parts of the United Kingdom.

### *Schedule 12*: *Breach, revocation and amendment of suspended sentence order, and effect of further conviction*

797. Part 1 of this Schedule and *paragraphs 3 and 4*, on statutory warnings, make similar provision to that dealing with community orders in Schedule 8. *Paragraph 6* provides that a magistrates' court can issue a summons for an offender to appear before a court (or a warrant for his arrest) if the offender has failed to comply with any community requirements of the order in cases where the suspended sentence order was made by a magistrates' court or which was made by the Crown Court and includes a direction that any failure to comply with the community requirements of the order is to be dealt with by a magistrates court. The summons will specify the court reviewing the order if the order contains provision for review. If the offender does not appear in response to a summons the court can issue a warrant for his arrest. *Paragraph 7* provides for the Crown Court to issue a summons or warrant for the offender to appear before it where the order was made by the Crown Court and does not include a direction that any failure to comply with the community requirements of the order is to be dealt with by a magistrates' court. If the offender does not appear in response to a summons, a warrant for his arrest can be issued.

798. *Paragraph 8* sets out the magistrates' court's powers where an offender breaches a suspended sentence by failing to comply with a community requirement or by committing a further offence anywhere in the United Kingdom. The presumption is that the suspended sentence will be activated, unless the court finds that it would be unjust to do so. If it activates the suspended sentence the court can set a shorter term or custodial period for the offender to serve if it wishes. If the court finds that it would be unjust to activate the suspended sentence it can keep the sentence suspended but amend the order to make the community requirements more onerous or to extend either the supervision or operational periods. The court must state the reasons for choosing this option. It must also take into account the extent to which the offender complied with the requirements

of the order and the facts of the subsequent offence. A magistrates' court can commit the offender to the Crown Court, including orders which were made by the Crown Court and include a direction that any failure to comply with the community requirements of the order is to be dealt with by a magistrates' court. If the proceedings occur in the Crown Court the determination of breach is to be made by the court and not a jury.

799. Under *paragraph 9* when the suspended sentence is activated, the court must make a custody plus order. That is, it has to set the licence conditions that will apply on the offender's release from custody at the end of custodial period of his sentence. The court may decide whether the new sentence is to take effect immediately or after any other sentence that the offender is serving (subject to the rules affecting consecutive sentences). *Sub-paragraph (3)* provides that an activated suspended sentence counts as having been imposed by the court which originally imposed the suspended sentence.

800. Under *paragraph 10,* if an offender has refused to comply with a mental health, drug or alcohol treatment requirement, and the refusal is believed by the court to be reasonable under the circumstances, it is not to count as breach. Also, the offender's consent must be obtained before amending a mental health, drug or alcohol treatment requirement in response to breach. *Paragraph 11* sets out which court deals with the suspended sentence if the offender is convicted of a further offence. Where the original sentence was passed by the Crown Court and the subsequent offence by a magistrates' court, the latter can remand the offender in custody or on bail to the Crown Court or give written notice to the Crown Court of the subsequent conviction.

801. Under *paragraph 12*, if it becomes apparent that the court has not dealt with the suspended sentence in cases where the offender has committed a new offence, a court with jurisdiction may issue a summons or warrant to the offender to appear before a court. A court with jurisdiction refers to the Crown Court if the suspended sentence was passed by the Crown Court, or a justice acting for the area if the suspended sentence was passed by the magistrates' court. A magistrates' court may not issue a summons except on information and may not issue a warrant except on information in writing and on oath. If the subsequent offence is committed in Scotland or Northern Ireland, and the original suspended sentence was passed in England or Wales, the Scottish or Northern Ireland court must give written notice of the conviction to the court that passed the suspended sentence. Summonses and warrants must direct the offender to appear before the court that imposed the suspended sentence.

802. *Part 3* deals with amending suspended sentence orders. *Paragraph 13* provides that the appropriate court can cancel the community requirements of a suspended sentence order on application of the offender or responsible officer. This may occur if the offender becomes very ill and cannot undertake the requirements. The appropriate court is explained in *sub-paragraph (4)*. *Paragraph 14* provides that the appropriate court can amend the suspended sentence order by substituting a new petty sessions area if the offender proposes to or has changed residence. The court may, and on the application of the responsible officer must, cancel or change any requirements of the order that are not available in the area to which the offender wishes to move. In particular, a programme requirement cannot be amended if it is not available in the new area. The appropriate court is the same as in *paragraph 12.*

803. Under *paragraph 15* an offender or his responsible officer can apply to have the community requirements of an order amended. The appropriate court can cancel a requirement or replace it with another requirement of the same kind, for example to alter the hours of a curfew or substitute one activity for another. The court cannot amend a mental health, drug or alcohol treatment requirement unless the offender consents. If the offender fails to consent, the court can revoke the order and re-sentence the offender. If it re-sentences him the court must take into account the extent to which the offender complied with the requirements of the order. The appropriate court has the same meaning as in paragraph 12. *Paragraph 16* provides that, where a community order includes a drug rehabilitation, alcohol treatment or mental health treatment requirement

and the medical practitioner or other person responsible for the treatment is of the opinion that the treatment should be extended beyond the period specified in the order, that the offender should receive different treatment, that the offender is not susceptible to treatment or that the offender does not require further treatment, he must make a report to the responsible officer. He can also report that he is unwilling to continue to treat (or direct the treatment) of the offender for any reason. The responsible officer must then apply to the court to have the requirement amended or cancelled.

804. *Paragraph 17* provides for the responsible officer to apply to the court to change a review without a hearing to a review with a hearing, and vice versa, in the case where a suspended sentence order contains a drug rehabilitation requirement.

805. The offender or the responsible officer can apply to the appropriate court (as defined in paragraph 13) under *paragraph 18* to extend the 12 months limit on unpaid work if it is in the interests of justice to do so. This might occur if the offender fell ill during the 12 months and was unable to finish all of his hours of unpaid work in time.

806. *Paragraphs 19 to 22* contain supplementary provisions. No application to cancel or amend the requirements a suspended sentence order, can be made if an appeal against the order is pending, except in the case of treatment requirements which the responsible officer has applied to the court to amend. Where a court is amending an order, and the application is not by the offender, the court must summon the offender to appear before the court and may issue a warrant if he does not appear. This does not apply if the court is cancelling a requirement. In amending any requirement the court must keep to the restrictions on the requirements that apply if the court was then making the order. *Paragraph 22* sets out arrangements for sending copies of the order to relevant parties.

### *Schedule 13* – *Transfer of suspended sentence orders to Scotland or Northern Ireland*

807. Schedule 13 enables suspended sentence orders to be complied with in Scotland and Northern Ireland. It contains four Parts. The first two relate to Scotland and Northern Ireland, respectively, and the third contains general provisions applicable to both. Part 4 is a small supplementary Part.

#### Parts 1 and 2

808. Parts 1 and 2 are very similar. *Paragraphs 1 and 6* enable the court to make the transfer. *Sub-paragraph (1)* of each paragraph requires the court to ensure that the requirements of the order can be complied with and supervision arranged in the area of Scotland or NI that the offender is transferring to. In practice this is done by the probation officer attached to the court in England and Wales which is making the transfer telephoning their equivalents in Scotland or Northern Ireland. The Scottish or Northern Ireland counterparts can turn down the transfer for any reason.

809. *Sub-paragraph (2)* is not a complete list of requirements available for transfer, it only contains those which have arrangements associated with them that the court has to confirm are available. These arrangements involve third parties, whose co-operation must be obtained before imposing them. For example, supervision does not need further arrangements because it only concerns the offender and the probation officer. A programme requirement, however, requires a place to be available on a suitable course.

810. *Sub-paragraph (3)* enables the court to require the order to be complied with in Scotland or Northern Ireland. *Sub-paragraph (4)* is a technical provision, such that any arrangements referred to above only have to be in place from when the order is transferred, not when it was first made. *Paragraph 1(5)* prevents the court from imposing an attendance centre requirement as part of transferred orders because they do not exist in Scotland.

811. *Paragraphs 1(6) and 6(5)* prevent transferred orders from containing a provision for court review, either as part of a drug rehabilitation requirement or of the suspended sentence order as a whole. As Scottish or Northern Ireland courts will not have the power to impose a suspended sentence, they will not have any training as to what the purpose of review is, and thus it is inappropriate to ask them to review it. Neither jurisdiction currently has any form of suspended sentence.

812. *Paragraphs 2 and 7* provide for the equivalent of the local probation board in Scotland or Northern Ireland to be specified in the order, and the equivalent of a responsible officer assigned. Accordingly, the requirement for the order to specify a petty sessions area (in England and Wales) is disapplied.

813. *Paragraphs 3 and 8* ensure the equivalent of the local probation board in Scotland or Northern Ireland and the local court in that area receive a copy of the order.

814. *Paragraphs 4 and 9* modify Chapter 4 of paragraph 23, the chapter which provides all of the requirements available as part of a suspended sentence order, such that it can apply to Scotland or Northern Ireland, respectively. *Sub-paragraph (3)* omits all of the provisions which state that the provider of a certain requirement have to be specified by the Secretary of State. This needs to be omitted because it would not include providers in Scotland and Northern Ireland, and thus those requirements would not be able to form part of a transferred order.

815. *Paragraph 5* is an interpretive provision.

## Part 3

816. Part 3 contains provisions for breach and amendment of transferred suspended sentence orders. In general terms, if an offender breaches a requirement of a transferred suspended sentence, the local Scottish or Northern Ireland court will determine whether or not the order has been breached. If it has, that court will require the offender to appear before the original court in England and Wales to deal with the consequences, as Scottish and Northern Ireland courts will not have any training or experience in suspended sentences. In most cases the response to breach will consist of activating the suspended prison sentence, which is a sentence of custody plus, of which Scottish and Northern Ireland courts will also have no experience. The home court can also send the case to the England and Wales court to determine breach as well as deal with the consequences if, for example, the case is for some reason complicated.

817. *Paragraph 10* applies Part 3 of the Schedule to such orders. *Paragraph 11* is an interpretive provision. *Paragraph 12* adapts Schedule 12, which covers breach, revocation and amendment of suspended sentence orders, so that it applies to suspended sentence orders that have been transferred to Scotland or Northern Ireland. Except for *sub-paragraph (3)* which concerns orders transferred to Scotland or Northern Ireland which are then transferred back to England and Wales. *Sub-paragraph (8)* prevents courts in England and Wales from dealing with the offender until it has been required to do so by the Scottish or Northern Ireland court. It is the "home" court, i.e. the Scottish or Northern Ireland court that will initially deal with the breach or amendment of a transferred suspended sentence order.

818. *Paragraph 13* provides for instigating court procedures in case of breach. This is equivalent to an information being laid at a magistrates' court in England and Wales. *Paragraph 14* provides court procedures which follow an information being laid. *Sub-paragraph (1)(b)* allows that court to require the original court to hear the breach as well as deal with the consequences. *Sub-paragraph (2)* deals with what happens after the Scotland or Northern Ireland court has certified a breach. It must require the offender to appear before the original court in England and Wales in order to have the breach dealt with. *Subsection (2)(b)* makes it clear that at the original court the breach certified in the Scottish or Northern Ireland court cannot be challenged again.

819. *Sub-paragraph (3)* is a provision that replicates a similar provision in Schedule 12. If the offender "breaches" by not complying with a treatment requirement, the court can determine that the non-compliance was reasonable, and thus the "breach" is not really a breach.

820. *Paragraph 15* provides for Scottish or Northern Ireland courts to amend transferred suspended sentence orders. These courts have all the powers that a court in England and Wales has over non-transferred suspended sentences, except that it cannot revoke the order and re-sentence the offender if he refused to comply with an amendment to a treatment requirement. In that case the Scottish or Northern Ireland court has to send the case back to the original court to deal with. *Sub-paragraphs (3) and (4)* require the offender to appear before the Scottish or Northern Ireland court if the responsible officer has applied to substitute one requirement for another. This is to give the offender the opportunity to object. It does not include occasions where the offender has himself made the application or where the application is just to cancel a requirement. It is assumed the offender has no objections in these cases.

821. *Paragraph 16* gives the Scotland or Northern Ireland court the option to decline to amend the order and send it back to the original court to deal with. *Paragraph 17* requires the court to ensure that any amendments to a transferred suspended sentence order can be complied with in the area of Scotland or Northern Ireland in which the offender lives. *Paragraph 18* applies the Schedule to any amended order as it applies to an unamended order. *Paragraph 19* set out the provides arrangements distributing copies of the amended order.

822. *Paragraph 20* provides for suspended sentence orders transferred to Scotland or Northern Ireland to be transferred back to England and Wales. This functions similarly to the original transfer, in that the court has to ensure that the requirements can be complied with and supervision arranged in the area of England and Wales that the offender is moving to.

### Part 4

823. *Paragraph 21* ensures the Scottish legal provisions which concern electronic monitoring apply to offenders on suspended sentence orders. *Paragraph 22* ensures that summonses issued in Northern Ireland and citations and warrants issued in Scotland can be executed anywhere in the UK.

### *Schedule 14* – ***Persons to whom copies of requirements to be provided in particular cases***

824. This Schedule sets out who is to receive copies of each different requirement, in addition to the persons mentioned in section 219.

### *Schedule 18*: ***Release of prisoners serving sentences of imprisonment or detention for public protection***

825. This Schedule amends the provisions of the Crime (Sentences) Act 1997 relating to the release of prisoners serving life sentences so that they also apply to prisoners serving the new sentence of imprisonment or detention for public protection. *Paragraph 2* inserts a new section 31A, which provides that after 10 years has elapsed following the release of an offender serving a sentence of imprisonment or detention for public protection (see sections 225 and 226), the offender may apply to the Parole Board for his licence to be terminated. If the Parole Board is satisfied that no further risk is posed then it must recommend to the Secretary of State that the licence be terminated. If the Parole Board concludes that the offender continues to pose a risk then it must reject the application and the offender may not submit another application until at least 12 months has elapsed.

### *Schedule 19: **The Parole Board: supplementary provisions***

826. The Schedule re-enacts Schedule 5 to the Criminal Justice Act 1991, which contains supplementary provisions about the Parole Board. The members of the Board must include representatives from certain professional fields. The Schedule also contains provisions about the payment of members, the funding of the Board and the keeping of proper records and accounts amongst other things.

### *Schedule 20: **Prisoners liable to removal from the United Kingdom: modifications of the Criminal Justice Act 1991***

827. Schedule 20 provides for an early removal scheme similar to that in sections 260 and 261 of this Act to be applied to those sentenced under the Criminal Justice Act 1991. The scheme is the same in substance as that set out in amendments sections 260 and 261 and any differences simply reflect the differences between the provisions of this Act and the Criminal Justice Act 1991. For example, in this Act the definition of the requisite period to be served before a prisoner may become eligible for early removal from prison is set out in terms of custodial periods only. For prisoners sentenced under the provisions of the 1991 Act the requisite period is defined as a proportion of the term of imprisonment - which includes the custodial and licence period.

### *Schedule 21: **Determination of minimum term in relation to mandatory life sentences***

828. This Schedule sets out the principles which a sentencing court must have regard to when assessing the seriousness of all cases of murder in order to determine the appropriate minimum term to be imposed.

829. *Paragraph 1* is definitional and is largely self-explanatory. Paragraphs 2 and 3 explain what is meant by racial or religious aggravation or aggravation by sexual orientation.

830. *Paragraphs 4, 5, 6 and 7* set out the starting points that a court should adopt when determining a minimum term. The starting point may be adjusted in accordance with the presence of aggravating or mitigating factors in order to arrive at the finally determined minimum term.

### *Paragraph 4*

831. This paragraph deals with the small numbers of exceptionally serious cases in which the court should normally start by considering a whole life term, and provides a number of examples of cases that should normally require consideration of a whole life order. The list is not intended to be exhaustive, but indicates that murders that fall within the given categories will normally require a whole life minimum term. However, in an individual case it could be appropriate for a court to commence the determination of the appropriate minimum term with the whole life starting point but, upon further consideration of the relevant circumstances of the case, ultimately decide that a whole life term is not required. In keeping with sentencing practice generally, it is entirely a matter for the sentencing court to determine the facts upon which it is to sentence.

### *Paragraph 5*

832. *Paragraph 5* deals with the murders which are not as serious as those that fall within paragraph 4 but are nevertheless particularly grave and require a starting point for determining the minimum term of 30 years. Like paragraph 4 this paragraph provides a non-exhaustive list of examples of cases that should normally require consideration of a 30 year starting point. This starting point may be adjusted up, or down, in accordance with the presence of aggravating or mitigating factors. A murder falling within the paragraph 5(2), may nevertheless be one that the court decides is exceptionally serious and more appropriately dealt with under paragraph 4(1) rather than 5(1).

833. Paragraph 5(2)(h) allows a court to adopt a 30 year starting point for an offender who is 18, 19 or 20 years old and, under current provision, subject to a sentence of mandatory custody for life.

### *Paragraphs 6 **and** 7*

834. The numbers of murders falling within paragraphs 4 and 5 will form a relatively small although significant proportion of all the murders that come before the courts. The majority of murders will therefore attract a starting point of 15 years under *paragraph 6*. *Paragraph 7* provides a separate starting point of 12 years for offenders aged under 18 at the time the offence was committed.

### *Paragraphs 8 to 12*

835. Once a starting point has been chosen, the court will then go on to consider factors that either increase or reduce the seriousness of the murder and make the necessary adjustments to arrive at the final minimum term. There is no restriction on the degree of adjustment that a court can make in consideration of aggravating or mitigating factors, as paragraph 8 explains. Although, therefore, there may be a few very exceptional cases in which starting points will be increased or decreased very substantially, it is expected that the vast majority of cases will tend to attract minimum terms that reflect the categorisation of cases set out in paragraphs 4 to 7.

836. *Paragraph 8* makes it clear that aggravating or mitigating factors cannot be double counted. If a murder, for example, fell within paragraph 5(2) because it was the murder of a police officer, the minimum term could not be increased beyond the starting point of 30 years on the basis that the case was aggravated by facts falling within paragraph 10 (f).

837. The list of factors that are to be regarded as aggravating set out at paragraph 10 is non-exhaustive and is provided by way of example. These examples are additional to those set out at paragraphs 4(2) and 5(2) so that any factor that does not determine the relevant starting point can be taken account under paragraph 8. Planning and premeditation requires inclusion at 10(a) because a court will want to take into account premeditation and planning of any degree and reliance on the reference at paragraph 4(2)(a)(i) would only include facts that amounted to a substantial degree of premeditation or planning. Other matters are included in paragraph 10, for example paragraphs (c) and (f), because they embrace but have a greater scope than facts that would fall within paragraphs 4(2) and 5(2). Paragraph 10 (g) covers circumstances in which the court is satisfied that, in those rare cases of convictions for murder in the absence of a body, the offender is adding to the grief of a victim's family by deliberately preventing the recovery of the body.

838. *Paragraph 11* sets out a number of factors that may be taken account of by the sentencing court as mitigating factors. Once again this list is not exhaustive and provides examples only. The list covers most of the mitigating factors that are likely to arise in cases of murder and is largely self-explanatory. As regards paragraph 11(a), it may not be commonly appreciated that the offence of murder does not require an intention to kill. In the case of offenders who are considerably younger than 18, paragraph 11(g) may have a very significant effect on the final determination of the minimum term.

839. *Paragraph 12* makes it clear that nothing in these principles affects the general provisions in the Act on the effect of previous convictions, offending while on bail and pleas of guilty.

### *Schedule 22* ***: Mandatory Life Sentences: Transitional Cases***

840. This Schedule deals with transitional matters. In particular it sets out arrangements to deal with:

a) convicted murderers serving minimum terms determined by the Secretary of State;

b) those already sentenced for murder but awaiting the determination of a minimum term;

c) minimum terms determined on or after commencement of section 269 in respect of offences committed before that date.

### *Paragraph 1*

841. *Paragraph 1* contains various definitions. These are self-explanatory save that it should be noted that the definition of "mandatory life sentence" excludes juveniles sentenced to mandatory detention during Her Majesty's Pleasure. This is because minimum terms for juveniles convicted of murder that were fixed by the Secretary of State are already subject to a review by the Lord Chief Justice established following the ruling of the European Court of Human Rights in the case of *V v UK* (Judgement of ECHR of 16th December 1999).

### **Existing prisoners notified by Secretary of State: Paragraphs 2, 3 and 4**

842. These paragraphs deal with prisoners who are already serving a life sentence subject to a minimum term, or whole life term, which has been fixed by the Secretary of State. In accordance with the ruling in the case of *Anderson,* and in seeking to afford the prisoners their rights under Article 6 of the Convention, this provision offers these prisoners an opportunity to apply to have their minimum term re-set by the High Court. Having reviewed a case, the High Court must reconsider the existing minimum term or whole life term. In so doing the court can order a period that is equal to that which was set by the Secretary of State or it may reduce the minimum term. It cannot however, increase the minimum term fixed by the Secretary of State.

843. Some prisoners serving life sentences will remain in prison although the minimum term fixed by the Secretary of State has expired. This group is excluded from the right to apply to the High Court, but paragraph 3(3) enables them to have their cases considered by the Parole Board.

844. Not all prisoners will necessarily wish to apply for a new minimum term. In this case the minimum term fixed by the Secretary of State in their case will remain effective.

845. *Paragraph 4* sets out in general terms the matters the court should have regard to when determining the appropriate minimum term in any individual case. In addition to the consideration of seriousness and time spent on remand required in every case under section 269, in these transitional cases the existing notified minimum term or whole life term will also be relevant. Paragraph 4(2) requires the reviewing court, when considering the seriousness of the offence, to have regard to both the principles set out in Schedule 21 and any judicial recommendations, made shortly after the original conviction, as to the appropriate minimum term to be served by the prisoner.

### **Existing prisoners not notified by Secretary of State: Paragraphs 5 to 8**

846. Since the judgement in *Anderson* ([2002] UKHL 46) the Home Secretary has not determined any minimum terms. Accordingly, there are a number of cases in which the prisoner has been found guilty of murder and sentenced to the mandatory life sentence but still awaits the determination of a minimum term. Paragraph 6 creates a duty on the part of the Home Secretary to refer these cases to the High Court for the determination of a minimum term under the provision at section 269.

847. In keeping with the provision for future cases, the reviewing court must take into guidelines account the new statutory principles and any relevant guidelines when considering the seriousness of the case for the purpose of determining the minimum

term. Any recommendations made by either the Lord Chief Justice or the trial judge also need to be taken into account by the High Court when determining the minimum term.

848. To ensure compatibility with Article 7 of the Convention, paragraph 8(a) prevents the High Court from determining the minimum term at a level greater than that which would have been imposed under the practice of the Secretary of State before the *Anderson* judgement. *Paragraph 8(b)* also makes it clear that no whole life term can be imposed unless such a term would, in the court's opinion, have been imposed by the Secretary of State.

### Sentences passed on or after commencement date in respect of offences committed before that date: Paragraphs 9 and 10

849. Some trials for murder after the commencement of these provisions will concern murders that were committed before commencement. Paragraphs 9 and 10 deal with such cases. The need to avoid imposing a sentence that is greater than that which would have been available at the time of the commission of the offence applies here as much as it does to the cases covered in the preceding paragraphs. Accordingly, paragraph 10 imposes a restriction equivalent to that in paragraph 8.

### *Paragraph 11*

850. *Paragraph 11* provides for any review or determination of a minimum term under either paragraphs 3 or 6 by the High Court to be undertaken by a single judge on the papers.

### *Paragraphs 12 to 18*

851. *Paragraph 12* requires a court reviewing an existing minimum term to give reasons for the order it makes and if the order specifies a minimum term that is shorter than that imposed by the Secretary of State to explain its reasons for doing so. Where a court determines the minimum term in the case of a convicted prisoner who has not been given a minimum term by the Home Secretary, paragraph 13 brings the duty to give reasons into line with that under paragraph 12.

852. *Paragraph 14* extends rights of appeal to the Court of Appeal and the House of Lords, if appropriate, to prisoners who have either had their minimum term reviewed or determined by the High Court under these transitional provisions. *Paragraph 15* extends section 36 of the Criminal Justice Act 1988 to these transitional arrangements and provides for a means by which the Attorney General can challenge a minimum term which he considers unduly lenient.

853. *Paragraph 16* ensures that the early release provisions apply consistently to both a minimum term in arising from a review of an existing minimum term by the High Court and those minimum terms fixed by the Home Secretary that remain effective if no application is made. *Paragraph 17* ensures that transferred prisoners may be dealt with under these transitional arrangements if necessary.

### *Schedule 23: Deferment of sentence*

854. This Schedule inserts new provisions about deferment of sentence into the Powers of Criminal Courts (Sentencing) Act 2000. In most cases, a court will pass sentence on an offender immediately after his conviction for the offence or offences for which he is before the court. However, the court also has the power to defer sentencing. As at present, the new provisions allow the court to defer sentencing for the purpose of enabling the court to have regard to the conduct of the offender and any change in his circumstances. However, it strengthens the deferred sentence by providing for reparative and other activity to be undertaken during the period of deferment, and extends "conduct" to include reference to how well the offender complies with such requirements. Progress will continue to act as a mitigating factor in the final sentence passed, including imposing a community sentence in lieu of a custodial one when clear

progress against undertakings has been made. Sentencing can be deferred only if the offender consents and undertakes to comply with any requirements set out by the court, and only where the court considers that deferment is in the interests of justice. The court cannot remand an offender if it also defers his sentence. As currently, sentence cannot be deferred for more than six months. The court has the power to issue a summons or a warrant to arrest the offender if he does not appear on the date for sentencing specified by the court. *Subsection (5)* of the new section prescribes who should receive a copy of the order deferring the passing of sentence.

855. Under new *section 1A* the court can include requirements regarding the offender's residence. If an offender is to undertake requirements the court may appoint a supervisor to monitor the offender's compliance with the requirements. The supervisor can be an officer of the local probation board or anyone else the court thinks appropriate. The person must consent to being a supervisor. The supervisor must provide the court with information as to the offender's compliance with the requirements, as it wishes.

856. Under new *section 1B*the court may deal with the offender before the end of the period of deferment if it is satisfied that the offender has failed to comply with one or more requirements. Currently, as there are no requirements attached to deferred sentences, the offender can only be returned to court early for sentencing if he commits another offence. *Subsection (2)* sets out the circumstances in which he can be returned to court early. *Subsection (3)* gives the court the power to issue a summons or warrant for the offender to appear before it.

857. Under new *section 1C* the court may deal with an offender before the end of the period of deferment if he commits another offence. *Subsections (2) and (3)* set out the powers of the Crown Court and magistrates' courts in these cases. If the offender is convicted of another offence during the period of deferment, the court may deal with the original deferred sentence at the same time as sentencing the offender for the new offence. If the original sentence was deferred by a Crown Court, it must be a Crown Court that passes sentence for both the offences. If the original sentence was deferred by a magistrates court, and the offender is brought before a Crown Court to be sentenced for the two offences, the Crown Court cannot pass a sentence greater than a magistrates court could have passed. That is, it cannot pass a sentence of greater than 12 months. The court has power to issue a summons or a warrant for the offender to appear before it.

858. New *section 1D* clarifies some of the legal detail surrounding the deferment of sentences. Deferment of sentence is to be regarded as an adjournment, and if the offender does not appear before the court when required to he is to be dealt with accordingly. When the court deals with an offender at the end of the period of deferment (or earlier if he does not comply with the requirements or commits another offence) it has the same powers as if the offence had just been committed. This includes committing him for sentence to the Crown Court. The court may issue a summons to someone appointed as a supervisor if that person refuses to appear before the court when the court wants to consider an offender's failure to comply with the requirements of the deferment or anything to do with the original offence.

### *Schedule 24:* ***Drug treatment and testing requirement in action plan order or supervision order***

859. This Schedule amends section 70 of the Powers of Criminal Courts (Sentencing) Act 2000. It introduces drug treatment, which may include testing, as a requirement available for inclusion in an action plan order. The Schedule also amends Schedule 6 to the Powers of Criminal Courts (Sentencing) Act 2000 to allow drug treatment, which may include testing, as a requirement available for inclusion in a supervision order.

860. The new requirement is available where the court is satisfied that the young offender is dependent on, or has a propensity to misuse, drugs and that this dependency or propensity is such as requires and may be susceptible to treatment. The Schedule strengthens the existing interventions available to the court to assist young offenders

with a drug misuse problem to address both their drug misuse and offending behaviour. The testing element of the requirement can only apply to those aged 14 years and over and can be included in an action plan order or supervision order only if the offender consents and the court has been notified by the Secretary of State that arrangements are in place for implementation.

### *Schedule 25*: ***Summary offences no longer punishable with imprisonment***

861. *Schedule 25* provides a list of summary offences which, following commencement of section 267, will cease to be punishable with imprisonment. In effect, this will mean that the maximum penalties for these offences will be the new generic community sentence and/or a fine. In connection to this, Part 2 of Schedule 32 makes the necessary consequential amendments to the relevant enactments. Part 7 of Schedule 37 contains associated repeals.

### *Schedule 26*: ***Increase in maximum term for certain summary offences***

862. *Schedule 26* makes the necessary consequential amendments so as to increase the maximum penalty for certain summary offences from a term of imprisonment of five months or less to a term of 51 weeks (equating to a full sentence of custody plus – see section 181).

### *Schedule 27*: ***Enabling powers: alteration of maximum penalties etc.***

863. *Schedule 27* makes the necessary changes to specific enabling powers contained within existing legislation so as to ensure that the offences that these powers may create have maximum penalties that are compatible with the new sentencing framework.

### *Schedule 28*: ***Increase in penalties for drug-related offences***

864. *Schedule 28* amends Schedule 4 to the Misuse of Drugs Act 1971 and related legislation to increase the penalties for offences committed in relation to Class C drugs. The provisions include an increase to the maximum penalties for trafficking Class C drugs from 5 to 14 years' imprisonment.

### *Schedule 30*: ***Disqualification from working with children***

865. Part 2 of the Criminal Justice and Court Services Act 2000 already requires the court to make an order disqualifying the offender from working with children on conviction for an "offence against a child", as defined in section 26 by reference to the list in Schedule 4 of the Act, where a sentence of imprisonment or detention for 12 months or more is imposed. In relation to adult offenders, a disqualification order must be made unless the court is satisfied that it is unlikely the individual will commit any further offence. In the case of offenders aged under 18, the court must make the order if it is satisfied that it is likely a further offence against a child will be committed.

866. *Paragraph 2* of this Schedule inserts new sections 29A and 29B into the Criminal Justice and Court Services Act 2000.

867. *New section 29A* extends the court's powers by adding a discretion to make an order if it is satisfied that it is likely a further offence against a child will be committed, even though the sentence threshold specified in the Act is not met. The test of whether the order should be made is whether the court is satisfied, having regard to all the circumstances, that it is likely that the individual will commit a further offence against a child. If the court makes a disqualification order, it must both state and record its reasons for doing so. These provisions add to but do not otherwise change the existing provisions in the Act relating to cases in which the sentencing threshold is met.

868. *New section 29B* has the effect that where a court was under a duty to consider the issue of a disqualification order, by virtue of convicting the offender of a relevant offence and

passing a sentence which met the threshold specified, but appeared not to have done so nor to have recorded its reasons for this, the prosecution has discretion at any time in the future to apply to a senior court for a disqualification order to be made. The court will then have to consider, on the basis of further evidence and argument if necessary, whether the test that the offender is likely to commit an offence is met and whether an order should be made. Where it considers the test is met in respect of an adult, it must make an order or, if it does not do so, must record the reasons for this decision. Where the offender is aged under 18 years, the court must make an order if it is satisfied that the offender is likely to commit a further offence against a child and must record its reasons for this decision. New section 29B applies to cases in which a court was under a duty to consider a disqualification order, i.e. to senior courts passing qualifying sentences on offenders convicted of an offence under Schedule 4 of in the Criminal Justice and Court Services Act 2000, after the implementation on January 11th 2001 of the relevant provisions in that Act.

### *Schedule 31*: ***Default orders: modification of provisions relating to community orders***

869. This Schedule must be read in conjunction with section 300 which gives the court to impose an unpaid work requirement or a curfew requirement, in lieu of imprisonment, where an offender has defaulted on the payment of a fine, and has a default order imposed on him.

870. *Paragraph 2* modifies the unpaid work provisions in section 199 so that the minimum number of hours which a person may be required to work as part of a default order is 20 hours and the maximum is laid out in the Table in paragraph 2 corresponding to the amount of the sum in default.

871. *Paragraph 3* makes similar modifications to the provisions of the curfew requirement under section 204 and lays out in a table the maximum number of days to which the offender subject to a default order can be subject, which correspond to the amount of the sum in default.

872. *Paragraph 4* modifies the enforcement, revocation and amendment provisions in Schedule 7 to make them apply to the default order. If an offender breaches his default order, the court can deal with him in any way in which the court which made the default order could deal with him for the original default. In other words, it can commit him to custody. *Paragraph 6* modifies Schedule 9 (transfer of community orders to Scotland or Northern Ireland) to allow default orders to be transferred to Scotland and Northern Ireland.

873. *Paragraph 5* provides the Secretary of State with an order-making power to amend the number of amounts of money specified in the tables under paragraphs 2 and 3 and the number of hours or days specified.

### *Schedule 32*: ***Amendments relating to sentencing***

874. This Schedule contains amendments related to the sentencing provisions in Part 12. Most do not seem to require detailed explanation.

875. *Paragraphs 40 to 43* amend the Repatriation of Prisoners Act 1984 which provides for UK nationals sentenced abroad to serve their sentences in the UK, and for foreign nationals sentenced in the UK to serve their sentences in their home country. The Act calculates the release date of repatriated prisoners based on the Criminal Justice Act 1991 and for life sentenced prisoners, the Crime (Sentences) Act 1997. The provisions in Chapter 7 of Part 12 of the Act replace these, and thus amendments to the 1984 Act are necessary. If life sentence prisoners repatriated to the UK have had no tariff or minimum period set, the Lord Chief Justice will be asked prior to repatriation to set a provisional tariff. The tariff will be formally set by the High Court once the prisoner has been repatriated to England and Wales. Release will work as currently. For all other

prisoners repatriated to the UK, the amount of time the prisoner has left to serve will be calculated in the same way as currently. The total length of sentence imposed is reduced by amount of time already served, plus remand or remission. The release date is then calculated on the remainder. The release date of all prisoners repatriated to the UK (except life prisoners) will be calculated in the same way as the release date for prisoners serving over 12 months in England and Wales who are not serving a sentence under sections 225 to 228. For example, a prisoner sentenced to 10 years abroad, who has already served two years before being repatriated, will have 8 years left to serve. Under Chapter 5 of Part 12 of the Act, release is after 4 years, followed by 4 more years on licence.

876. *Paragraph 125* substitutes a new Schedule 3 in the Powers of Criminal Courts (Sentencing) Act 2000. Schedule 3 to the PCC(S)A deals with breach, revocation and amendment of a number of community orders. Most of them are replaced by the generic community sentence in this Act. Curfew and exclusion orders are being retained as stand-alone orders for offenders aged 10-15. Curfew orders are governed by sections 37 to 40 of the PCC(S)A and exclusion orders are governed by sections 40A to 40C of that Act. The provisions on exclusion orders are inserted by section 46 of the Criminal Justice and Court Services Act 2000, which is not yet in force. Paragraphs 78 to 82 of Schedule 25 to the Act make the changes which limit the availability of those orders to offenders under 16.

877. The new Schedule 3 therefore deals with breach, revocation and amendment of curfew orders and exclusion orders for young people up to the age of 16. The new Schedule 3 does not make any substantive changes to the way in which the existing Schedule 3 operates for those aged under 16.

### *Schedule 33*: ***Jury service***

878. *Schedule 33* amends the principal statute governing jury service, the Juries Act 1974, to abolish (except in the case of mentally disordered persons) the categories of ineligibility for, and excusal "as of right" from, jury service, currently set out in Parts 1 and 3 of Schedule 1 to that Act. This means that certain groups of people who currently must not, or need not, do jury service will, when these provisions are brought into force, be required to do so unless they can show good reason not to. *Schedule 33* also makes amendments to the category of those disqualified from jury service, as set out in Part 2 of Schedule 1 to the Juries Act 1974, to reflect developments in sentencing legislation, including those made by the Act itself.

### *Paragraphs 2, 3, 14* ***and*** *15*

879. These provisions have the effect of removing the status of "ineligibility" for jury service, and entitlement to "excusal as of right" from jury service, from a number of people; they will, as a result, in future be regarded in all cases as potential jurors. Under the Juries Act 1974, as it currently stands, the judiciary, others concerned with the administration of justice, and the clergy, are "ineligible" for jury service and therefore barred from serving as jurors. That bar will be lifted. Others, including people over 65, members of parliament, medical professionals and members of certain religious bodies, are currently entitled to refuse to serve as jurors. That entitlement will be removed. If any person affected by these changes does not wish to serve as a juror, he or she will now be required to apply for excusal or deferral under section 9 or 9A of the 1974 Act, showing "good reason" why he or she should not serve as summoned.

880. *Paragraph 2 of Schedule 33* replaces section 1 of the Juries Act 1974 with a new version, removing the status of ineligibility for jury service currently in section 1 of the 1974 Act, with a saving for mentally disordered persons only. *Paragraph 15* substitutes a new version of Schedule 1 to the 1974 Act, and correspondingly removes the first three groups of persons ineligible (the judiciary, others concerned with the administration of justice, and the clergy), leaving only mentally disordered persons with that status.

*Paragraph 14 of Schedule 33* makes consequential provision to remove references to these groups of ineligible people in the context of the jury summoning offences in section 20 of the Juries Act 1974.

881. *Paragraph 15* also replaces the categories of those who are disqualified from jury service with a new list for Part 2 of Schedule 1 to the Juries Act 1974. These are people who have served, or are serving, prison sentences or community orders of varying degrees of seriousness. The period of time during which they are to be disqualified varies accordingly. A number of amendments have been made to Part 2 to reflect recent and forthcoming developments in sentencing legislation. Juveniles sentenced under section 91 of the Powers of Criminal Courts (Sentencing) Act 2000 to detention for life, or for a term of five years or more, will be disqualified for life from jury service. People sentenced to imprisonment or detention for public protection, or to an extended sentence under *section 227 or 228* of the Act are to be disqualified for life from jury service. Anyone who has received a community order (as defined in *section 177* of the Act) will be disqualified from jury service for ten years.

882. *Paragraph 3 of Schedule 32* repeals section 9(1) of the Juries Act 1974. This subsection provided that certain groups of people listed in Part 3 of Schedule 1 to the 1974 Act should be "excused as of right" from jury service: that is, they were entitled to refuse to do jury service if they so wish. These groups include people over 65 years of age, members of parliament, members of medical and similar professions, people with religious objections to doing jury service, and (in specified circumstances) members of the armed forces. No one will in future be entitled to excusal as of right from jury service, as is currently provided. Part 3 has been omitted from the substituted Schedule 1 in *paragraph 15*.

### *Paragraphs 4 to 11*

883. These paragraphs make provision consequential on the repeal of Part 3 of Schedule 1 to the Juries Act 1974. Full-time serving members of the armed forces are at present entitled to excusal as of right from jury service if, but only if, their commanding officer certifies that their absence would be prejudicial to the efficiency of the service in question. With the abolition of excusal as of right, service personnel who do not wish to do jury service will, like everyone else, have to apply under section 9 or 9A of the 1974 Act and show "good reason" why they should not serve as summoned. A commanding officer's certificate is, however, to be regarded in future as conclusive evidence of good reason for the purposes of these provisions, so that on its production a jury service summons will be deferred; if there has already been a deferral or if the commanding officer certifies that absence would be prejudicial for a specified period of time, then service personnel will be excused altogether from the obligation imposed by the summons. But that is without prejudice to the position should a further summons be issued on a future occasion.

884. *Paragraph 12*: Sections 9A and 9 of the Juries Act 1974 deal, respectively, with discretionary deferral and excusal. If a person who has been summoned to do jury service can show that there is a "good reason" that his summons should be deferred or excused, then discretion exists to defer or excuse. The discretion currently rests with the Jury Central Summoning Bureau, a part of the Lord Chancellor's Department, which administers the jury summoning system on behalf of the Crown Court in England and Wales. With the abolition of most of the categories of persons ineligible for jury service, and of the availability of excusal as of right, many of these cases will now fall to be dealt with as applications for excusal or deferral under sections 9 and 9A. New section 9AA, introduced by this paragraph, places a statutory duty on the Lord Chancellor (in whom responsibility for jury summoning is vested by section 2 of the 1974 Act) to publish and lay before Parliament guidelines relating to the exercise by the Jury Central Summoning Bureau of its functions in relation to discretionary deferral and excusal.

885. *Paragraph 13:* Section 19 of the Juries Act 1974 gives an entitlement to jurors to be paid, amongst other things, a subsistence allowance during the period they are serving on a court case. This paragraph will enable the Court Service of the Lord Chancellor's Department (which administers the Crown Court, and the payment of jurors' subsistence allowances) to pay this allowance otherwise than by means of cash. Some court facilities enable staff to obtain refreshments by non-monetary means, such as a voucher or an electronic 'swipe card'; this paragraph will enable them to extend the same means to jurors.

### *Schedule 34: Parenting Order attached to Referral Order*

886. Schedule 34 makes provision about the interaction of parenting orders, made under sections 8 to 10 Crime and Disorder Act 1998 and referral orders made under Part 3 of the Powers of Criminal Courts (Sentencing) Act 2000.

887. *Removal of restriction in Crime and Disorder Act 1998.* This removes from section 8 of the Crime and Disorder Act 1998 the restriction currently on a court for the making of a Parenting Order alongside a Referral Order.

888. *Supplemental provisions relating to Parenting Orders.* This amends section 9 of the Crime and Disorder Act 1998 (which makes supplemental provision relating to Parenting Orders) so that it is possible to make a parenting order and a referral order in respect of the same offence.

889. *Sub-paragraph (2)* substitutes a new subsection (1) into section 9. The old subsection provided that a parenting order could not be made in respect of the same offence. The new subsection provides that the normal duty on the court to make a parenting order (or explain why it would not help to prevent the offender from committing another offence) where a person under the age of 16 is convicted of an offence does not apply where the court makes a referral order in respect of the offence.

890. *Sub-paragraph (3)* inserts a new subsection (2A) into section 9. This provides that where the court does decide to make a Parenting Order with a Referral Order, the court must obtain and consider a report by a probation officer, a local authority social worker, or a member of a youth offending team. The report should indicate what the requirements of the Parenting Order might include, the reasons why it would be desirable, and also, if the offender is under age 16 years, information about the family's circumstances and the likely effect of the Order on those circumstances.

891. *Sub-paragraph (4)* inserts a new subsection (7A) which defines a Referral Order an order imposed under section 16(2) or (3) Powers of Criminal Courts (Sentencing) Act 2000.

892. *Removal of Restriction in Powers of Criminal Courts (Sentencing) Act 2000.* This removes the restriction in section 19(5) of the Powers of Criminal Courts (Sentencing) Act 2000 preventing the court from imposing a parenting order and a referral order in respect of the same offence.

893. *Panel to refer case back to Youth Court where parent or guardian fails to comply.* This inserts a new subsection (2A) into section 22 of the Powers of Criminal Courts (Sentencing) Act 2000. A court making a referral order may require a parent or guardian to attending the meetings of the youth offender panel under Section 20 of the Powers of Criminal Courts (Sentencing) Act 2000. Where the parent or guardian fails to comply with such an order, the new subsection provides the power to the panel to refer the case back to the offender's youth court. This would then allow the court the opportunity to decide whether it should impose a Parenting Order.

894. *Arrangements when a panel refers a parent or guardian to the youth court.* These insert new provisions into section 28 and Schedule 1 Powers of Criminal Courts (Sentencing) Act 2000. These provisions set out the arrangements when a youth offender panel refers a parent or guardian to the appropriate youth court using the power set out in the new

section 22(2A). The panel must make a report to the court explaining why the parent is being referred to it and the court can require the parent to appear before it by means of the issue of a summons, or a warrant for arrest. Where the parent then appears before the youth court, the court may make a Parenting Order if both of two conditions are satisfied. The first is that the court is satisfied that the parent has failed to comply with an order made by the court under section 20 to attend the youth referral panel, without reasonable excuse. The second is that the court believes that it is desirable in the interests of preventing further offences being committed by the offender. The provisions also set out that a Parenting Order means an order requiring the parent to comply for up to twelve months with requirements the court considers to be desirable in the interests of preventing further offences by the offender and to attend a counselling or guidance programme for up to three months. The counselling or guidance programme can include or consist of a residential course provided the court is satisfied that this is likely to be more effective than a non-residential course and that any interference with family life is proportionate. The provisions also state which of the provisions of the Crime and Disorder Act relating to parenting orders apply to a parenting order made in these circumstances and provide for a right of appeal to the Crown Court against the making of a parenting order in these circumstances.

### *Schedule 38: Transitory, transitional and savings provisions*

895. *Paragraph 1* relates to section 61 of the Criminal Justice and Court Services Act 2000, which (among other things) abolishes the sentences of detention in a young offender institution and custody for life and which is not yet in force. If provisions of Part 12 of the Act come into force before section 61 comes into force, this paragraph enables an order under section 333(1) to modify the provision of the Act in relation to things done before section 61 comes into force. For example, it might be necessary to provide for a reference to a sentence of imprisonment to include a reference to a sentence of detention in a young offender institution, or for a reference to an offender aged 18 or over to have effect as a reference to an offender aged 21 or over.

896. *Paragraph 2* provides a transitional provision preserving the authority of any sentencing guidelines issued by the Court of Appeal prior to the repeal of section 80 to 81 of the Crime and Disorder Act 1998 and the establishment of the Sentencing Guidelines Council.

897. *Paragraph 4* contains a transitory provision providing that any drug treatment and testing order made under section 52 of the Powers of Criminal Courts (Sentencing) Act (before that section is repealed by this Act) need not include a review provision if the order is for less than 12 months. A community order under the Act including a drug rehabilitation requirement must include a review provision if it is over 12 months, and may include one if the period is less than 12 months.

898. *Paragraph 5* makes temporary modifications of the provisions as to drug testing in section 65 of the Criminal Justice Act 1991, pending repeal of that section under this Act.

899. *Paragraph 6* would enable a shorter version of intermittent custody to be introduced before the sentencing limit on magistrates' courts is increased from 6 months to 12 or 18 months.

## HANSARD REFERENCES

900. The following table sets out the dates and Hansard references for each stage of the Act's passage through Parliament.

| *Stage* | *Date* | *Hansard Reference* |
|---|---|---|
| **House of Commons** | | |

| *Stage* | *Date* | *Hansard Reference* |
|---|---|---|
| Introduction | 21 November 2002 | Vol 394 Col 800 |
| Second Reading | 4 December 2002 | Vol 395 Cols 912-1014 |
| Committee | 17 December 2002; 19 December 2002; 7 January 2003; 9 January 2003; 14 January 2003; 16 January 2003; 21 January 2003; 23 January 2003; 28 January 2003; 30 January 2003; 4 February 2003; 6 February 2003; 11 February 2003; 13 February 2003; 25 February 2003; 27 February 2003 and 4 March 2003 | Hansard Standing Committee B |
| Report and Third Reading | 2 April 2003, 19 May 2003 and 20 May 2003. | Vol 402 Cols 925-1038; Vol 405 Cols 688-814 and 865-983 |
| Commons Consideration of Lords Amendments | 18 November 2003 | Vol 413 Cols 643-744 |
| Commons Insistence on Disagreeing to Certain Lords Amendments to Words so Restored to the Act and Commons Consequential Amendments to the Act | 19 November 2003 and 20 November 2003 | Vol 413 Cols 876-903 and 1025-1036 |
| **House of Lords** | | |
| Introduction | 21 May 2003 | Vol 648 Col 835 |
| Second Reading | 16 June 2003 | Vol 649 Cols 558-654 |
| Committee | 30 June 2003; 7 July 2003; 14 July 2003; 15 July 2003; 17 July 2003; 15 September 2003; 18 September 2003; 6 October 2003; 8 October 2003; 14 October 2003 and 15 October 2003 | Vol 650 Cols 601-672 and 697-718; Vol 651 Cols 12-27, 36-80, 98-124, 645-699, 715-754; 768-823, 837-846, 1009-1025 and 1039-1090; Vol 652 Cols 687-734, 737-754 and 1081-1139; Vol 653 Cols 22-76, 296-362, 377-412, 768-840, 858-886, 890-930, 945-1018 and 1037-1052 |
| Report | 29 October 2003; 30 October 2003; 4 November 2003; 5 November 2003 and 11 November 2003 | Vol 654 Cols 283-335, 352-374, 419-425, 440-494, 691-766, 800-864, 880-910 and 1234-1319 |
| Third Reading | 17 November 2003 | Vol 654 Cols 1774-1829 |

| *Stage* | *Date* | *Hansard Reference* |
|---|---|---|
| Lords Consideration of Commons Reasons for Disagreeing to Certain Lords Amendments and Commons Amendments to words so Restored to the Act, and Commons Amendments in Lieu of a Certain Lords Amendment Disagreed to. | 19 November 2003 | Vol 654 Cols 1939-2010 |
| Lords Consideration of Commons Insistence on Disagreeing to Certain Lords Amendments to Words so Restored to the Act and Commons Consequential Amendments to the Act | 20 November 2003 | Vol 654 Cols 2050-2084 and 2105-2112 |
| **Royal Assent** – 20 November 2003 | | House of Lords Hansard Vol 654 Col 2114 |
| | | House of Commons Hansard Vol 413 Col 1037 |

Adapted and published by GRANGIS under the OGL Licence 3.0.

www.nationalarchives.gov.uk/doc/open-government-licence/version/3/

GRANGIS - UK PUBLISHING 2022.
Thank you for taking the time to leave us a review regarding this version

★★★★★

For further inquiries, contact us at:
www.grangis.com / contact@grangis.com

www.ingramcontent.com/pod-product-compliance
Lightning Source LLC
LaVergne TN
LVHW060212210926
848481LV00008B/2712